Pension Scheme Taxation and Retirement Planning

Pension Scheme Taxation and Retirement Planning

Alec Ure
Gavin Moffat

A Day = 6 April 2006

 Tottel
publishing

Tottel Publishing, Maxwelton House, 41–43 Boltro Road, Haywards Heath, West Sussex, RH16 1BJ

A CIP Catalogue record for this book is available from the British Library.

ISBN 978 1 84766 288 0

Typeset by Phoenix Photosetting, Chatham, Kent
Printed and bound in Great Britain by
Athenæum Press Limited, Gateshead, Tyne & Wear

Preface

Much has changed in the world of pensions over the last few years. Economic trends, increasing longevity, investment volatility and regulation have all served to turn pensions from something of a niche subject into something discussed in pubs and at dinner parties, sometimes to the chagrin of any actuaries or financial advisers who happen to be present. Over the space of five years we have seen three new Pensions Acts come into being, and each new Finance Act has brought further changes to the new pension tax regime. We are now almost three years on since the adoption of the new pension tax regime, and it is perhaps no longer appropriate to refer to it as 'new'. The main principles have had a decent chance to bed down. For the most part, recent changes to the regime have involved fine tuning and clearing up some of the unintended consequences. Nonetheless, politically motivated changes are not unheard of, from the introduction of taxable property rules in 2006 to the November 2008 pre-budget report freezing the annual and lifetime allowances in 2011 for five years. In this book we have sought to provide the reader with a complete picture of the tax regime including changes up to and including Finance Act 2008, and to highlight the implications of the tax rules that will need to be borne in mind when making decisions and giving advice, whether at a scheme level or on an individual basis.

For the majority of pension scheme members, the high contribution allowances and generous benefit limits should mean that the tax rules will have only a limited impact on them. This book is therefore divided into two parts. The first deals with the tax provisions faced by all schemes and their members. The second concentrates on those issues of particular interest to high earners and those with high value pension funds.

While the tax rules should have little impact on the ordinary scheme member, there are provisions that will be of benefit to many, especially when compared to the rules that existed before 2006. The relaxed rules on membership, tax-free lump sums, transfers and timing and nature of benefit will all be of interest to those involved in scheme design. It seems likely that this will become an increasingly important area as greater focus is placed on pensions as part of the remuneration package. Longer working lives may call for increased pension flexibility, and the advent of 'soft compulsion' in 2012 will see up to an estimated 7 million new members enrolled into workplace pension schemes.

For those concerned with the administration and governance of pension schemes, the chapters on reporting, compliance and investment rules will be of importance. The requirements of the regime are not onerous, but those with the statutory duty of scheme administrator need to give them due attention or face the consequences.

Preface

The modern workplace is becoming an increasingly global one, and pension rules have often struggled to keep pace with this. The current tax regime offers significant advantages over the pre-2006 position, and we have therefore devoted a chapter to overseas considerations. The tax regime has given us the new acronym of QROPS (qualifying recognised overseas pension scheme), and there are an increasing number of such schemes registered with HMRC. Both QROPS and migrant member relief, where UK tax relief is granted on contributions to overseas arrangements, are covered, as well as some of the cross-border provisions arising from the EU Pensions Directive.

SSAS, SIPP and FURBS were the pre-2006 acronyms associated with pensions for senior executives, directors and high net worth individuals. The current tax regime introduces us to new acronyms for such vehicles – IRPS and EFRBS (investment regulated pension schemes and employer-financed retirement benefit schemes). The tax treatment of such arrangements has changed significantly. IRPS are subject to the taxable property provisions in particular, and this would cover what were once SSASs and SIPPs. Any scheme that is not a registered pension scheme (and this covers the pre-2006 equivalent of UURBS and FURBS) is treated as an EFRBS. The tax treatment of a funded EFRBS is so unfavourable that there is virtually no benefit in operating one, although transitional protection does exist for pre-2006 schemes. These matters are covered in part two of this book.

Other matters covered in part two include the very important annual and lifetime allowances that high earners may find themselves up against, and for those who had already accrued large pension funds by April 2006, there is a chapter dealing specifically with the transitional protection for such rights. Although the post-2006 regime was dubbed 'tax simplification', the transitional protection provisions are anything but. The rules surrounding enhanced protection are sometimes very intricate, perhaps necessarily so since enhanced protection completely exempts a person from the lifetime allowance charge. It is therefore very important to ensure enhanced protection rules are not infringed or the consequences could be financially painful. We also look at some tax planning measures in part two, including excepted group life policies, which seem to be gaining increasing favour with employers as a tax-efficient means of providing life cover for their top earners.

It is our hope that, in buying this book, the reader gains an insight into all the relevant taxation aspects of pensions and is better equipped for effective retirement planning.

Alec Ure
Alec Ure & Associates

Gavin Moffatt
SBJ Benefit Consultants Ltd

Contents

Contents

Table of statutes

Paragraph references printed in **bold** type indicate where the Act is set out in part or in full.

Table of statutory instruments

Those paragraph numbers in **bold** type indicate where a Statutory Instrument is set out in part or in full.

Table of cases

List of Abbreviations

APPS	Appropriate personal pension scheme
ASP	Alternatively secured pension
AVCs	Additional voluntary contributions
BCE	Benefit crystallisation event
BIM	HMRC's Business Income Manual
BOJ	'Best Of Judgment' assessment
CBBR	Clearing Bank Base Rates
CEIOPS	Committee of European Insurance and Occupational Pension Supervisors
CGT	Capital Gains Tax
CT	Corporation Tax
DB	Defined benefit schemes
DC	Defined contribution, or money purchase, schemes
DCA	Department of Constitutional Affairs
DWP	Department for Work and Pensions
EEA	European Economic Area
EC	European Commission
ECJ	European Court of Justice
EFRBS	Employer-financed retirement benefit schemes
EGLP	Expected group life policy
EIM	HMRC's Employment Income Manual
EU	European Union
FSA	Financial Services Authority
FSMA	Financial Services and Markets Act 2000
FURBS	Funded unapproved retirement benefit schemes
GAD	Government Actuary's Department
HMRC	Her Majesty's Revenue and Customs
HMRC APSS	HMRC Audit and Pension Scheme Services
HMRC SPSS	Savings, Pensions, Share Schemes
IHT	Inheritance tax
IM	Inspector's manual
IORPS, and IORPS Directive	Directive 2003/41/EC of the European Parliament and the Council on the activities and supervision of institutions for occupational retirement provision, which was adopted on 3 June 2003
IPCC	Independent Police Complaints Commission
IRPS	Investment-regulated pension scheme
LAM	HMRC's Life Assurance Manual
LLP	Limited Liability Partnership
NAO	National Audit Office
NAPF	National Association of Pension Funds

NI	National Insurance
NIM	HMRC's National Insurance Manual
NRD	Normal retirement date
OEIC	Open-ended investment company
PAYE	Pay As You Earn
PSTR	Pension Scheme Tax Reference
QROPS	Qualifying Recognised Overseas Pension Scheme
RACs	Retirement annuity contracts
RAS	Relief at source
RAT	Rate applicable to trusts
REITS	Real Estate Investment Trusts, under Finance Act 2006, Pt 4
RNUK	Relevant non-UK scheme
RPI	Retail Prices Index
RPSM	Registered Pension Schemes Manual
SAYE	Save As You Earn
SCO	HMRC's Special Compliance Office
SIPPS	Self-invested personal pension scheme
SSAS	Small self-administered scheme
S2P	State Second Pension
TSEM	HMRC's Trusts, Settlements and Estates Manual
UK	United Kingdom
UK-REITS	UK real estate investment trusts
UURBS	Unfunded unapproved retirement benefit schemes
VAT	Value added tax

Part One
The main tax rules

Chapter 1

Introduction

1.1 This book serves to update and replace *Taxation of Pension Benefits* (Fourth Edition) and *Retirement Planning for High Net Worth Individuals* (Seventh Edition), by combining the two titles into one publication.

Her Majesty's Revenue and Customs (HMRC's) discretionary powers were removed by the *Finance Act 2004*, which came into effect on 6 April 2006 (A-Day). They were replaced by direct statute law and secondary legislation combined with published guidance.

Although the tax simplification regime is now firmly in place, the Government is continuing to make changes to both the new pensions tax legislation and to HMRC practice in respect of registered pension schemes. Some of these changes affect all members of registered pension schemes and some are of greater importance to high earners. The latter changes include the introduction of investment-regulated pension schemes (IRPS) and revised rules for overseas schemes and for employer-financed retirement benefit schemes (EFRBS). Sadly, this means that the concept of true simplification has been eroded.

In view of the Government's late decision to introduce two new pensions tax sub-regimes, chiefly in the area of investments (one to cover the majority of most members of registered pension schemes, one for high earners) in place of a single one, the contents of this book are divided into two Parts:

- Part One describes the main tax rules which apply to all registered pension schemes

- Part Two describes the main considerations for high net worth individuals.

BACKGROUND TO THE CURRENT REGIME

1.2 The considerable number of legislative changes and changes in practice over the past twenty years or so resulted in the existence of eight different benefit regimes. This created considerable administrative problems,

1

not only for pension schemes practitioners, trustees and managers, but also for HMRC and the other regulatory bodies who are involved in such schemes.

Not the least of the above problems were the complexities which arose from the constant necessity to conduct checks on retained benefits. These checks were necessary in order to test current scheme benefits against the prevailing HMRC limits for the tax regime which applied to each individual circumstance.

First moves for change

1.3   Although the landmark moves for change are by now largely historic, the ongoing reforms continue to make reference to the aims and aspirations of past committees and reports. The most significant events are summarised below:

- 1993: the Goode Report, by Professor Roy Goode, was published by the Pension Law Committee in September 1993. It identified the significant problems associated with the multiplicity of tax regimes, and contained some early plans for change.

- 1998: the National Association of Pension Funds (NAPF) published a report based on its ongoing review of UK pension provision. This was accompanied by proposals which had been put forward by the Department of Social Security (now the Department for Work and Pensions (DWP)).

- 2000: Paul Myners published his Government-commissioned report into institutional investment on 16 May 2000. The report called for the removal of (approximately) 50 existing barriers to investment growth, and recommended greater familiarity with investment issues, independent custody and shareholder activism. The report is constantly under review and remains a key source of reference.

- 2001: the Sandler Review was published on 9 July 2001. The report recommended a simplification of products and advice, and significant reductions in costs and overheads. The Financial Services Authority, (FSA) also contributes to such recommendations under ongoing reviews of practice.

- 2002: the Pickering Report was published on 11 July 2002 for the DWP. The review had involved a wide consultative process into UK pension provision. The report supported pensions simplification, although it contained some indication of ongoing complexities, particularly in the field of contracting out. It also recommended some easier methods for employers, commercial providers and citizens to accumulate retirement benefits.

- 2002: the HMRC/Treasury Simplification Team published its first report entitled *Simplifying the Taxation of Pensions: Increasing Choice and Flexibility for All* on 17 December 2002.

- 2003 to date: the HMRC/Treasury Simplification Team published a successor report entitled *Simplifying the Taxation of Pensions: The*

Government's Proposals on 10 December 2003. The document contained the main structure of the post A-Day tax regime. The Chancellor of the Exchequer at the time approached the National Audit Office (NAO) to provide an independent evaluation of the assumptions used in order to establish the numbers of people who would be affected by the proposed new lifetime allowance. The originally proposed lifetime allowance of £1.4 million as at A-Day was raised to £1.5 million for the tax year 2006/2007.

THE MAIN LEGISLATION

Finance Acts

1.4   The key statute is the *Finance Act 2004*. The relevant sections of the Act are ss 149–284, and the relevant Schedules are Schs 28–36.

The Act has undergone various amendments and extensions since it came into effect. The most significant changes were inserted by the *Finance Act 2006*, and they have particular effect on high net worth individuals.

The main amending statutes are:

- the *Finance Act 2005*, ss 101 and 102, and Sch 10;

- the *Finance (No 2) Act 2005*, which restored some of the provisions of the original Finance Bill 2005 (which was shortened in its original construction before the general election in that year, and included the blocking of capital gains tax avoidance by temporary non-residents and trustees). Additionally, the second Act contained rules on the disposal of assets overseas by residents and non-residents;

- the *Finance Act 2006*, which:

    – contained amendments in respect of tax-free cash lump sums;

    – imposed a charge to inheritance tax (IHT) on certain death benefits;

    – imposed investment restrictions and taxable property charges on investment-regulated pension schemes (IRPS), being schemes or arrangements in which there is an element of direct or indirect member control over investment activity;

- the *Finance Act 2007*, which:

    – abolished tax relief on premiums paid on personal fixed term life assurance policies provided via personal or occupational pension schemes where the only benefit payable is a lump sum on death or critical illness;

    – imposed restrictions on pension schemes which invest in UK real estate investment trusts (UK-REITS);

    – relaxed the timing of the payment of lump sums;

    – introduced changes to alternatively secured pensions (ASP);

- introduced changes to the categories of persons who can establish and register a pension scheme;

- the *Finance Act 2008*, which:

  - contained amendments in respect of tax-free cash lump sums

  - imposed a charge on tax-relieved pension savings which are diverted into inheritance tax using scheme pensions and lifetime annuities in other circumstances than ASP;

  - contained further amendments to the rules which apply to residential property held by SSAS and SIPPS, and a relaxation of the definition of an IRPS;

  - permitted regulations to be made to provide for the commutation of small stranded pots of less than £2,000 in occupational pension schemes;

  - provided for IHT relief from A-Day in respect of certain overseas schemes, in line with the exemptions which apply to UK registered schemes;

  - prevented the avoidance of spreading contributions for tax relief purposes by means of interposing a new company and financing it to pay the contribution

  - required contributions to be physically alienated from the employer, in the relevant accounting period they are paid.

Additionally, the regulatory-making powers which are contained in the *Finance Act 2004* have been used for the purpose of bringing in a large number of regulations and orders. The effect of these regulations and orders is described under the relevant chapters below. The main statutory instruments and orders are listed in **Appendix 2**.

Statutes under Tax Law Rewrites

1.5   The following Tax Law Rewrites have been completed. Many have highlighted, amongst other things, the multitude of taxation legislation which applied to tax-advantaged pension schemes:

- the *Capital Allowances Act 2001* – effective from April 2001;

- the *Income Tax (Earnings and Pensions) Act 2003* – effective from April 2003. This Act included the important repeal of Schedule E by way of a grouping of employment income, pensions and social security income within 'earnings';

- the *Income Tax (Pay as You Earn) Regulations 2003* – effective from April 2004;

- the *Income Tax (Trading and Other Income) Act 2005* – effective from April 2005;

- the *Income Tax Act 2007* – effective from April 2007.

SUMMARY OF THE CURRENT TAX REGIME

1.6   The main features of the current tax regime are summarised below, and cross-references are provided to the detailed explanations of the subject matter which is contained in the chapters of this book.

The pre A-Day legislation will remain of importance for some years to come, in view of the transitional protections which are described in **Chapter 11** and with further regard to any outstanding actions or enquiries which apply to pre A-Day events. Accordingly, **Appendix 1** contains tables which summarise the main pension tax rules which applied before A-Day.

There are modification powers under the *Finance Act 2004* for the purpose of providing transitional protection for schemes if their documentation has not been amended to comply with the new tax rules. The *Pension Schemes (Modification of Rules of Existing Schemes) Regulations 2006 (SI 2006/364)* override existing scheme documentation. The regulations include, amongst other things, a rule of construction and they give trustees discretion over whether or not to make a payment which would otherwise fall to be treated as an unauthorised payment.

The statutory period by which schemes must be amended in order to comply with the current legislation ends on 6 April 2011 (*Finance Act 2004, Sch 36, Pt 1, para 3*). However, trustees, scheme managers and employers should seek guidance on whether or not they should change their documents at an earlier date. In order to achieve this, it is necessary to ensure that all the latest documentation changes, including those which may have been announced by way of company or trustee minutes or resolutions, are made available to the scheme's legal advisers.

The main features of the current tax regime are given below.

Eligibility

1.7   The legislation provides much greater access to registered pension scheme membership than under earlier regimes for tax-advantaged schemes. Not only may members include the employed and self-employed, but there is also an opportunity for migrants to become members. Individuals may also concurrently be members of any type or any number of schemes (for example, occupational pension schemes and personal pension schemes). Details are given in **Chapter 2**.

Tax-relievable allowances

1.8   The *Finance Act 2007* removed the pre A-Day limits regime. It was replaced by a limit on the aggregate amount of contributions/fund growth on which tax relief will be given on an annual basis, and by a limit on the aggregate amount of lifetime savings on which tax relief will be given. These two allowances are referred to in the legislation as the annual allowance and the lifetime allowance. They are described in detail in **Chapter 10**.

The Government intent was that the relatively generous level of the lifetime allowance would prove to be an incentive to pension saving for individuals who were previously restricted by short service to small benefit provision. The full impact of change is not yet known, but there has been a clear increase in the number of new money purchase (defined contribution, or DC) schemes and in the number of defined benefit (DB) schemes which have converted to DC schemes. The number of closures of DB schemes has also increased, partly due to the tight statutory regime which applies to such schemes under DWP rules and related legislation.

Tax-relievable contributions

1.9   Tax-relievable contributions may be paid at much higher levels than pre-A-Day limits by most members and employers, and scheme income and gains continued to be generally tax-free.

Further information is given in **Chapters 3** and **5** respectively.

Benefit style

1.10   The sponsor and/or provider are now free to determine the nature and structure of benefits to be provided. Multiple-employer schemes are also permitted, whether or not those employers are associated. The main aim is to provide greater member mobility and more flexible benefit provision. To some extent the relaxations were driven by the need to comply with *Directive 2003/41/EC* of the European Parliament and the Council on the activities and supervision of institutions for occupational retirement provision, which was adopted on 3 June 2003 (IORPS). Its objective is to allow pension funds to benefit from the internal market principles of free movement of capital and free provision of services.

There is flexible provision to take pensions, including whilst remaining in service. For DC schemes, pensions may be secured, alternatively secured or unsecured.

Further information concerning benefits and overseas considerations is provided in **Chapters 4** and **9** respectively.

Transferability of member rights

1.11   Transfers may be made freely between registered schemes, and also from UK registered schemes to overseas schemes which are regulated as pension funds in their country of establishment (if they undertake to comply with information-reporting requirements). Again, the changes were partly driven by the need to comply with the EU IORPS.

Further information about these significant relaxations concerning transfers and overseas considerations is provided in **Chapters 6** and **9** respectively.

Investments

1.12   Many of the restrictions which applied to investments which could be made by tax-advantaged schemes before A-Day, including the removal of the bar on investment in residential property for most schemes, have disappeared. There are, however, special rules which apply to IRPS. Otherwise, the current legislation generally relies on the 'prudent man principle' to be applied by investment managers, trustees and scheme managers, in keeping with EU guidelines.

Further information about the investment rules, and IRPS, is given in **Chapters 5** and **12** respectively.

Transitional protection

1.13   An important facility, which chiefly benefits high earners, is the provision of transitional protection for their pre A-Day rights and entitlements. A member may apply for enhanced protection or primary protection from the lifetime allowance. There are also available protections for certain tax-free lump sums.

Further information about the transitional protection rules is given in **Chapter 11**.

Registration

1.14   The rules which apply to scheme registration are described in **Chapter 2**. Most actions must be conducted online.

Reporting and self-assessment

1.15   A codified system exists for reporting various events, and for self-assessment. Again, most actions must be conducted online. The rules which apply to reporting and self-assessment are described in **Chapter 7**.

Compliance, and unauthorised member payments

1.16   There must be strict compliance with legislative requirements and published codes of practice and guidelines. Tax charges, penalties, sanctions and unauthorised member payment charges may be incurred in the event of non-compliance. The compliance requirements extend to trustees, managers, administrators, fund managers, pension scheme promoters and scheme advisers, as appropriate.

Further information concerning compliance and unauthorised member payments is provided in **Chapters 8** and **14** respectively.

Non-registered schemes – EFRBS

1.17   Under the legislation which prevailed before A-Day, funded or unfunded schemes which were not approved (FURBS and UURBS) received certain tax and national insurance concessionary treatment. The current legislation effectively removed these tax advantages, with some transitional protection for accrued rights as at A-Day.

Non-registered funded schemes are known as employer-financed retirement benefit schemes (EFRBS) under the *Finance Act 2004*.

Further information concerning FURBS, UURBS and EFRBS is provided in **Chapter 15**.

Overseas issues

1.18 *The Finance Act 2004* brought in many changes concerning overseas matters. The main impact was that transfers can now generally be made from UK registered schemes to overseas schemes, and migrants who come to the United Kingdom will receive tax reliefs on their contributions in place of the former corresponding relief provisions.

Further information about overseas matters is provided in **Chapter 9**.

HMRC Registered Pensions Schemes Manual (RPSM)

1.19 The HMRC website contains a comprehensive Registered Pensions Schemes Manual (RPSM). This manual contains guidance for trustees, employers, members and scheme managers on the various subjects covered by the current tax rules. It is a very large document, with a significant number of links. It also contains a useful glossary of terms.

Chapter 2

Registration, providers and membership

THE MAIN PROCEDURE

2.1   All new schemes must register with HMRC Audit and Pension Scheme Services (HMRC APSS) if they wish to receive the tax reliefs (see **Chapter 3** and *Finance Act 2004, s 153*) which are given to registered pension schemes. The forms must, with a few exceptions, be completed online. The procedures are described in HMRC's RPSM (see **1.18**). They are summarised in this chapter and are available with detailed links on the HMRC website. The main forms and maintenance procedures are described in **Appendix 3**. The scheme administrator (see **2.3**) must apply for registration, and may not devolve that duty. The scheme administrator may arrange for a scheme practitioner to be appointed (see **2.4** and **Appendix 3**).

Most applications are processed within one working day of receipt (online applications are processed instantly), and tax relief will be available on contributions from the date on which HMRC acknowledges the registration of the scheme. The scheme administrator will receive a success message which includes the Pension Scheme Tax Reference (PSTR) – see RPSM02306020 – and HMRC's acknowledgement of the registration will be placed on the scheme administrator's Pensions Notice board within Pension Schemes Online.

Changes to details concerning scheme administrators and practitioners should be reported by using the 'pension schemes online' service, which can be found at http://www.hmrc.gov.uk.

CORE INFORMATION

2.2   The registration procedure requires core information to be provided to HMRC, which then has 12 months to raise any queries with regard to the registration. After that period the scheme will be treated as registered for the future unless it is found that there is evidence of deliberate fraud or a withholding of information at the time of the original application. In addition to the information required for tax purposes, contracting-out forms are available on the website to accompany applications, where appropriate.

The core information requirements of registration are:

● the legal structure of the scheme (a trust is not essential);

● the size of scheme membership in bands of 0,1–10, 11–50, 51–10,000 and over 10,000 (HMRC considers that small schemes may carry more risk than large ones);

- the establisher of the scheme (HMRC considers that schemes which are established by a connected employer may carry more risk than 'off-the-shelf' products);

- details of the administrator;

- the degree of member control over assets;

- registration for relief at source (RAS), where applicable;

- registration with the Pensions Regulator, where there is more than one member;

- election to contract out of the State Second Pension (S2P), where required;

- registration of a stakeholder plan, where applicable (such a plan must register for tax relief and, if appropriate, to operate relief at source on contributions to the scheme. It must also make an application or election to contract-out of the State Second Pension (S2P) and apply to the Pensions Regulator for stakeholder registration).

Following the application process, registration of a scheme will appear online and the administrator will be able to authorise a practitioner or practitioners to carry out administrative tasks if so wishes.

SCHEME ADMINISTRATOR

2.3   The main responsibilities of the scheme administrator concerning scheme registration are described in RPSM02101010. He should register to use Pension Schemes Online by first obtaining an activation token and I.D. online. He must submit to HMRC a fully completed application in the form specified by HMRC. In practice, this will all be one online form. Applications may not be made before the scheme has been established. The relevant maintenance forms and completion notes are listed in **2.6**.

The scheme administrator must be resident in either:

- the UK;

- another **EU member state;** or

- another state in the EEA (ie Liechtenstein, Iceland or Norway).

If more than one person is appointed as the scheme administrator, each is jointly and severally liable for any tax charges on the scheme administrator.

For deferred annuity contracts and assigned policies, the scheme administrator must be resident as stated above. If no scheme administrator has been formally appointed, HMRC regards the person who controls the management of the pension scheme (policy or contract) as the scheme administrator of that scheme.

Once the scheme has been registered, the scheme administrator can authorise HMRC to deal with one or more practitioners acting on their behalf (see **2.4** and RPSM02307000).

HMRC requires that the administrator understands the responsibilities and functions imposed upon him by the legislation, and requires him to declare that he will discharge those functions at all times. This is a far-reaching commitment as it applies whether the administrator is resident in the United Kingdom or overseas. The main information contained in the declaration is that:

- the scheme is fully compliant with the legislation in its application to a registered pension scheme;

- the information provided by the administrator during the application process is correct and complete;

- the administrator is aware that any false statements are likely to lead to penalties and/or prosecution.

SCHEME PRACTITIONER

2.4 The main responsibilities of the scheme practitioner will be those which are covered in his letter of appointment and list of services which is given to the scheme administrator or trustees. He can register to use Pension Schemes Online by first obtaining an activation token and I.D. online. He can conduct most activities, other than scheme registration, on behalf of the scheme administrator (see **Appendix 3**).

The relevant maintenance forms and completion notes are listed in **2.6**.

APPLYING FOR REGISTRATION

2.5 The relevant forms and completion notes are provided on HMRC's website in PDF format. The list of forms details which forms will still be accepted on paper. The main forms and completion notes can be found on: www.hmrc.gov.uk/pensionschemes/tax-simp-forms.htm

In addition to the schemes and arrangements described in **2.16**, it is also necessary to register buy-out policies, *section 32* contracts (*Finance Act 1981, s 32*) and assigned policies. Buy-out policies and *section 32* contracts are deferred annuities (ie they will provide an annuity to the member at some time in the future). Individual policies which are already held under a **registered pension scheme** and are earmarked for the provision of a member's benefits may be assigned to the member and will fall within the category of deferred annuity contracts. See RPSM02104010.

In the case of deferred annuities the **scheme administrator** does not have to complete the entire registration application process on-line, but he must make the required declarations (*Finance Act 2004, s 270*). Further details are given in RPSM02306150.

The current versions of the registration forms are shown below:

Form number	Version		Description
APSS100	08/08	XXK	Application for pension scheme tax registration
APSS100 Notes	04/08	50K	Completion Notes for APSS 100
APSS101	08/08	59K	Election to contract out
APSS101 Notes	08/08	53K	Completion Notes for APSS 101
APSS102	01/08	77K	Election for Industry-wide money purchase schemes
APSS102 Notes	01/08	45K	Completion Notes for APSS 102
APSS103	01/08	81K	Relief at Source details
APSS103 Notes	01/08	63K	Completion Notes for APSS 103
APSS103A	03/06	59K	Relief at Source details- specimen signatures
APSS109	03/06	63K	Notification of succession to a 'split' scheme
APSS109 Notes	03/06	34K	Supplementary page for Question 3
APSS110	03/06	61K	Notification of succession to a sub-scheme

Approved and exempt-approved schemes as at A-Day were automatically treated as registered schemes. This applied to:

- schemes approved under the *Income and Corporation Taxes Act 1988* (ICTA 1988), Ch 1, Pt XIV, being approved retirement benefit schemes and additional voluntary contribution schemes;

- personal pension schemes approved under ICTA 1988, Ch IV, Pt XIV, being approved personal pension schemes, approved stakeholder schemes and approved group personal pension schemes;

- retirement annuity contracts or retirement annuity trust schemes approved before 1 July 1988 under ICTA 1988, Ch III, Pt XIV, being insurance contracts for the self-employed or employees who did not qualify for approved scheme membership;

- public sector schemes, being relevant statutory schemes for members of the public service, Parliament and national assemblies;

- schemes with split approval under ICTA 1988, s 661, but only in respect of the part of the scheme approved under ICTA 1988, Ch I, Pt XIV;

- old code schemes, being schemes which were formally approved superannuation funds before 1970 with frozen contributions since 5 April 1980;

- deferred annuity contracts of a specified nature.

This applied in all cases unless the scheme elected to opt-out or subsequently has its registration withdrawn.

MAINTENANCE FORMS AND COMPLETION NOTES

2.6   The relevant maintenance forms and completion notes are also provided on HMRC's website in PDF format. The list of forms details which forms will still be accepted on paper. The current versions of the registration forms are shown below:

Form number	Version	Description
APSS150 (65K) [This form must only be used by Scheme Administrators of registered pension schemes to authorise a practitioner to act on their behalf].	03/06	Authorising and de-authorising a Practitioner
APSS151 (45K)	09/07	Add Scheme Administrator
APSS152 (59K)	03/07	Amend scheme details
APSS153 (59K)	03/07	Change of Scheme Administrator/Practitioner user details
APSS154 (54K)	03/07	Associate Scheme Administrator to scheme
APSS155 (91K)	04/08	Election to vary a contracting-out or appropriate scheme certificate.
APSS155 (43K)	04/08	Notes for completion of PS155
APSS161 (60K)	03/06	Pre-register as Scheme Administrator/ Practitioner
APSS203 (63K)	03/06	Authorisation of Scheme Administrator(s) to view Lifetime Allowance certificate(s)
APSS209 (60K)	03/06	Request by Scheme Administrator for Lifetime Allowance certificate details
APSS413 (54K)	08/06	Notice of Appeal and Application to Postpone Payment

REGISTRATION REJECTED

2.7   If an application is rejected (see RPSM02101030), HMRC will give the reason for the decision. The **scheme administrator** has the right of appeal against that decision (*Finance Act 2004, s 156*) within 30 days. An appeal may be heard before the General Commissioners or the Special Commissioners

OPTING OUT OF REGISTRATION

2.8   Under the provisions of the *Finance Act 2004, s 153* a scheme may opt out of automatic registration. If a scheme did not opt out before A-Day, it will have been treated as a registered scheme. If it did opt out, a 40% charge would have been applied on the market value of the fund (which means the assets and/or other sums which are held for the purpose of the scheme as at A-Day). Opting out would also have negated the pensions business status of any life assurance provision under the scheme at the beginning of the company's period of account in which the opt-out took place.

The scheme administrator is responsible for payment of the 40% charge, and where more than one person acts as the scheme administrator each person is jointly and separately liable for the tax payment. Thereafter the scheme will have been treated as an EFRBS (see **Chapter 15**).

SCHEMES THAT DO NOT APPLY FOR REGISTRATION

2.9   Where an occupational **pension scheme** does not wish to be registered (see RPSM02101040) it will not qualify for the tax reliefs shown in **Chapter 3**. It is likely to be treated as an EFRBS (see **Chapter 15**).

REGISTRATION WITHDRAWN

2.10   The effect of HMRC withdrawing the registration of a scheme is described in **Chapter 14**. The administrator may appeal against such a decision (see **2.7**). Registration may only be withdrawn by HMRC, there is no provision for voluntary de-registration. Registration can only be withdrawn from an entire pension scheme, not from an **arrangement** or arrangements within the scheme. See RPSM02105010.

SCHEMES WHICH LOST APPROVAL BEFORE 6 APRIL 2006

2.11   Any scheme which had lost approval before A-Day may seek to become a registered pension scheme at any time from that date onwards if its scheme administrator applies for registration for the scheme and satisfies the registration conditions.

REGISTERING A NON-UK BASED PENSION SCHEME

2.12   A **pension scheme** which is set up outside the UK may register with HMRC (RPSM02102050). The same conditions apply as to a UK-based scheme, including the residence of the **scheme administrator.** The scheme administrator must make the same declarations as apply for a UK-based scheme, as described in **2.3**.

SCHEME DOCUMENTATION

2.13   The governing scheme documentation will need to be in place before registration can be sought. There are no requirements under the *Finance Act 2004* for HMRC to be provided with documents which govern the scheme provisions, except where it determines that it needs to have sight of documentation for a specific purpose. There is also wide freedom in the choice of scheme design, and schemes can be set up by one or more written instruments or agreements. This means that a pension scheme may be established by a trust instrument, deed poll, contract or board's resolution.

MODIFICATION POWERS

2.14   The Finance Act 2004 contains modification powers (see **1.6**) which largely preserve the way in which the scheme rules were applied before A-Day, in conjunction with the tax approval rules that applied before that date. However, consideration must also be given to the requirements of the *Pensions Act 1995, s 67*, in respect of any amendments to scheme documentation. The Pensions Regulator's Code of Practice dated 24 January 2007 provides guidance on the modification of subsisting rights. From 6 April 2006 employers with more than 150 employees were required to consult before making certain changes to:

- benefit accrual;

- defined contributions levels of payment to occupational pensions schemes; or

- changing the level of contributions to personal pension schemes.

(the threshold reduced to 100 from 6 April 2007 and 50 from 6 April 2008).

The code also applies to anyone seeking to modify an occupational pension scheme, and to the trustees of such a scheme. The parties will normally need to obtain the informed consent to any protected or detrimental modification of the benefits of the members affected.

NOTIFYING HMRC OF CHANGES SINCE REGISTRATION

2.15   HMRC must be notified if certain changes are made to the documentation and/or structure registered schemes (see **Chapter 7**). These include:

- where the scheme changed its rules and it was previously treated as more than one scheme before A-Day (this will include schemes which were split approved prior to A-Day)

- where the legal structure of the scheme changed from one to another of the following categories:

    - a single trust under which all of the assets of the scheme are held for the benefit of all members of the scheme;

    - an annuity contract – two party contract between scheme establisher and member;

    - a body corporate – e.g. a registered company;

    - other – e.g. deed poll;

    - a change in the number of members so that they now fall in to a different band (see **2.2**);

    - a change in the country or territory in which it is established;

> – where the scheme become, or ceased to become, an occupational
> pension scheme.

PROVIDERS

2.16 A scheme must be an occupational pension scheme or, with effect
from 6 April 2007 (*Finance Act 2007*, and the *Financial Services and Markets
Act 2000 (Regulated Activities) (Amendment) Order 2006 (SI 2006/1969)*,
established by a person with permission under the *Financial Services and
Markets Act 2000* to establish in the UK a personal pension scheme or a
stakeholder pension scheme. Before 6 April 2007 non-occupational pension
schemes had to be established by:

- an insurance company;

- a unit trust scheme manager;

- an operator, trustee or depositary of a recognised EEA collective
  investment scheme;

- an authorised open-ended investment company (OEIC);

- a building society;

- a bank; or

- an EEA investment portfolio manager.

An occupational pension scheme may be established by:

- an employer (if membership of the scheme is open to its own or any
  other employees – such a scheme is an occupational pension scheme,
  even if other people may also join the scheme);

- more than one employer (if the membership of the scheme is open to
  their own or any other employees – such a scheme is an occupational
  pension scheme, even if other people may also join the scheme); or

- Government departments or Ministers and UK parliamentary bodies
  (such a scheme will be a public service pension scheme).

An employer will be recognised as a sponsoring employer where one or more
of its employees are members and the scheme benefits for those members are
directly related to their employment with the employers in question.

MEMBERSHIP

2.17 Registered pension schemes may be open to all, whatever the
employment (including self-employment) or residence status (see **Chapter 9**)
of the individual concerned. A member may concurrently be a member of any
type or any number of schemes (for example, occupational pension schemes
and personal pension schemes). Non-associated multi-employer schemes can
clearly benefit from economies of scale.

A member may also be a member of any type or any number of schemes, such
as occupational pension schemes and personal pension schemes.

ADHERING COMPANIES

2.18   There are no longer any HMRC requirements about the way that any employer is allowed under the scheme rules to participate in an occupational pension scheme or about its degree of association) (if any) with the principal or adhering employers (see RPSM02102020).

Chapter 3

Tax reliefs on contributions and assets, and tax charges

INTRODUCTION

3.1   The tax reliefs and exemptions which are given to registered schemes and arrangements make them an attractive means of saving for retirement for members and their dependants and other beneficiaries.

The post A-Day regime has transformed the tax reliefs which are available on aggregated member and employer contributions and the lifetime savings of scheme members. These matters are dealt with in **3.2** to **3.12** and **3.13** to **3.25** respectively.

The accumulated fund of a registered scheme in respect of income and gains is almost entirely tax-free. These matters are dealt with in **3.26**.

The tax charges which may be incurred in certain circumstances are summarised in **3.27**.

RPSM02103010 provides an 'at a glance' list of the main reliefs and exemptions as follows:

- contributions by members and payments made on behalf of members (except employer payments) up to the higher of £3,600 and 100% of earnings;

- increase in pension benefits promised in **defined benefit arrangements** within the **annual allowance**;

- employer contributions;

- investment income – free of income tax;

- investment gains – free of capital gains tax;

- lump sum benefits, in specified circumstances, are free of income tax;

- pension business – such of a company's life assurance business as is referable to contracts entered into for the purposes of a registered pension scheme, or is the re-insurance of such business.

MEMBER CONTRIBUTIONS

General principles

3.2   There are no formal limits on the amount of member contributions which may be paid by a member or other person in respect of a member, only on the amount on which the member may enjoy tax relief. Full relief is available on member contributions up to a level of 100% of the individual's annual allowance (see **Chapter 10**), or £3,600 if that is the higher figure.

Contributions may also be made by third parties (see **3.13**) in respect of a person who has no earnings (for example, a minor or a spouse who is not working), and *in specie* (see **3.4**).

Additionally, the following qualify as contributions made by or on behalf of a member (*Finance Act 2004, ss 188(4); 188(6) and 195*):

- Pension credit rights from a non-registered pension scheme. These are rights which have been derived from a **pension sharing order** or provision following divorce or dissolution of a civil partnership. They increase a member's rights under a registered pension scheme. As they will not have previously received tax relief, they can be treated as a contribution on behalf of the member. The member can claim relief on them up to the annual limit on relief.

- An amount recovered from a member by his employer in respect of minimum payments made to a registered pension scheme (in accordance with the *Pension Schemes Act 1993, s 8(3)*, or the *Pension Schemes (Northern Ireland) Act 1993, s 4(3)*).

- Transfers of certain shares in a SAYE option scheme or share incentive plan. The maximum permitted timescales for transferring the shares are:

  – for shares in a SAYE option scheme, 90 days after the member exercised their right to acquire the shares, and

  – for shares in a share incentive plan, 90 days after the member directed the trustees of the share incentive plan to transfer ownership of the shares to the member.

The value given to the contribution for tax relief purposes is the market value of the shares at the date they were transferred to the pension scheme.

Transfers-in and pension credit rights from a registered pension scheme are not regarded as member contributions.

Where members of appropriate personal pension schemes (APPSs) have contracted out of the state scheme (S2P) HMRC will make a contribution equivalent to the amount of the minimum contributions as before. The amount of the minimum contributions payable by HMRC is determined in accordance with DWP legislation

Tax-relievable contributions

3.3 In order to qualify for tax relief on **relievable pension contributions** the individual must be an **active member** of a **registered pension scheme**, and a **relevant UK individual** in the tax year in which the contribution is paid:

A **relevant UK individual for a tax year** is a person who:

- has **relevant UK earnings** chargeable to income tax for that tax year;

- is resident in the UK at some time during that tax year;

- was resident in the UK at some time during the five tax years immediately before the tax year in question and was also resident in the UK when he joined the pension scheme; or

- has for that tax year general earnings from overseas Crown employment subject to UK tax, or is the spouse or civil partner of an individual who has for the tax year general earnings from overseas Crown employment subject to UK tax (both as defined by the *Income Tax (Earnings and Pensions) Act 2003, s 28*).

Relevant UK earnings are:

- employment income such as salary, wages, bonus, overtime, commission which is chargeable to tax under the *Income Tax (Earnings and Pensions) Act 2003, s 7(2)*;

- income chargeable under the *Income Tax (Trading and Other Income) Act 2005, Pt 2*, that is income derived from the carrying on or exercise of a trade, profession or vocation (whether individually or as a partner acting personally in a partnership);

- income arising from patent rights and treated as earned income under the *Income and Corporation Taxes Act 1988, s 833 (5B);*

- general earnings from an overseas Crown employment which are subject to tax in accordance with the *Income Tax (Earnings and Pensions) Act 2003, s 28.*

UK earnings which are not taxable in the UK under double taxation agreements (*Income and Corporation Taxes Act 1988, s 788*) do not count towards the annual allowance.

In-specie contributions

3.4   Although member contributions to a **registered pension scheme** must be monetary, it is permissible to agree to pay a contribution in such form and then to settle the debt by way of a transfer of asset(s). RPSM05101045 gives the following explanation of how this can be effectively achieved:

'An example will probably aid understanding here. If an individual wishes to pay a contribution they cannot do this by merely saying 'take this asset and whatever it is worth that is my contribution'. What they must do is to say that I wish to pay a contribution of, say, £10,000. If the scheme agrees, this debt may be paid by the member through a transfer of an asset of that value. If the asset is of a lower value the balance will be paid in cash.

If the contribution is being made to a registered pension scheme that operates relief at source (RAS) the amount of cash contribution specified should, if applicable, be the net amount after the individual exercises his right to deduct from the payment the basic rate RAS relief (see RPSM05101310).The basic rate relief will be recoverable by the **scheme**

administrator in the normal way from HMRC and if appropriate the individual can claim higher rate relief via his self assessment return.'

Non-relievable contributions

3.5   The following contributions are not tax-relievable on the individual:

- contributions paid after age 75;

- employer contributions;

- age-related rebates or minimum contributions by HMRC to a contracted-out pension scheme;

- life assurance premiums (see **3.6**).

LIFE ASSURANCE PREMIUMS

3.6   Under the *Finance Act 2004, Sch 18,* tax relief was removed from member contributions to personal life assurance policies which are set up as pensions (which are sometimes referred to as 'pension term assurance'). The Act contained a measure of protection for existing policies:

- A policy may continue if it was issued in respect of insurance made before 6 December 2006.

- A policy issued in respect of insurance made before 1 August 2007 may continue as long as the proposal was received before 14 December 2006 or, if the scheme included pension rights before 13 April 2007. There are slightly different dates which apply in respect of an occupational pension scheme in the unlikely event that this restriction would apply to such a scheme.

Any variations to a protected policy so as to increase its term or benefits will invalidate any protection.

The withdrawal of relief does not apply to life assurance premiums paid by members under an occupational pension scheme as long as the life assurance was a group policy and the other members covered by the policy are not connected with the individual paying the premiums (ie a spouse, relative or civil partner). AVCs made to group schemes to buy extra life assurance cover should still attract tax relief.

Life assurance premiums paid by an employer for the benefit of his employees may continue as before.

METHODS OF GIVING TAX RELIEF ON CONTRIBUTIONS

3.7   Relief on contributions is normally given through the PAYE system. Retirement annuity contracts and pension annuity contracts were brought within PAYE on 6 April 2007. There are some differing methods of claiming tax reliefs, which are available only in specified circumstances and depend on the method chosen by the scheme. The different methods are described under their relevant headings below.

Relief at source

3.8   Under relief at source (RAS) the member's contribution is paid net of basic rate of tax, and the scheme administrator claims the payment back from HMRC as a credit to the member's fund. (*Finance Act 2004, s 192, and the Registered Pension Schemes (Relief at Source) Regulations (SI 2005/3448)*).

As is the case for stakeholder schemes, higher-rate taxpayers will need to use the self-employment tax regime in order to claim the additional relief which is due to them. This is also appropriate for persons who have no UK earnings or whose UK earnings are less than the basic amount of £3,600 – in other words they must claim back through the self-assessment system.

RAS can be applied for at the same time as a pension scheme applies for registration

Net pay arrangement

3.9   The net pay arrangement has been in place for many years (*Finance Act 2004, s 193*), and the present method is unchanged. This is the procedure whereby an employer deducts the contribution from an individual's employment taxable income before operating PAYE. This contribution is now termed a '**relievable pension contribution**'. The employer pays the gross contribution into the pension scheme.

Tax relief is enjoyed by the individual at his marginal rate of income tax without needing to make an additional claim unless, exceptionally, full relief cannot be given through the operation of net pay. Therefore, if a member makes a relievable pension contribution of £100 the employer will deduct £100 from the individual's employment income and pay £100 into the pension scheme.

A person who contributes under a net pay arrangement can claim tax relief under self-assessment, PAYE coding or a repayment claim.

Relief on making a claim

3.10   This approach means that no relief is given to the member when the contribution is paid. The individual makes gross contributions to the scheme and claims tax relief on his relievable pension contributions. Therefore, where an individual makes a relievable pension contribution of £100, £100 will be paid to the scheme. The individual then claims the tax relief from HMRC. Relief is given by way of a deduction from the individual's total income.

Gross contributions are only available to ongoing **retirement annuity contracts** (RACs) where the RAC does not operate the relief at source system.

PUBLIC SERVICE PENSION SCHEMES

3.11   Some members of public service pension schemes, such as general practitioners and dentists, are taxed on some of their **relevant UK earnings** under *Income Tax (Trading and Other Income) Act 2005, Pt 2*, through being self-employed. If they choose to pension these earnings in a registered pension scheme set up in accordance with National Health Service Acts they will be unable to use the net pay arrangement to obtain tax relief on their contributions. The member should make a claim from tax relief to HMRC, through his self-assessment tax return if possible.

MIGRANT MEMBER RELIEF

3.12   An individual who joins a registered pension scheme who has been resident in the UK at some time within the last five years may be granted tax relief under the *Finance Act 2004, s 189* against his UK chargeable earnings (see **Chapter 9**).

EMPLOYER CONTRIBUTIONS

General principles

3.13   As is the case with member contributions, there are no statutory limits on the amount of employer contributions that can be paid, only on the amount of the tax reliefs that are available (see **Chapter 10**). Tax relief is given on contributions which are paid on behalf of a member by any employer, corporate body or legal entity, but if the contribution is made by anyone other than the employer itself it will be deemed to have been made by the scheme member (who should receive any tax relief which is due). BIM46000, in particular BIM46055 and BIM46060, address the matter of tax reliefs for multi-employer schemes (see below).

Where a company is a member of a group registered pension scheme, relief will be given in respect of its contribution amount to the scheme:

- although the levels of contribution may not reflect the individual circumstances of a particular employer, this does not prevent a deduction being allowed if payments are apportioned between the employing companies on a reasonable basis;

- where, say, the parent company pays the contributions and each employing subsidiary is recharged an appropriate amount relating to its employees, the intra-group recharge may be accepted as being a contribution paid by the employer in the period of account in which the parent company paid the contribution.

In the case of non-group schemes:

- the payment of a pension contribution is part of the normal costs of employing staff, and so it will usually be allowable expenditure;

- the above also applies where the contribution is to a multi-employer scheme for companies that are not in the same group (eg an industry-wide scheme), even though employees elsewhere in the industry may benefit from the payment.

Tax-relievable contributions

3.14   Tax relief is given on employer contributions to a registered pension scheme against the employer's trading receipts. The contributions may include the cost of any management expenses which the employer pays to the scheme.

RPSM05102010 gives the following guidance:

'Tax relief on employer contributions to a **registered pension scheme** is given by allowing contributions to be deducted as an expense in computing the profits of a trade, profession or investment business, and so reducing the amount of an employer's taxable profit.

In the case of a trade or profession, employer contributions will be deductible as an expense provided that they are incurred wholly and exclusively for the purposes of the employer's trade or profession *Income and Corporation Taxes Act 1988, s 74(1)(a)* – corporation tax and *Income Tax (Trading and Other Income) Act 2005, s 34* – income tax. Where the employer is a company with investment business the employer contributions will be deductible as an expense of management *Income and Corporation Taxes Act 1988, s 75.*

The pension tax legislation amends the normal rules as to what is an allowable deduction and as to the timing of a deduction. The details of these amendments can be found on RPSM05102020, but briefly the 2 main points are:

- pension contributions are not treated as capital payments if they otherwise would be; and

- a deduction can only be given for the period in which the contribution is paid.

The HMRC officer dealing with the Income Tax/Corporation Tax return of the employer will consider questions as to whether the contribution is an allowable expense. More specific guidance about whether contributions to registered pension schemes are an allowable expense is in the Business Income Manual at BIM 46001.

As a contribution needs to meet the 'wholly and exclusively' rule if tax relief is to be given in computing the profits of a trade or profession for tax purposes, special consideration needs to be given in making any risk assessment to:

- schemes with multiple employers – see RPSM05102160; and

- contributions paid in respect of members who are controlling directors or are connected to a controlling director – see RPSM05102170.

Tax relief can only be given on contributions that have actually been paid. The amount shown in the profit and loss account in respect of obligations in respect of defined benefit schemes may be substantially different from the amount of contributions paid to the scheme. But it is only the amount actually paid that can be considered for tax relief.

There are transitional provisions for some employers who received tax relief before 6 April 2006 for a contribution actually paid after 5 April 2006 – see RPSM05102150.

Tax relief on large contributions may be spread forward into future tax years – see RPSM05102060 to RPSM05102130.

Detailed guidance on the deduction in computing trading profits for employer's contributions to a registered pension scheme can be found in the Business Income Manual at BIM 46000 onwards.

Detailed guidance on the deduction in computing profits for employer's contributions to a registered pension scheme by an Investment Company is in the Company Taxation Manual at CTM08340 onwards.'

Deductible expenses

3.15   RPSM05102020 states that employer contributions will not be treated as capital payments if they otherwise would be for the purposes of Case I or II of Schedule D or in computing trading profits for the purposes of the Income Tax (Trading and Other Income) Act 2005. The contributions can only be deducted for the period of account in which they are paid. It is not possible to carry contributions back or forward to other periods.

Employers with investment business

3.16   Tax relief on employer contributions is given as an expense of management of the employer's investment business under *Income and Corporation Taxes Act 1988, s 75.*

This section was modified so that:

- relief is available where, ordinarily, a contribution would not be allowed under *s 75* because the contribution represents an expense of a capital nature; and

- the contribution can only be referred to the accounting period in which it is paid.

Employers who are life insurance companies

3.17   Tax relief on employer contributions is given as an expense under *Income and Corporation Taxes Act 1988, s 76.*

This section was modified so that:

- the contributions are brought into account in step 1 of *s 76(7)* if they would not otherwise be (and so are not regarded as capital expenses); and

- the contributions can only be referred to the accounting period in which they are paid.

The Life Assurance Manual (LAM) Chapter 12A contains further details about *s 76.*

THE SPREADING RULES

3.18   The *Finance Act 2004* retained the main spreading rules which were in place as at A-Day. The relevant statutory references are the *Finance Act 2004, ss 197* and *198.* Pre A-Day periods of spread continue to apply until the spread has run its course or the employer ceases business, whichever first occurs.

RPSM05102000 provides links to numerous examples of how to calculate periods of spread. In brief, a large contribution may be spread for tax deduction purposes over two or more accounting periods. The main criterion is that contributions exceeding 210% of an amount paid in a preceding accounting year must be considered for spreading. The spread is applied to the amount by which the contribution paid in the current accounting period exceeds 110% of the amount of the contribution paid in the previous accounting period.

Major exceptions are:

- spreading will not apply to any payment which has not exceeded £500,000;

- on a cessation of business, where a period of spread is already in place, the relief may be allowed in an earlier accounting period of the employer choice;

- contributions which are paid to fund cost of living increases for pensioners, or to meet future service liabilities for new entrants, are excluded from spreading.

The *Finance Act 2008, s 90,* prevented the avoidance of spreading by means of interposing a new company and financing it to pay the contribution, with effect from 10 October 2007.

Employer contributions must be physically alienated from the employer, in the relevant accounting period. If they are paid in a later the tax relief is only granted for that period.

The Accounting period

3.19   Spreading means that the relief which is due to an employer on the contribution is not given entirely in the chargeable period in which the payment is made. Instead, part of the relief due is spread forward into future periods. The chargeable period means a period of account where a contribution relates to a trade or profession, and an accounting period where it relates to an investment business or to the basic life assurance and general annuity business of a life insurance company.

DEFICIENCY PAYMENTS

3.20   Statutory payments by employers to cover deficiencies in the assets of a registered pension scheme under the *Pensions Act 1995, s 75,* are deemed to be relievable contributions. Further details on granting relief are provided in RPSM05102040.

LEVY PAYMENTS

3.21   Levy payments under the *Pensions Act 2004, Pt 2,* by employers are not strictly contributions. However, the *Pension Protection Fund (Tax) Regulations 2006 (SI 2006/575)* deem them to be so, meaning that tax relief is available on any levy payments and the relief will not be spread.

IN-SPECIE CONTRIBUTIONS

3.22   As is the case for member contributions (see **3.4**), contributions into registered pension schemes by employers may be made other than in cash form. From a tax efficiency viewpoint, an investor who wishes to make contributions into a registered scheme could find it more beneficial to transfer assets than to first realise those assets into cash for the purpose of making a payment. However, again, the payments must be expressed as cash sums. For example:

- ABC Property Developers Limited ('ABCPDL') agrees with the trustees of the ABCPDL pension scheme to pay a monetary amount into the pension scheme

- ABCPDL offers to meet its obligation by effecting a transfer of assets into the pension scheme, of market value equal to the debt.

- The Trustees of the scheme are agreeable to accepting the transfer of assets in settlement of the debt.

- The transfer of assets is made and treated as a contribution into the scheme.

The 'payment' must be made within the employer's relevant accounting period for the tax relief to be given. Records should therefore be kept of the arrangement by the parties for the future.

Where RAS applies to the scheme (see **3.8**), the contribution should be paid net of RAS. The basic rate relief will be recoverable by the scheme administrator in the normal way from HMRC and if appropriate the individual can claim higher rate relief via the self-assessment return.

It should be noted that certain transactions may attract capital gains tax and stamp duty at the time of transfer.

CONTRACTING-OUT

3.23   Any minimum payments which an employer makes to a contracted-out money purchase occupational pension scheme under the *Pension Schemes*

Act 1993, s 8, or the *Pension Schemes (Northern Ireland) Act 1993, s 4,* will qualify for tax relief. This does not include any amount recovered by the employer from the member in respect of minimum payments.

MIGRANT MEMBERS

3.24   Employer contributions to a qualifying overseas pension scheme in respect of a migrant member may be allowed against the employer's profits only when the benefits are paid to the relevant member (see **Chapter 9**).

HMRC has stated that it will look at the ratio of the overall amounts paid by way of contributions and pay in respect of the work done when considering the granting of relief. For example, part of a contribution may not receive relief if an Inspector considers that an excessive level of remuneration has been paid.

RESTRICTIONS ON TAX RELIEF

3.25   RPSM05102140 provides examples of circumstances in which tax relief may be restricted on employer contributions. The relevant regulations are the *Registered Pension Schemes (Restriction of Employers' Relief) Regulations 2005 (SI 2005/3458).*

In summary, HMRC may restrict tax relief where:

1.   any of the member's benefits are dependent on the non-payment of a benefit that he was expecting to receive from an EFRBS;

2.   payment of benefits to the member from an EFRBS would reduce the transfer value of any rights in a registered pension scheme.

The manual states that the process for 1 and 2 is to calculate the *pension input amount* (see **Chapter 10**) for each of the member's arrangements under the scheme in relation to the employer's period of account in which the contributions are paid. The amount of the restriction on the relief is an amount equal to the aggregate of the pension input amounts for the period of account in question in respect of each arrangements under the scheme relating to the member. Where the pension input period is being calculated in the case of *cash balance arrangements* and *defined benefit arrangements*, the amount of any *relievable pension contributions* paid by or on behalf of the member during the period of account in question is deducted from the closing value of the pension input amount. In the case of the *other money purchase arrangements*, the pension input amount is established by taking into account only the employer's contributions paid in respect of the member during the period of account in question.

Additionally, RPSM05102170 addresses the matter of contributions for directors or individuals connected to a controlling director. It states that, broadly, it will be accepted that a contribution will be treated as wholly and exclusively for the purposes of the trade, and so will be tax relievable, if it is paid in respect of a controlling director or a connected employee in line with a contribution that would have been made for an unconnected employee in a similar situation. Further detail, including the possibility of an Inspector challenging the allowability of a contribution, is given in BIM46000 onwards.

FUND ASSETS AND YIELD

3.26   **Chapter 4** describes the current investment rules. The funds of registered pension schemes receive considerable tax reliefs similar to the tax reliefs which applied to exempt approved schemes prior to A-Day. The investment yield of such schemes is free of income tax and capital gains tax, and lump sum benefits are free of tax subject to the limits described in **Chapter 4**.

Special tax consequences arise in respect of schemes (IRPS) investing in taxable property which includes residential property and personal chattels. These are detailed in **Chapter 12.**

The main tax reliefs and exemptions are:

- any income received by a registered scheme in respect of its investments, deposits or other activities are free of tax (*Finance Act 2004, s 186*);

- any profits or gains arising in respect of transactions in certificates of deposit are free of tax (*Income and Corporation Taxes Act 1988, s 56*);

- any underwriting commissions which are applied for the purpose of a registered scheme are free of any charge (*Finance Act 2004, s 186(1)(b)*);

- any profits from sale and repurchase agreements (Repos) and manufactured payments are free of tax (*SI 1995/3036*);

- there is no capital gains tax on gains on the disposal of investments (*Taxation of Chargeable Gains Act 1992, s 271*), including income from futures and options (*Finance Act 2004, s 186(3)*).

Income from futures contracts and options contracts are deemed to all be from investments as is any income derived from transactions relating to futures contracts or options contracts (*Finance Act 2004, s 186(3)*).

POTENTIAL TAX CHARGES

3.27   In general, there will be no tax charges under the registered scheme regime, with the following exceptions:

- in connection with any trading activities by the trustees;

- on any income which is derived from investments or deposits held as a member of a property investment LLP.

A property investment LLP is a limited liability partnership whose business consists wholly or mainly in the making of investments in land and the principal part of whose income is derived therefrom. Income, including any relevant stock lending fees, will be assessable to income tax. A gain arising from the acquisition or disposal of an investment is a chargeable gain liable to capital gains tax.

Charges will arise where unauthorised payments etc are made. These charges are described in **Chapters 8** and **14**, as appropriate.

VAT

3.28   It is possible to offset VAT incurred on scheme expenses for employers and trustees. Specialist advice is recommended. A summary of the main rules is given below.

Generally, VAT incurred in connection with investment activities cannot be reclaimed by the employer (unless the employer is the sole trustee). However, it can be reclaimed as input tax by the scheme if it makes taxable supplies or is otherwise VAT registrable and has a right to deduct input tax. The following are examples of costs related to investment activity:

- advice in connection with making investments;

- brokerage charges;

- rent and service charge collection for property holdings;

- producing records and accounts in connection with property purchases, lettings and disposals, investments etc;

- trustees services, ie services of a professional trustee in managing the assets of the fund;

- legal fees on behalf of representative beneficiaries in connection with changes in pension fund arrangements;

- custodian charges

VAT on management costs is regarded as the employer's business costs and can be reclaimed. These costs include:

- making arrangements for setting up a pension fund;

- management of the scheme, eg collection of contributions and payment of pensions;

- advice on a review of the scheme, and implementing any change to the scheme;

- accounting and auditing, insofar as they relate to the management of the scheme, eg preparation of annual accounts;

- actuarial valuations of the assets of the fund;

- general actuarial advice connected with the fund's administration;

- providing general statistics in connection with the performance of a fund's investments, properties etc;

- legal instructions and general legal advice including drafting of trust deeds insofar as they relate to the management of the scheme.

If the employer pays any of the above costs on behalf of the scheme it will be able to claim input tax in respect of the VAT incurred provided it holds a tax invoice made out in the company/business's name unless it is partially or fully exempt.

Chapter 4

Benefit rules and benefit crystallisation events

INTRODUCTION

4.1   The concept of imposing limits on the benefits payable by tax-advantaged pension schemes largely disappeared with A-Day (6 April 2006) and the introduction of the new pension tax regime under the *Finance Act 2004*. The exception to this is where transitional provisions contained in the *Pension Schemes (Modification of Rules of Existing Schemes) Regulations 2006 (SI 2006/364)* apply to a scheme and have not yet been disapplied by the trustees or managers of the scheme. These regulations operate so as to continue some of the pre A-Day limits, most notably the earnings cap, and are primarily designed to protect against a potential leap in scheme liabilities as a result of the removal of the old limits. The regulations are due to expire on 6 April 2011, and so trustees and managers of schemes, together with sponsoring employers, may wish to revisit scheme rules before then.

The new regime divides payments from registered pension schemes into authorised payments and unauthorised payments. If a payment is unauthorised, it does not mean it cannot be paid; it means that the payment is subject to a range of unauthorised payment charges which can in some cases be quite severe. **Chapter 14** provides more information on unauthorised payment charges.

Authorised payments have a more favourable tax treatment, and so it is important that member and survivor benefits paid from registered pension schemes should conform with the rules for authorised member payments contained in sections 164–171 of FA 2004. The tax treatment of authorised member payments varies. Depending on the payment, it can be tax-free, subject to income tax, or subject to the lifetime allowance charge (see **Chapter 10**). The main rules governing authorised member payments are:

- the pension rules;

- the lump sum rules;

- the pension death benefit rules;

- the lump sum death benefit rules.

The payment of a benefit from a registered pension scheme may be subject to the lifetime allowance of the person receiving the benefit or to the lifetime allowance of the person in respect of whom it is paid in the case of a death benefit. The payment of such a benefit, or the first payment of such a benefit if it is a pension, is known as a benefit crystallisation event (BCE).

4.1 *Benefit rules and benefit crystallisation events*

This chapter looks at the rules for authorised member payments, the minimum age for payment, pension sharing and the benefit crystallisation events.

PENSION RULES

4.2 There is no overall limit on the amount of pension which can be paid under the new regime, and the pre A-Day requirement that a member must have left employment for a benefit to be paid is removed (with the exception of ill health retirements and protected low pension ages in **4.30** below).

Pension can only be paid in one of the following forms post A-Day:

- Scheme pension (this *must* be paid under a defined benefit arrangement).

- Lifetime annuity.

- Unsecured pension before age 75 (income withdrawal or short-term annuity).

- Alternatively secured pension (ASP) after age 75 (income withdrawal).

Pensions will normally be taxed as earnings under the *Income Tax (Earnings and Pensions) Act 2003*.

Scheme pension

4.3 Scheme pension must be paid under a defined benefit arrangement and may be paid under a money purchase arrangement. It must meet the following conditions:

- It must be payable by the scheme administrator or by an insurance company selected by the scheme administrator.

- It must be payable in at least annual instalments until the member's death or until the later of the member's death and a guaranteed period of up to ten years.

- The level of scheme pension must not decrease from one year to the next except in permitted circumstances.

- If it is paid under a money purchase arrangement, the member must first have had the choice to select a lifetime annuity.

The permitted circumstances in which a scheme pension may decrease are:

- Reduction of an ill-health pension upon full or partial recovery.

- A reduction applying to all pensions in payment.

- Reduction between the ages of 60 and 65 to take account of integration with the state pension (bridging pension).

- Pension sharing order or provision.

- Forfeiture of pension under provisions allowed by the *Pensions Act 1995*.

- Court order.

- Abatement under a public service pension scheme.

- Certain other circumstances relating to the Pension Protection Fund, contracted-out rights affected by the *Gender Recognition Act 2004* and admission to the Royal Hospital at Chelsea.

Effect of reduction of pension

4.4   If the level of a pension decreases other than in permitted circumstances, future instalments will be subject to unauthorised payment charges.

Furthermore if the level of a pension in payment is reduced to below 80% of its original level, any tax-free lump sum paid in connection with the pension will become an unauthorised payment. Care must therefore be taken in any matter which involves the reduction or cessation of a pension in payment.

Lifetime annuity

4.5   A lifetime annuity may be paid under a money purchase arrangement. It may be purchased before age 75 either from uncrystallised funds or unsecured pension funds and after age 75 from an alternatively secured pension fund. It must meet the following conditions:

- It must be payable by an insurance company.

- The member must have had an opportunity to select the insurance company (open market option).

- It must be payable until the member's death or until the later of the member's death and a guaranteed period of up to ten years.

- It must not decrease in payment except where the variation relies on investment performance, tracks an investment index or tracks the Retail Prices Index. A lifetime annuity may also be reduced in consequence of a pension sharing order.

- No payment, either directly or indirectly, of a capital sum may be given on the member's death, with the exception of an annuity protection lump sum death benefit.

Where a guaranteed annuity is provided, it may be assigned during the guarantee period either by the terms of the member's will, or by the personal representatives, to allow:

- a testamentary disposition or the rights of those entitled on an intestacy; or

- an appropriation of the annuity to a legacy or a share or interest in an estate.

There is no firm definition of the meaning of the term 'annuity' in the legislation. Ultimately, the decision must be one of legal opinion if there is any uncertainty in the minds of the trustees or administrator as to the appropriate risk of a product.

Compulsory insurance

4.6   It was originally stated in the *Finance Act 2004, Sch 28, para 2(1)* that pensions had to be secured with an insurance company for any schemes which had less than 50 members. After consultation it was decided to drop this requirement, and it was removed by *Sch 10* to the *Finance Act 2005*.

Unsecured pension

4.7   Unsecured pension is only available under money purchase arrangements. It may take the form of a short-term annuity, purchased with pension scheme funds and payable for no more than five years (and not beyond age 75). However, unsecured pension is more likely to take the form of income withdrawal.

The maximum amount of income withdrawal that may be drawn annually is 120% of a notional annuity rate calculated using tables drawn up by the Government Actuary's Department (GAD). The GAD rates are based on a single-life, non-escalating annuity for a person of the same age and gender as the member. Withdrawal rates vary with gilt yields published in the *Financial Times*.

The minimum amount of income withdrawal that may be drawn annually is nil. This makes it possible to draw a lump sum from a money purchase arrangement without actually having to draw any income, although the funds will have been crystallised for lifetime allowance purposes.

Withdrawals may be taken in regular instalments (eg monthly) or paid as one or more lump sums in the year. The amount of income drawn can be varied at any time subject to any restrictions in scheme rules. Most providers will be flexible in this regard, but income withdrawal offered by an occupational pension scheme may have limitations.

Income withdrawal payments are subject to income tax under PAYE.

Unsecured pension may not normally start before age 50, or age 55 from 6 April 2010. The exception to this is if rights are brought into payment on grounds of ill health. Income withdrawal may continue until age 75 at which point it would be treated as alternatively secured pension (see **4.11**) if it is not used to purchase an annuity at that time.

Note that there is a second lifetime allowance test whenever someone with unsecured pension reaches age 75 or buys an annuity with the unsecured pension fund before age 75. See **Chapter 13**.

A pension commencement lump sum may be paid in connection with unsecured pension. The lump sum amount is one third of the amount designated for unsecured pension, ie 25% of the funds being crystallised. The amount to be tested against the lifetime allowance is the sum of the lump sum and the funds designated for unsecured pension.

Funds designated for income withdrawal may be transferred from one arrangement to another. See **Chapter 6** for more information.

Flexibility

4.8   The post A-Day tax regime permits significant flexibility in how members may draw benefits from money purchase arrangements, whether they are occupational schemes or personal pensions. The new rules permit partial vesting and benefits may be vested in different ways. For example, it is permissible to use some funds to buy a guaranteed lifetime annuity, a 5 year short term annuity, or designate funds within the arrangement for income withdrawal and still leave a proportion of the benefits in the arrangement as uncrystallised. This may be a useful consideration in retirement planning, where funds could be used in part to buy an annuity if market conditions are favourable while any portion of the fund that remains uncrystallised could be returned tax-free on death before age 75. This flexibility is recognised in HMRC's *Registered Pension Schemes Manual*.

RPSM09100390: Authorised benefits: Member choice (or member designation):

'The legislation allows a registered pension scheme to give its members certain choices over when and in what manner they draw benefits. In particular, where benefits are held in a money purchase arrangement, they can be drawn before age 75 direct from the scheme as an unsecured pension (either direct from the scheme through income withdrawal or through the purchase of a short-term annuity contract with an insurance company).

Where dealing with the payment of an unsecured pension the legislation refers to this member choice as "designation" (i.e. the member can designate when and how they draw their benefits within guidelines).

The precise options open to a member of a registered pension scheme as to how and when they take their benefits will depend on the type of scheme (i.e. whether **money purchase** or not) and the degree of flexibility the scheme is prepared to offer its members.

For example, a member of an **occupational pension scheme** that provides **defined benefits** is likely to have a more limited choice over when they can draw their benefits and no option over the format. (Under a **defined benefits arrangement** the pension can only be paid in one way, as a **scheme pension**.) Whereas a member who holds their benefits in one or more money purchase arrangements within a registered pension scheme is likely to have a number of options over the time of payment and the form of those benefits.

The member may also be allowed to phase in their entitlements held under an **arrangement** over time. This is dealt with in RPSM09100400.

The precise options available to a member will be specified in the scheme rules.'

Income withdrawal rate reviews

4.9   The maximum income withdrawal level must be reviewed every five years, or earlier at the member's request on the anniversary of the start of income withdrawal. An anniversary review may be favourable for the member if gilt yields have improved at that time. If a review is carried out on an anniversary, a five year review will not be needed until five years after the anniversary review.

The maximum income withdrawal level must also be reviewed if a subsequent income withdrawal designation is made, if part of the income withdrawal fund is used to buy a lifetime annuity or if the income withdrawal fund is split under a pension sharing order.

Transitional provisions

4.10 In the case of someone who commenced taking income withdrawals before 6 April 2006 (income drawdown), income withdrawal is treated as starting on 6 April 2006. Providers had until 5 April 2008 to apply the new withdrawal limits to such funds.

Funds already designated for income withdrawal before 6 April 2006 will need to be ringfenced from any other funds in the same arrangement that are designated for income withdrawal after 6 April 2006.

Funds designated for income withdrawal before 6 April 2006 are exempt from the second lifetime allowance test (see **Chapter 13**) under transitional provisions. As long as such funds accept no new income withdrawal designations, they will not be subject to a lifetime allowance test upon the member reaching age 75 or earlier purchase of an annuity or transfer to a qualifying recognised overseas pension scheme.

Alternatively secured pension

4.11 Alternatively secured pension (ASP) is the same as for income withdrawal under age 75 with three important differences.

- The GAD rate applicable will be the rate for a 75 year old no matter how old the member actually is.

- A minimum amount of 55% of the GAD rate must be drawn each year (a change introduced in the *FA 2007* amid Treasury fears of possible tax abuse), and the maximum amount that may be drawn is 90% of the GAD rate.

- The minimum and maximum income limits must reviewed every year instead of every five years.

If less than the 55% minimum amount is drawn, the scheme administrator is liable for a 40% tax charge on the difference between the 55% minimum and the amount actually drawn.

The first review year starts on the member's 75th birthday and the scheme administrator must review the maximum level of income on each subsequent anniversary or up to 60 days before the anniversary. If a member uses part of his ASP fund to buy a lifetime annuity, the maximum withdrawal amount will not be reduced until after the next review.

It is possible to transfer ASP funds from one arrangement to another, but if this is done the transferred amount must be ringfenced within the receiving arrangement, and the administrator of the receiving arrangement must be notified of the member's minimum and maximum withdrawal amounts and the sum already drawn during the year.

As an alternative to annuitisation ASP appears unattractive unless someone has a genuine objection to the mortality pooling that comes with purchasing an annuity, or even just an objection to leaving money to an insurance company.

LUMP SUM RULES

Pension commencement lump sum

4.12   Under the post-A-Day tax regime a pension commencement lump sum must only be paid in connection with a pension coming into payment. The pre A-Day possibilities for cash only schemes no longer exist except where provided for under transitional protection. Similarly, members who had continued rights pre A-Day will no longer be able to take a lump sum at retirement and defer drawing the associated pension.

Pension commencement lump sums must be paid within the period of six months before and twelve months after the date on which the connected pension commences. Entitlement cannot arise after the age of 75, but a pension commencement lump sum may still be paid after age 75 if entitlement arose before then and it is paid within twelve months. How the lump sum is calculated depends on whether the arrangement it comes from is a defined benefit or money purchase arrangement.

In a money purchase arrangement the lump sum is expressed as one third of the annuity purchase price, where a lifetime annuity is provided, or one third of the sums designated for income withdrawal. This equates to 25% of funds being vested, but expressing it in such a manner ensures the lump sum calculation is tied to the amount of funds actually crystallised at the time.

Calculation of the pension commencement lump sum is more complicated under a defined benefit arrangement. The lump sum is calculated according to the formula $\frac{1}{4} \times (LS + AC)$ where:

- LS is the amount of lump sum actually taken; and

- AC is the amount crystallised by the scheme pension coming into payment (normally 20 times the initial rate of scheme pension in a defined benefit arrangement).

In a defined benefit arrangement where a lump sum is provided by the commutation of pension, the maximum amount of lump sum depends on the commutation rate used within the scheme. The lump sum formula may more usefully be expressed as:

$(20 \times \text{full pension} \times \text{commutation factor})/(20 + 3 \times \text{commutation factor})$

Therefore a £10,000 pa pension in a defined benefit scheme with a commutation rate of, say, £14 per £1 pa may be partially commuted for a lump sum of up to:

$(20 \times 10,000 \times 14)/(20 + 3 \times 14) = £45,161$

The residual pension will be $10,000 - 45,161/14 = £6,774.21$ pa.

Note that the lump sum will always be $6^2/_3$ times the residual pension in a defined benefit arrangement unless transitional protection applies.

If a person has taken a lump sum prior to A-Day, this will be taken into consideration for the purpose of calculating the maximum lump sum that may be taken from the same arrangement after A-Day. Additionally, any person who has taken a lump sum prior to A-Day, but deferred his or her pension until after A-Day, will not be permitted to take a further tax-free lump sum in relation to that employment.

Lump sums from AVCs

4.13   Any rights derived from additional voluntary contributions (AVCs) that were not commutable before A-Day because they were started after 8 April 1987 may be commutable post A-Day subject to scheme rules permitting.

Where money purchase AVCs have been paid under a defined benefit scheme, the entire AVC fund may be used first to provide a pension commencement lump sum before it is necessary to commute defined benefit pension, subject again to scheme rules permitting.

Two or more schemes relating to the same employment

4.14   Prior to A-Day the HMRC maximum lump sum was based on final remuneration and service in an employment. Where two occupational pension schemes related to the same employment, it was possible to draw the lump sum entirely from one scheme. This was useful if one of the schemes was defined benefit and the other money purchase, as the member could avoid commuting valuable defined benefit pension and take his lump sum, up to the maximum permitted, from his money purchase scheme instead.

Payment of pension commencement lump sum under the post A-Day rules is linked to the pension being brought into payment, not the member's service with an employer. It is therefore no longer possible to draw lump sum from a separate scheme of the same employment in the way it was before A-Day. This is, however, still possible if a member has both defined benefit and money purchase rights *in the same scheme*, for example by having benefits in two sections under the same scheme.

Overall lump sum limit

4.15   Unless transitional protection applies the maximum pension commencement lump sum that may be taken tax-free is limited to 25% of the available lifetime allowance. This is calculated according to the following formula:

¼ × (CSLA − AAC × CSLA/PSLA)

where

CSLA is the standard lifetime allowance at date of vesting

AAC is the aggregate of the amounts crystallised by previous benefit vestings

PSLA is the standard lifetime allowance at each respective previous crystallisation event.

The following examples from the HMRC Registered Pension Schemes Manual illustrate this.

RPSM09104550: Pension commencement lump sum: Maximum amount: Available portion (extract):

Example 1 − calculating the available portion of the member's lump sum allowance

John has £450,000 of **uncrystallised funds** in a **money purchase arrangement**. He does not have an enhanced **lifetime allowance**. In the 2010/11 tax year he decides to use all the funds held in the **arrangement** to provide an **unsecured pension** and the maximum **pension commencement lump sum** permitted.

Before paying out benefits the **scheme administrator** writes to John telling him that he will crystallise £450,000 for lifetime allowance purposes, which represents 25% of the **standard lifetime allowance** for that tax year (25% of £1.8 million). The scheme administrator also asks John to:

1. provide a statement confirming his anticipated available lifetime allowance at the time he wishes to draw benefits, expressed as a percentage of the standard lifetime allowance for that current tax year, based on statements he will have been provided by other scheme administrators, where benefits have been crystallised previously under other **registered pension schemes**, and.

2. confirm whether or not he is entitled to an enhanced lifetime allowance.

John has used up 85% of his lifetime allowance previously. John confirms that he will have 15% of the standard lifetime allowance of £1.8 million available when he draws benefits. He also confirms he is not entitled to an enhanced lifetime allowance.

The scheme administrator applies the percentage available (15%) to the standard lifetime allowance for that year (£1.8 million), and divides this by four to obtain the available portion of the lump sum allowance.

So 15% × £1.8 million = £270,000.

This figure divided by four gives £67,500.

The permitted maximum is therefore capped at £67,500.

The scheme administrator will also have identified a **chargeable amount** of £180,000 (£450,000 − £270,000). This can be paid as a **lifetime allowance excess lump sum** (minus the **lifetime allowance charge** due).

RPSM09104560: Pension commencement lump sum: Maximum amount: Available portion (extract):

Example 2 – calculating the available portion of the member's lump sum allowance

Chris has £450,000 of **uncrystallised funds** in a **money purchase arrangement**. He is also entitled to an enhanced **lifetime allowance** of 150% of the **standard lifetime allowance**. (So he has a lifetime allowance enhancement factor of 0.5). Chris has not protected any lump sum rights in existence on 5 April 2006.

In the 2010/11 tax year Chris decides to use all the funds to provide an **unsecured pension** and the maximum **pension commencement lump sum**. In this tax year his lifetime allowance is £2.7 million (£1.8 million + {£1.8 million × 0.5}).

Chris has already used up 90% of the standard lifetime allowance. So at the point he will draw benefits, he will have an available lifetime allowance of 60% of the standard lifetime allowance (150% – 90%). This means Chris can crystallise £1.08 million (60% of £1.8 million) before exceeding his available lifetime allowance.

Before Chris draws benefits the **scheme administrator** writes to him asking him for details of previous crystallisations under other schemes and whether or not he is entitled to an enhanced lifetime allowance.

Chris provides the scheme administrator with the number on the HMRC certificate confirming his entitlement to an enhanced lifetime allowance as evidence of his entitlement. He also tells the administrator that he has already used 90% of the standard lifetime allowance.

The scheme administrator uses this information to work out whether or not Chris has enough available lifetime allowance to cover the amount crystallising under their scheme at that time. The scheme administrator can also use this information to identify what Chris's available portion of the lump sum allowance actually is.

The scheme administrator now knows that Chris has used up 90% of the current £1.8 million standard lifetime allowance at the point benefits are crystallising for lifetime allowance purposes. This means that previous crystallisations, adjusted by reference to the changes in standard lifetime allowance level, or 'AAC', represent £1.62 million (90% of £1.8 million).

So the scheme administrator knows that the available portion of the lump sum allowance is a quarter of £180,000 (£1.8 million – £1.62 million). This is £45,000.

The permitted maximum for Chris is therefore £45,000 (not the applicable amount of £112,500).

But no **chargeable amount** arises, as the amount crystallising is covered by his available lifetime allowance.

Protected lump sums

4.16   Many members of defined benefit schemes will enjoy a higher level of tax-free lump sum under the new rules if their rules provide the necessary flexibility. Members of most personal pension schemes will effectively enjoy a continuation of their existing entitlements, namely 25% of their fund values. Members of occupational money purchase schemes are less likely to benefit from the 25% limit, as their existing 3n/80ths or uplifted 80ths final salary formula may have been higher due to lower levels of contributions. However, paras *31–34, Sch 36, Finance Act 2004,* offer protection for accrued lump sums greater than 25% in cases where all the following conditions are met:

(a)   the relevant member must become entitled to all pensions payable to him under the scheme on the same date;

(b)   the pension scheme must have been an approved occupational pension scheme (meaning approved under *Ch I, Pt XIV, ICTA 1988,* a relevant statutory scheme, a Parliamentary fund, a *section 32* policy or a former superannuation fund under *s 208, ICTA1970*);

(c)   the value of the member's uncrystallised lump sum rights on 5 April 2006 must have exceeded 25% of the value of his uncrystallised rights on 5 April 2006;

(d)   where the lump sum entitlement at A-Day exceeded £375,000, notice of intention to rely on either primary or enhanced protection must *not* have been given;

(e)   the member must not have requested and received a transfer of his benefits out of the scheme on or after 6 April 2006.

If all pension rights of a member are transferred out of his scheme post A-Day protection will be lost unless the transfer is part of a block transfer (see **4.20**) or rights are transferred to a buy–out policy upon scheme wind-up. If a partial transfer occurs, the protected lump sum in the ceding scheme must be reduced by one quarter of the transfer value.

Valuing lump sum rights at 5 April 2006

4.17   To assess whether lump sum protection applies to a member's rights within an arrangement, it is necessary to value the member's uncrystallised lump sum and pension rights in the arrangement as at 5 April 2006. This can prove to be a complicated matter due to the need to have regard to pre A-Day HMRC limits.

The percentage of lump sum rights is determined by use of the formula:

$\text{VULSR/VUR} \times 100$

where:

VULSR is the value of uncrystallised lump sum rights on 5 April 2006

VUR is the value of uncrystallised rights on 5 April 2006

VUR is calculated as a member's fund value in the case of a money purchase arrangement, and as 20 times the annual pension in the case of a defined benefit arrangement. VULSR is the member's lump sum rights under the scheme rules. In both cases it is to be assumed that the member had become entitled to payment of the benefits on 5 April 2006, that he was in good physical and mental health, and that he had reached either age 60, or any earlier age which was specified at 10 December 2003 as the minimum age at which benefits could be paid without reduction. For the purpose of the formula above, pension and lump sum rights must not exceed the relevant HMRC limit as at 5 April 2006.

For example, if an active member was subject to the pre '87 regime with:

- 30 years potential service to his normal retirement date; and

- 20 years service accrued to 5 April 2006

then the HMRC maximum lump sum at 5 April 2006 is the higher of:

$3/80 \times 20 \times$ Final Remuneration, and

$20/30 \times (120/80 \times$ Final Remuneration – Lump Sum Retained Benefits)

In view of the member's service and his relevant tax regime, the uplifted 80ths scale applies. This gives a maximum lump sum of 120/80, less lump sum retained benefits, multiplied by the formula:

N/NS

where:

N is service accrued to 5 April 2006

NS is potential service to normal retirement date

(20 years and 30 years respectively in this example – see para **8.37** of the Practice Notes IR12 (2001)).

However:

(a) retained benefits can be ignored if the member's P60 earnings from pensionable employment did not exceed £50,000 in the tax year 2004/05, whether or not he is a controlling director (where pensionable service ceased during 2004/05, a pro rata calculation applies);

(b) where pensionable service ceased before 6 April 2004, retained benefits can be ignored if P60 earnings in the last complete tax year before date of leaving did not exceed £25,000;

(c) retained benefits may be ignored in other circumstances where an easement under the Practice Notes IR12 (2001) already applies;

(d) lump sum retained benefits need only be taken into account for pre '87 members, not for '87 – '89 regime members or for post '89 regime members.

Deferred pensioners will have their maximum lump sum revalued up to 5 April 2006 in line with increases in the Retail Prices Index (paras 10.15 to 10.18 of the Practice Notes IR12 (2001)). Active members are treated as having left service on 5 April 2006.

Where a lump sum is calculated as 2.25 times the initial pension payable and the arrangement is a money purchase arrangement, the notional pension for the purpose of the 2.25 times pension calculation may be derived by dividing the member's fund at 5 April 2006 by 20 or by the appropriate income drawdown factor published by the Government Actuary's Department and applicable at 5 April 2006. See the following example from the HMRC Registered Pension Schemes Manual.

Example of valuing lump sum rights

4.18

RPSM03105130:

'Valuing lump sum rights: Example 3

Facts: Sam has uncrystallised rights in a personal pension with a value of £1.3 million on 5 April 2006. She also has uncrystallised rights in a retirement benefit scheme of her current employer. She has 1989 rights in the scheme. At 5 April 2006, she has 15 years' pensionable service and pensionable earnings of £105,600 (due to the 'earnings cap' which is lower than her actual salary of £175,000). Her normal retirement date is 5 April 2010. The personal pension benefits are not a retained benefit as they relate to a wholly concurrent employment.

Step 1: Calculate Sam's lump sum rights under paragraph 25, schedule 36 Finance Act 2004.

Sam's rights in the personal pension are worth £1.3 million but £50,000 of these are 'protected rights' which cannot be paid as lump sums. Her uncrystallised lump sum rights are therefore 25% of £1,250,000, giving £312,500.

Her crystallised lump sum rights in the retirement benefit scheme are the greater of

– 3/80 × 15 (years) × £105,600 = £59,400, and

– 2¼ × the initial gross pension from the scheme.

She has money purchase rights in the scheme valued at £700,000 on 5 April 2006. This is the value determined by paragraphs 8 and 9 schedule 36 Finance Act 2004. To determine the amount of annual pension payable from the scheme, the capital value (£700,000) could be divided by 20, or an annuity rate taken from the GAD tables on 5 April 2006 could be applied to the capital value. In this example, the divisor of 20 is used giving an annual pension of £35,000. Multiplying the pension by 2¼ gives £78,750 which is the greater lump sum of the two calculations above.

Step 2: Calculate Sam's uncrystallised lump sum rights under paragraph 26 schedule 36 Finance Act 2004 (the HMRC limit test).

In this instance the calculation of the rights in the retirement benefit scheme is the same as at Step 1.

If the GAD tables had been used to determine the annual pension payable, the calculations at Step 1 and 2 may have produced different results. If the valuation assumption in paragraph 25(7) schedule 36 Finance Act 2004 applied, Sam would be deemed to be 60 (her normal retirement age) and that age would have been used in Step 1 for the GAD calculation. Her actual age (55) would be used for the GAD calculation at Step 2.

Where the lump sum value requires an annual pension figure, the same method (GAD table or divisor of 20) must be used in Steps 1 and 2. If the pension is a defined benefit pension the divisor of 20 must be used.

Summary – Sam's uncrystallised lump sum rights are £391,250 (£312,500 plus £78,750).

Valuing lump sums – more than one scheme relating to the same employment

4.19   The amount of lump sum rights that may be protected must not exceed HMRC limits as at 5 April 2006. Similarly, in working out the amount of a member's pension rights for the 25% test, HMRC limits must not be exceeded. The situation is particularly complicated if a member has rights under more than one arrangement relating to the same employment. In this case, where the aggregate lump sums or pension rights exceed HMRC limits, each benefit must be reduced in proportion to the excess of aggregate rights. This may mean that some lump sums which were thought to benefit from protection actually do not, and vice versa. The following examples, reproduced from the HMRC Registered Pension Schemes Manual, illustrate this.

RPSM03105560 – Technical Pages: Protecting pension rights from tax charges: Lump sums: Scheme specific protection: Example 1 valuation where lump sum is over HMRC limit

Valuing lump sum benefits exceeding 25%: lump sum benefits on 5 April 2006 exceed HMRC limits: example 1

Asif has pension and lump sum rights for a single employment on 5 April 2006. His total pension rights are £210,000 and total lump sum rights are £60,000. These rights are held in three schemes. His rights are held in a single **arrangement** under each scheme.

Asif's maximum permitted lump sum for the employment under HMRC limits was calculated as £54,000. His maximum permitted pension under HMRC limits was greater than £210,000.

Therefore VULSR must be adjusted whilst VUR remains the same.

The position before adjustment was as follows

Scheme 1 – pension rights of £60,000; lump sum £15,000; lump sum percentage 25%

Scheme 2 – pension rights of £60,000 ; lump sum £20,000; lump sum percentage 33.33%

Scheme 3 – pension rights of £90,000; lump sum £25,000; lump sum percentage 27.78%

The reduction in Asif's lump sum rights from £60,000 to £54,000 must be apportioned amongst the three schemes. The legislation specifies that the apportionment is as follows.

Scheme lump sum – (excess lump sum × scheme lump sum/total lump sums)

So for scheme 1 the apportionment would be

£15,000 – (£6000 × £15,000/£60,000) = £13,500

After adjustment, Asif's lump sum percentage from each of the three schemes becomes

Scheme 1 – pension rights of £60,000; lump sum £13,500; scheme percentage 22.5%

Scheme 2 – pension rights of £60,000; lump sum £18,000; scheme percentage 30%

Scheme 3 – pension rights of £90,000; lump sum £22,500; scheme percentage 25%

So after the required adjustment, only the rights in Scheme 2 qualify for protection as the lump percentage exceeds 25% of the uncrystallised pension rights in that scheme.

Rights in schemes 1 and 3 may be taken at 25% because the normal rules for pension commencement lump sums in Schedule 29 Finance Act 2004 apply to the rights under those two schemes.

RPSM03105570 – Technical Pages: Protecting pension rights from tax charges: Lump sums: Scheme specific protection: Example valuation where pension is over HMRC limit

Example of valuing lump sum benefits exceeding 25%: pension benefits on 5 April 2006 exceed HMRC limits

An adjustment to the value of an individual's uncrystallised pension rights also triggers a re-calculation of the lump sum percentage available in multiple schemes.

Lesley has pension and lump sum rights in two schemes for a sole employment on 5 April 2006. She has total pension rights of £200,000 and her lump sum rights are £44,000. Her rights are held in a single arrangement under each scheme. The £44,000 is less than her maximum permitted lump sum under HMRC limits but her maximum permitted pension under HMRC limits is valued at £160,000.

The position before adjustment was as follows

Scheme A – pension rights of £80,000; lump sum £20,000; lump sum percentage 25%

Scheme B – pension rights of £120,000; lump sum £24,000; lump sum percentage 20%

The reduction in Lesley's pension rights from £200,000 to £160,000 must be apportioned between the two schemes.

In scheme A, the value of the pension rights is adjusted as follows, £80,000 – (£40,000 × £80,000/£200,000) which gives a figure of £64,000.

In scheme B, the value of the pension rights is adjusted as follows, £120,000 – (£40,000 × £120,000/£200,000 which gives a figure of £96,000.

After adjustment, Lesley's lump sum percentages from the two schemes become

Scheme A – pension rights of £64,000; lump sum £20,000; lump sum percentage 31.25%

Scheme B – pension rights of £96,000; lump sum £24,000; lump sum percentage 25%

So after the required adjustment, the rights in Scheme A qualify for protection, as the lump sum percentage exceeds 25% of Lesley's uncrystallised pension rights in that scheme.

Block transfers

4.20   Block transfers provide an easement to the loss of lump sum protection (and low normal pension age protection) for an individual's rights on making a transfer, the main purpose being to avoid unnecessary restrictions on genuine corporate reconstructions. If a member with a protected lump sum becomes a member of another pension arrangement as a result of a block transfer, he will not lose his lump sum protection. Successive block transfers can be made without affecting protection. It is therefore important to understand the conditions applicable to a block transfer. HMRC describe a block transfer as follows:

'A transfer is a block transfer if it involves the transfer in a single transaction of all the sums and assets representing accrued rights under the scheme from which the transfer is made which relate to the member and at least one other member of that pension scheme. To be a single transaction

● all of the sums and assets must be transferred from the transferring scheme to only one receiving scheme. Two or more partial transfers to two or more different schemes cannot be a transfer in a single transaction; and

● the transaction must be made under a single agreement for a single transfer between the two schemes.

It is not necessary that all of the sums and assets are all physically passed from the transferring scheme to the receiving scheme on the same day – there may be legal or administration reasons why this is not possible. However they should all be transferred in relation to the agreement to transfer and within a reasonable timescale.

There is no restriction on the type of registered pension scheme receiving the transfer. So a personal pension scheme can receive a block transfer as long as the other block transfer conditions are met.'

Note that for protection to continue to apply, the member, whose rights are transferring under the block transfer, must not have been a member of the receiving scheme for more than 12 months before the date of transfer. This is a point that is sometimes overlooked and will be very important if employees' deferred pension rights in one scheme are being transferred to a successor scheme in the same employment.

Payment of protected lump sum

4.21   Once it comes to be paid, the amount of a protected lump sum is calculated according to the following complicated formula:

$VULSR \times CSLA/FSLA + ALSA$, where

$ALSA = ¼ \times (LS + AC - VUR \times CSLA/FSLA)$

VULSR is the value of uncrystallised lump sum rights on 5 April 2006

CSLA is the current standard lifetime allowance (i.e. at the time of paying the lump sum)

FSLA is the lifetime allowance for 2006/07 (£1.5 million)

LS is the amount of lump sum actually taken

AC is the amount crystallised by bringing the annual pension into payment, and

VUR is the value of uncrystallised rights under the scheme on 5 April 2006.

If ALSA (additional lump sum amount) is a negative number, it is taken to be nil.

The formula set out above reflects an amendment made by the *Finance Act 2008*. Prior to the amendment, ALSA was only taken into account in the formula if relevant benefit accrual had occurred post A-Day. Relevant benefit accrual is, in the case of a money purchase arrangement, the payment of a contribution and, in the case of a defined benefit arrangement, the payment of pension above a certain level that is not easily ascertained and which consequently led to the amendment of the formula.

If use of the protected lump sum formula leads to a figure that is actually less than the normal formula for calculating a pension commencement lump sum, the normal calculation can be used instead.

Note that post A-Day scheme administrators are not obliged to pay the maximum protected lump sum. If scheme rules permit they may pay a lump sum of up to the protected amount.

Stand-alone lump sum

4.22 The *Taxation of Pension Schemes (Transitional Provisons) (Amendment No 2) Order, SI 2006/04* provides rules for the calculation of stand-alone lump sums. A stand-alone lump sum is a tax-free lump sum which constitutes the whole of a person's rights under a pension scheme on 5 April 2006. It includes not just the scenario of a cash only scheme but also the situation where the maximum HMRC approvable lump sum is greater than the value of the commutable pension rights on 5 April 2006. As long as there is no relevant benefit accrual post A-Day (which would be the case if there were no further pensionable service under a defined benefit arrangement and no further contributions paid under a money purchase arrangement) the lump sum may be paid tax-free whatever its value has grown to by investment growth or revaluation.

Protected lump sums – interaction with overall lump sum limit

4.23 The maximum amount of pension commencement lump sum that can be paid is normally limited to 25% of the available lifetime allowance (see **4.15**). Protected lump sums which are greater than 25% override the above restriction, meaning that a member who does not register for primary or enhanced protection may continue to have a lump sum entitlement greater than £375,000 if that entitlement was greater than 25% of the value of his rights at A-Day. The protection conditions in paras 31–34, Sch 36, *Finance Act 2004* must be met.

Short service refund lump sum

4.24 Where a member of an occupational pension scheme has less than two years' qualifying service, refunds of contributions made by the member will be permitted, and will be taxed at 20% on the first £10,800 and at 40% on any excess (*FA 2004, Ch 5, s 205*). See **4.25** below if interest is paid on a refund of contributions.

Scheme administration member payment

4.25 A short service refund lump sum may only be paid up to the amount of member contributions actually made. If a refund of member contributions is paid from a money purchase scheme, it may incorporate investment gains or losses. If the sum paid to the member is higher than the amount of his contributions due to investment gains, or if interest is otherwise added to the refund payment, the investment gain or interest would not fall within the parameters of a short service refund lump sum. However, the investment gain or interest could still be an authorised payment if it falls within the parameters of a scheme administration member payment. See the following extract from the Registered Pension Schemes Manual.

RPSM09104740 – Technical Pages: Member benefits: Lump sums: Short service refund lump sum: Interest on payment

Interest paid on the short service refund lump sum

The definition of a short service refund lump sum includes an upper limit equal to the amount of actual contributions made by the member to the scheme. But the scheme rules may provide for the refund to consist of other monies on top of the actual contributions being refunded. The **scheme administrator** must determine the nature of the payment according to the scheme rules. The interest may be paid as a separately calculated amount or may form part of the lump sum payment.

Interest as a separately calculated amount

A registered pension scheme's rules may provide for interest to be paid in addition to the contributions being refunded. The interest may arise simply because of a delay in making a payment or may be a payment over and above the computed lump sum for some other reason. If it qualifies to be treated as a **scheme administration member payment** (see below) for tax purposes, a payment of interest on top of the refunded contributions is an authorised payment.

A scheme administration member payment is a payment for the administration or management of the scheme. Such payments should be made on an arm's length, commercial basis. So any interest paid by a scheme on a refund of contributions should be no more than a reasonable commercial rate if it is to be a scheme administration member payment. Any excess will be an **unauthorised member payment** and taxed accordingly – see RPSM04104020 and RPSM04104040.

Interest payments associated with a short service refund lump sum that meet the definition of scheme administration member payment are taxable under section 369 Income Tax (Trading and Other Income) Act 2005 (formerly Case III Schedule D). The scheme administrator should make the payment without deducting income tax, and the recipient should include the interest in a self-assessment tax return or notify their HMRC income tax office of liability if they do not receive a notice to make a return.

Interest as part of the lump sum

If the contributions to be refunded are less than the statutory maximum then schemes may be able to provide for interest to be paid as part of the lump sum. For example, the lump sum may be computed with reference to an interest rate. If the interest is part of the lump sum, and the lump sum paid is within the statutory maximum, the tax treatment set out in section 205 Finance Act 2004 applies.

Serious ill-health lump sum

4.26 Serious ill-health commutation will still be permitted for registered pension schemes, out of uncrystallised benefits. The administrator must obtain written medical evidence that the member's life expectancy is less than one year and must notify HMRC. There will be no tax liability on the payment if the lifetime allowance is not exceeded. However, if a member in circumstances of serious ill health with a life expectancy of less than a year fails to exercise an option to wholly commute their benefits, the value of the benefits foregone may be liable to inheritance tax.

Triviality

4.27 Trivial commutation is still permitted but this is no longer on a scheme-by-scheme basis. The aggregate of all existing pension benefits must be within 1% of the prevailing lifetime allowance and there is only a 12-month opportunity in which to commute. All rights under a scheme must be extinguished by the lump sum triviality payment and income tax will be charged on 75% of the commuted value under PAYE. Tax is chargeable on 100% of the commuted value if it relates to pension which has already been brought into payment. Where too much income tax has been deducted under PAYE, a special form (P53A) can be used to reclaim overpayments.

A trivial commutation lump sum is only payable between the ages of 60 and 75 and if some lifetime allowance remains available to the member (although the lump sum itself does not count towards the lifetime allowance).

Since, generally, all entitlements of the member under the scheme must be extinguished by the payment of a trivial commutation lump sum, this means that it would also be necessary to commute dependants' pensions or to establish them as a separate arrangement under the scheme.

It is intended to introduce easements to the triviality rules under an amendment made by the *Finance Act 2008*. This would once again permit triviality payments to be made on a scheme-by-scheme basis, but only from occupational pension schemes and where the following conditions are met:

(a)   The payment does not exceed £2,000,

(b)   The member is between ages 60 and 75,

(c)   The member is not a controlling director,

(d)   The payment extinguishes all of the member's rights under all related schemes, and

(e)   The member had not transferred any rights out of any related schemes within the previous three years.

These measures are still in draft form. It is also intended to introduce further provisions to permit the commutation of small 'stranded pots' in certain limited circumstances. Regulations are expected to come into force in late 2008.

A trivial commutation payment may also be made where an occupational pension scheme is winding up and the commutation payment is less than 1% of the lifetime allowance. The following additional conditions must be met:

(a)   Some lifetime allowance remains available,

(b)   The commutation payment extinguishes the member's benefits under the scheme,

(c)   The payment is made before the member's 75th birthday,

(d)   The employer is not contributing to another scheme in respect of the member, and

(e)   The employer gives an undertaking to HMRC not to make any further contributions in respect of the member within a year of the date of payment.

Note, however, that where a winding-up lump sum is to be paid, there is no aggregation requirement and the minimum age limit of 60 does not apply.

Excessive lump sums

4.28   HMRC gives the following explanation of the treatment of the payment of excessive lump sums:

'RPSM09104030: What happens when the limits on authorised lump sums are exceeded? (extract):

If a registered pension scheme makes a lump sum payment that does not fit into any of the seven authorised member lump sum payment definitions it is an **unauthorised** member payment, and will be taxed as such (see RPSM04104020 and RPSM04104040).

Where a scheme makes a payment that meets the definition of an authorised lump sum payment, but the amount paid simply exceeds the limit specified in the legislation, this does not mean that the whole payment becomes unauthorised in all cases.

For the following lump sum payments

a pension commencement lump sum,

a stand-alone lump sum – see RPSM03105155 and RPSM03105202,

a short service refund lump sum,

a refund of excess contributions lump sum, and

a winding-up lump sum (which is capped to 1% of the standard lifetime allowance at the time of payment),

the part of the payment that is within limits will still represent an authorised lump sum payment, as appropriate. Any excess will not be treated as being part of that lump sum payment, and will become either

another form of authorised lump sum payment or scheme administration member payment (where it falls within the relevant definition), or an unauthorised member payment, and be taxed as such.

With the other forms of authorised member lump sum payments, either

the limit is an integral part of the definition (so if the limit is breached the whole payment falls out of the definition, as with payment of a trivial commutation lump sum), or

there are no limits as such, although the amounts paid are tested for lifetime allowance purposes (as with payment of a serious ill-health lump sum or lifetime allowance excess lump sum).'

PENSION AGES

Normal minimum pension age

4.29   Pensions payable to members of registered pension schemes must not come into payment before the member has reached normal minimum pension age. This is currently age 50 but will increase to age 55 with effect from 6 April 2010. The exception to this is where a pension is brought into payment on grounds of ill health. An ill-health pension is subject to the following rules:

- the member must have left the employment to which the pension relates; and

- the administrator must obtain proper medical evidence that the member is incapable of continuing in his current occupation.

An ill-health pension may cease, where scheme rules permit or require, if the member recovers sufficiently to return to his original job.

Protected low retirement age

4.30   Transitional provisions exist to protect low normal retirement ages that members of registered pension schemes may have been entitled to on 5 April 2006. However, if benefits are taken before normal minimum pension age under this protective measure, an abatement of 2.5% per annum must be applied to the lifetime allowance. This is applied in respect of individuals who have a protected pension age lower than 50.

The nature of protection depends on whether the scheme in question was a personal pension scheme or an occupational pension scheme. See below.

Personal pension schemes

4.31   Members of personal pension schemes and retirement annuity contracts may retain their low normal retirement age if:

- there was an unqualified right to take a pension before age 50;

- they become entitled to all uncrystallised pension and/or lump sum rights under the scheme on the same day;

- they cease any relevant employment on drawing benefits; and

- they held one of the following occupations: athlete; badminton player; boxer; cricketer; cyclist; dancer; diver (saturation, deep sea and free swimming); footballer; golfer; ice hockey player; jockey – flat racing; jockey – national hunt; member of the Reserve Forces; model; motor cycle rider (motocross or road racing); motor racing driver; rugby league player; rugby union player; skier (downhill); snooker or billiards player; speedway rider; squash player; table tennis player; tennis player (including real tennis); trapeze artiste; wrestler.

If a member is entitled to a protected low retirement age and transfers his benefits out of the scheme, he will lose the right to his protected low retirement age. However, the right to a low retirement age will be retained if the transfer is part of a block transfer (see **4.20**).

Occupational pension schemes

4.32   Members of occupational pension schemes or deferred annuity contracts with a low normal retirement age will be able to retain that right if:

- the member had the right on 5 April 2006 to take a pension and/or lump sum before the age of 55;

- the right is unqualified (in that no other party need consent to the individual's request before it becomes binding upon the scheme or contract holder);

- the provision to take benefits before age 55 was set out in the governing documentation of the retirement benefit scheme or deferred annuity contract on 10 December 2003;

- the member becomes entitled to all of his uncrystallised pension and/or lump sum rights under the scheme on the same day;

- the member has left the employment to which the scheme relates;

- the member either:

  – had the right under the scheme or contract on 10 December 2003, or

  – acquired the right in accordance with the scheme provisions as they were on 10 December 2003 upon joining the scheme after that date

On transferring out of the pension scheme a member will normally lose his right to a protected low retirement age. However, where the transfer is part of a block transfer, members with a right to a low normal retirement age may continue to hold that right under the new arrangement.

The lifetime allowance abatement (see **4.30** above) will not apply if an individual is taking his benefits from one of the following schemes:

- The Armed Forces Pension Scheme,

- The British Transport Police Force Superannuation Fund,

- The Firefighters' Pension Scheme,

- The Firemen's Pension Scheme (Northern Ireland),

- The Gurkha Pension Scheme,

- The Police Pension Scheme,

- The Police Service of Northern Ireland Pension Scheme,

- The Police Service of Northern Ireland Full Time Reserve Pension Scheme, or

- A scheme established solely for the receipt of additional voluntary pension contributions from members of the schemes above.

PENSION DEATH BENEFIT RULES

General rules

4.33 There is generally no limit on the amount of dependant's pension that can be paid from a registered pension scheme. The payment of a dependant's pension does not count as a benefit crystallisation event and is therefore not subject to the lifetime allowance. Dependants' pensions are, however, subject to income tax under PAYE.

It is no longer a necessity that a dependant's pension payable to a surviving spouse is payable for the life of the spouse (or until earlier remarriage).

Dependants' pensions from defined benefit arrangements are generally unrestricted. The exception to this is a dependant's pension payable on death in retirement, where death occurs after age 75 and the member's pension commenced after 5 April 2006. In this case the dependant's pension must not exceed the level of the member's pension at date of death plus 5% of any retirement lump sum taken.

On the death of a member of a money purchase arrangement before retirement, a dependant may choose to purchase an annuity or to take income withdrawals. On the death of the member after retirement a dependant may continue to take income withdrawals if the member had been taking income withdrawals, or purchase an annuity. If the member was in receipt of an annuity at date of death, the terms of the annuity could provide for payment of a dependant's annuity.

A ten-year guarantee may be provided on members' pensions from defined benefit schemes and on lifetime annuities.

Where a scheme provides for a dependant's pension, it may be possible, depending on scheme rules, to convert it into a lump sum death benefit before the dependant becomes entitled to it.

In order to receive a dependant's pension, the recipient must meet the definition of dependant set out the *Finance Act 2004*.

Meaning of dependant

4.34   A person who was married to, or who was a civil partner of, the member at the date of death is a dependant. A dependant may also be someone who was married to, or who was a civil partner of, the member at the time when the member's pension commenced as long as the rules of the scheme provide for this.

A child of the member is a dependant if he has not reached the age of 23 or, if he has reached that age, he was in the opinion of the scheme administrator dependent on the member because of physical or mental impairment.

A person who is not a child of the member, not married to the member and not a civil partner of the member may still be a dependant if, in the opinion of the scheme administrator, at the date of the member's death:

● He was financially dependent on the member,

● His financial relationship with the member was one of mutual dependence, or

● He was dependent on the member because of physical or mental impairment.

Transitional protection – children's pensions

4.35   Although children's pensions must normally cease by age 23, transitional provisions ensure that a right to a child's pension continues after A-Day and the pension would be payable until the later of the child reaching age 23 and ceasing full-time education or vocational training. For this to apply, one of the following three conditions must be met:

Condition 1

● The pension was in payment to a child of the member on 5 April 2006 or the member had died on or before 5 April 2006 and a pension was due to come into payment to the child; and

● The rules of the pension scheme allowed a pension to be paid to a child of the member following the death of that member until the child ceased full-time education or vocational training.

Condition 2

● The pension was in payment to a member on 5 April 2006;

● The rules of the pension scheme allowed a pension to be paid to a child of the member following the death of that member until the child ceased full-time education or vocational training; and

● The child was born on or before 5 April 2007.

Condition 3

● The rules of the pension scheme on 10 December 2003 allowed an irrevocable election to be made designating part of the sums or assets representing the member's rights as available for the payment of a pension to a child of the member following the death of that member until the child ceased full-time education or vocational training; and

- Such an election had been made by the member and accepted by the scheme administrator on or before 5 April 2006.

LUMP SUM DEATH BENEFIT RULES

General rules

4.36   As with dependants' pensions there is no limit to the amount of lump sum death benefit that may be paid from a registered pension scheme. However, the lump sum will either be subject to the lifetime allowance, if it is paid in respect of uncrystallised rights, or will be subject to a special tax charge, if it is paid in respect of crystallised rights.

A registered pension scheme may pay lump sum death benefits to any person in most circumstances. However, where a trivial commutation lump sum death benefit is concerned, the payment must be made to dependants (see **4.39**). If lump sum death benefits are not paid directly to the legal personal representative, that person must be notified of the payment. It is also a requirement that the amount of the lifetime allowance used up is declared, and a charge of 55% on any excess over the lifetime allowance will fall on the beneficiary.

Lump sum death benefits may not, with one exception, be payable on death after age 75. The one exception is where a member or dependant in receipt of alternatively secured pension dies after age 75 and there are no other dependants. In this case a tax-free lump sum may be paid to a charity nominated by the member or by the scheme administrator.

The type of lump sum death payable will depend on whether the arrangement from which it is paid is defined benefit or money purchase.

Defined benefit arrangements

4.37   A defined benefit lump sum death benefit may be paid tax-free up to the level of the deceased member's lifetime allowance where the following conditions are met:

- The member had not reached age 75 at date of death;

- It is paid in respect of a defined benefit arrangement;

- It is paid before the end of the period of two years beginning with the earlier of the day on which the scheme administrator first knew of the member's death and the day on which the scheme administrator could first reasonably be expected to have known of it; and

- It is not a pension protection lump sum death benefit or a trivial commutation lump sum death benefit (see **4.39**).

A defined benefit lump sum death benefit will usually be in the form of a death in service lump sum from an occupational pension scheme (eg four times salary), but the definition could also cover the case where a dependant's pension is instead commuted for a lump sum before it becomes payable.

A five-year guarantee expressed to be payable as a lump sum would also fall under the definition of a defined benefit lump sum death benefit. Note, however, that if the five year guarantee is expressed as a continuation of pension instalments and is commuted for a lump sum, HMRC may view this as an unauthorised payment.

A pension protection lump sum death benefit may be paid in respect of crystallised rights where the following conditions are met:

- The member had not reached the age of 75 at the date of death;

- It is paid in respect of a defined benefit arrangement;

- It is paid in respect of a scheme pension to which the member was entitled at the date of his death; and

- The member has specified that it is to be treated as a pension protection lump sum death benefit (i.e. instead of a defined benefit lump sum death benefit).

The amount of a pension protection lump sum death benefit must not exceed the amount crystallised by the pension coming into payment less instalments of pension already received. The lump sum is not subject to the lifetime allowance but is instead subject to a 35% tax charge. It is therefore unlikely that schemes would pay such a lump sum when a defined benefit lump sum death benefit can be paid tax-free. The only situation where this would be paid in preference to a defined benefit lump sum death benefit is where a member's lifetime allowance has been exhausted. In this case the 35% tax charge would be preferable to the 55% tax charge that would otherwise arise. The member must make an election for it to be treated as such.

Money purchase arrangements

4.38   If death occurs before any benefits have been drawn, a member's entire fund value can be paid as an uncrystallised funds lump sum death benefit. An uncrystallised funds lump sum death benefit may be paid tax-free up to the level of the lifetime allowance and must meet the following conditions:

- The member has not reached age 75 at the date of death;

- It is paid in respect of a money purchase arrangement;

- It is paid before the end of the period of two years beginning with the earlier of the day on which the scheme administrator first knew of the member's death and the day on which the scheme administrator could first reasonably be expected to have known of it; and

- It is paid in respect of uncrystallised funds.

While this is similar to the position that applied for personal pensions before A-Day, it is a significant easement for occupational money purchase pension schemes, which were limited to four times final remuneration plus a return of member contributions prior to A-Day. Occupational money purchase schemes may now pay a death in service lump sum of whatever may have been insured under the scheme (eg four times salary) plus an unrestricted return of the member's fund, subject to scheme rules permitting and subject to the lifetime allowance.

There are two types of lump sum death benefit that may be paid from a money purchase arrangement after benefits have come into payment.

An unsecured pension fund lump sum death benefit may be paid if a member or dependant was in receipt of income withdrawal at the date of death and was under age 75. The value of the remaining income withdrawal fund may be paid as a lump sum subject to a 35% tax charge.

An annuity protection lump sum death benefit may be paid if the member was under age 75 and was in receipt of a lifetime annuity at the date of death. A lump sum may be paid up to the limit of the initial amount crystallised by the lifetime annuity coming into payment less any instalments already taken. The lump sum is subject to the 35% tax charge.

If a five year guarantee is purchased with a lifetime annuity from a money purchase arrangement and it is payable as a lump sum, this would seem to fall under the definition of an annuity protection lump sum death benefit and could therefore be subject to the 35% tax charge unless it can be structured in another way. However, note that transitional protection provides that where an annuity was purchased before A-Day and there was an attaching right for payment of the guarantee balance as a lump sum, that lump sum can continue to be paid tax-free on death after A-Day within the guarantee period and regardless of whether the pensioner was over age 75 at date of death.

Trivial commutation lump sum death benefit

4.39   A trivial commutation lump sum death benefit may be paid if the following conditions are met:

- The member had not reached the age of 75 at the date of death;

- It is paid to a dependant entitled under the pension scheme to pension death benefit in respect of the member;

- It is paid before the day on which the member would have reached age 75; and

- It extinguishes the dependant's entitlement under the pension scheme to pension death benefit and lump sum death benefit in respect of the member.

If the lump sum paid exceeds 1% of the lifetime allowance, only the amount up to the 1% limit can be treated as a trivial commutation lump sum death benefit. A trivial commutation lump sum death benefit can be paid from either a defined benefit arrangement or a money purchase arrangement and is wholly subject to income tax under PAYE (no 25% tax-free amount).

Funeral grant

4.40   The rules of some occupational pension schemes allow a one-off tax-free payment to be made upon the death of a member in order to fund funeral expenses. Where the member was over the age of 75 at the date of death, such a payment would not be an authorised lump sum. The *Taxation of Pension Schemes (Transitional Provisions) Order 2006 (SI 2006/572)* created a new authorised payment, called a life cover lump sum, to provide protection in these circumstances. The conditions that have to be met are:

- The registered pension scheme was, immediately before A-Day, a retirement benefit scheme approved for the purposes of *Chap I, Pt XIV ICTA 1988*;

- The member had a right under the pension scheme to a life cover lump sum on 5 April 2006;

- The rules of the pension scheme on 10 December 2003 included provision conferring such a right on some or all of the persons who were then members of the pension scheme, and such a right was either then conferred on the member or would have been had the member been a member of the scheme on that date;

- The rules of the scheme in relation to life cover lump sums have not been changed since 10 December 2003; and

- The member was in receipt of benefits from the scheme on or before 5 April 2006 or entitled to one or more life cover lump sums amounting to £2,500 or less.

The payment is tax-free by virtue of *s 636 A, Income Tax (Earnings and Pensions) Act 2003*. It is not listed as being included in the lifetime allowance as it is not defined as a relevant lump sum death benefit for the purpose of benefit crystallisation events (*s 216* and *Sch 32, Finance Act 2004*).

PENSION SHARING

Pre A-Day pension debit and credit

4.41   Pension sharing on divorce operates so as to reduce a member's pension rights by a pension debit, and to award the ex-spouse with a pension credit. Before A-Day a pension debit counted against the HMRC maximum benefit a member was allowed to accrue under the pre A-Day tax regime. The pension credit was ignored in assessing the HMRC maximum benefit of the ex-spouse.

Post A-Day pension credit

4.42   The position changed on 6 April 2006. If a person acquires a pension credit post A-Day it will count towards that person's lifetime allowance.

However, in a case where the pension being shared is one that has been brought into payment on or after 6 April 2006, the person receiving the pension credit can apply for an uplift to his or her lifetime allowance. Since the pension being shared will already have been tested against the lifetime allowance once before, when it was brought into payment, it would be unfair to test it against a lifetime allowance a second time. The uplift is calculated according to the formula APC/SLA, where:

- APC is the appropriate amount of the pension credit rights at the date they were acquired (ie that part of the original member's cash equivalent transfer value which was split in favour of the ex-spouse), and

- SLA is the standard lifetime allowance at the time when the pension credit rights were acquired.

For example, if £1 million worth of pension rights are shared in the 2007/08 tax year in the proportion 50:50, the pension credit recipient can claim an uplift of £500,000/£1,600,000 = 0.3125, which is rounded up to two decimal places, 0.32. If the person with pension credit draws benefits in the 2010/11 tax year when the lifetime allowance is £1.8 million, his or her lifetime allowance will be increased to £1.8 million × 1.32 = £2,376,000.

To receive this uplift the recipient of pension credit must notify HMRC on form APSS201 by 31 January five years after the 31 January following the tax year in which the pension sharing order took effect.

A similar uplift is available for anyone who acquired pension credit before 6 April 2006, given that pre A-Day pension credit did not count against HMRC limits. The uplift is available whether or not the pension credit relates to rights which were already in payment. The uplift is calculated according to the formula IAPC/SLA, where:

- IAPC is the appropriate amount of the pension credit rights at the date they were acquired (i.e. that part of the original member's cash equivalent transfer value which was split in favour of the ex-spouse), and

- SLA is the standard lifetime allowance for the 2006/07 tax year (ie £1,500,000).

To determine the amount of IAPC it is increased in line with increases in the Retail Prices Index from the month in which the pension credit was acquired up to April 2006.

Anyone seeking an uplift for pre-A-Day pension credit must notify HMRC on form APSS201 on or before 5 April 2009. Note, however, that this uplift is not available for pre A-Day pension credit if the person with pension credit is also relying on primary protection.

Post A-Day pension debit

4.43   For those subject to a pension debit before A-Day, the good news is that this does not count towards the post A-Day lifetime allowance, despite the fact that it counted towards pre A-Day HMRC limits. This means that someone with a pension debit acquires scope to fund his or her benefits up to their original level. However, if any transitional protection is being relied on that requires the calculation of HMRC maximum benefits on 5 April 2006, the pension debit may have to be taken into account for those purposes.

For the seriously wealthy this means divorce may not necessarily be all bad news post A-Day. If 100% of pension rights are given away post A-Day as part of a divorce settlement, the person giving the rights away will be able to fund up to the lifetime allowance once again essentially benefiting from contribution tax relief twice.

BENEFIT CRYSTALLISATION EVENTS

4.44   Testing of the lifetime allowance and other limits under the new tax regime is triggered by the occasion of a benefit crystallisation event (BCE). Each person's lifetime allowance is reduced by the amount crystallised by each BCE that occurs in respect of him or her.

The *Finance Act 2004, s 216* identifies ten different testing events. It is not possible to avoid paying the lifetime allowance charge by leaving monies and/or assets in a registered scheme or taking them overseas. The events are as follows:

Event 1

This is triggered by the designation of sums or assets held under a money purchase arrangement as available for the payment of unsecured pension.

The amount crystallised is the aggregate of the amount of the sums and the market value of the assets designated.

Event 2

This is triggered by an individual becoming entitled to a scheme pension.

The amount crystallised is **RVF × P** (see **4.45**).

Event 3

This is triggered by an individual in receipt of scheme pension becoming entitled to payment of the scheme pension, otherwise than in excepted circumstances, at an increased annual rate which exceeds by more than the permitted margin the rate at which it was payable on the day on which he became entitled to it.

The amount crystallised is **RVF × XP** (see **4.45**).

Event 4

This is triggered by an individual becoming entitled to a lifetime annuity purchased under a money purchase arrangement.

The amount crystallised is the aggregate of the amount of such of the sums, and the market value of such of the assets, representing the individual's rights under the arrangement as are applied to purchase the lifetime annuity (and any related dependant's annuity).

Event 5

This is triggered by an individual reaching the age of 75 when prospectively entitled to a scheme pension or a lump sum (or both) under a defined benefit arrangement under any of the relevant pension schemes.

The amount crystallised is **(RVF × DP) + DSLS** (see **4.45**).

Event 5A

This is triggered by an individual reaching the age of 75 having previously designated sums or assets under a money purchase arrangement for the provision of unsecured pension.

The amount crystallised is the aggregate of the sums and the market value of the assets representing his unsecured pension fund under the arrangement less the aggregate of the amounts crystallised by BCE 1.

Event 6

This is triggered by an individual becoming entitled to a pension commencement lump sum, a serious ill-health lump sum or a lifetime allowance excess lump sum.

The amount crystallised is the amount of the lump sum (paid to the individual).

Event 7

This is triggered by a person being paid a defined benefit lump sum death benefit or an uncrystallised funds lump sum death benefit.

The amount crystallised is the amount of the lump sum death benefit.

Event 8

This is triggered by the transfer of sums or assets held for the purposes of, or representing accrued rights under, a pension scheme so as to become held for the purposes of, or to represent rights under, a qualifying recognised overseas pension scheme in connection with the individual's membership of that pension scheme.

The amount crystallised is the aggregate of the amount of any sums transferred and the market value of any assets transferred.

Event 9

Any event prescribed in regulations by HMRC as being a BCE. The amount crystallised by an event under BCE 9 will also be prescribed by regulations.

Key to terms in the BCE formulae

4.45   The following meanings apply to the relevant formulae in **4.44** above:

- in benefit crystallisation event 2, '**P**' is the amount of the pension which will be payable to the individual in the period of 12 months beginning with the day on which the individual becomes entitled to it (assuming that it remains payable throughout that period at the rate at which it is payable on that day);

- in benefit crystallisation events 2, 3 and 5, '**RVF**' is the relevant valuation factor (20, unless a different factor has been agreed with HMRC);

- in benefit crystallisation event 3, '**XP**' is (subject to the above) the amount by which the increased annual rate of the pension exceeds the rate at which it was payable on the day on which the individual became entitled to it, as increased by the permitted margin;

- in benefit crystallisation event 5, '**DP**' is the annual rate of the scheme pension to which the individual would be entitled if, on the date on which the individual reaches 75, the individual acquired an actual (rather than a prospective) right to receive it;

- in benefit crystallisation event 5, '**DSLS**' is so much of any lump sum to which the individual would be entitled (otherwise than by way of commutation of pension) as would be paid to the individual if, on that date, the individual acquired an actual (rather than a prospective) right to receive it.

Chapter 5

Investment rules

INTRODUCTION

5.1   The intent of the HMRC and Treasury Simplification Team's report entitled *Simplifying the Taxation of Pensions: The Government's Proposals*, which was published on 10 December 2003, was to introduce a single set of investment rules for all post A-Day registered schemes. In practice, this concept has been significantly eroded with the introduction of taxable property rules (see **2.4**). In a further development, the *Occupational Pension Schemes (Investment) Regulations 2005 (SI 2005/3378)* revoked the *Occupational Pension Schemes (Investment) Regulations 1996 (SI 1996/3127)* – see **5.5**. This chapter deals with the investment rules which apply to all registered schemes from A-Day. The additional taxable property charges which apply to IRPS are dealt with in **Chapter 12**.

The post A-Day investment rules have brought UK legislation more into line with the *IORPS Directive 2003/41/EC*, and they rely to a large extent on the prudent man principle. Also, consideration must be given to an appropriate level of scheme liquidity. Effectively, of course, the UK has always applied sound principles in governing the investment activity of exempt-approved pension schemes as such schemes are subject to trust law and specialised pensions legislation. As the new tax regime does not require registered schemes to be governed by trust law the prudent man principle has become of paramount importance to benefit protection.

General principles to follow

5.2   The *Finance Act 2004, s 161,* includes investments in the category of 'payments' where they are held by or for a connected person. The list of payments which involve investment activity is:

- transfers of assets or transfers of money's worth;

- payments made for benefits provided in connection with an investment;

- payments or benefits even where a pension scheme has been wound up since the acquisition of the investments;

- payments made to connected persons (that is connected to a member or sponsoring employer);

- assets filled by a person connected to a member or sponsoring employer;

- any increase in the value of an asset, or reduction in the liability of an asset which relates to a person connected to a member or sponsoring employer.

The investment powers of trustees and managers of registered pension schemes may be drawn up very widely. Nevertheless, there are general principles to follow if tax charges and penalties are to be avoided:

- taking value out of a pension scheme for unauthorised reasons is prohibited, and subjected to penalties and charges;

- the 'prudent man' principle must be followed;

- attempts to liberate pensions from registered pension schemes in contravention of legislation and practice will be penalised;

- members who suffer loss as a result of unauthorised payments may be entitled to reimbursement of their loss if they were not instrumental in the cause of the loss;

- administrators who would otherwise be penalised in circumstances where a loss of a member's benefits has been caused in whole or in part may apply for an exemption if they were provided with false information;

- the use of assets by a member or connected person may be chargeable to a benefit-in-kind charge;

- the non-commercial use of assets may be subject to charge;

- value-shifting of assets will be subject to charge;

- administrators will be liable to tax on any wasting assets acquired by the pension scheme.

Transitional protection

5.3   In the few areas where the post-A-Day regime is more onerous than the pre A-Day regime transitional arrangements permit existing investments to be retained subject to the standing rules at the time. This protection will be lost if changes are subsequently made to the investment (eg to an existing loan agreement of a property lease).

PERMITTED INVESTMENTS

The main rules which apply

5.4   The following types of investment may be considered by registered pension schemes, if their rules so permit. These investment powers may extend to all areas described below, and any others which the scheme permits, subject to any special conditions which apply. The special conditions are described under the relevant headings in the remainder of this chapter:

(a)   loans, other than member loans;

(b)   borrowing;

(c)   transactions between an employer's or member's business and the scheme;

(d)   investment in land and buildings;

(e)   loans to the employer or other party that is unconnected to the member;

(f)   investment in property, including in some circumstances residential property;

(g)   disposals of assets on a commercial basis other than in order to avoid tax charges which should lawfully be incurred;

(h)   purchases of assets by scheme members or connected persons from the scheme on a commercial basis;

(i)   sale of assets by a member to a registered scheme on an arm's-length basis;

(j)   investment in quoted or unquoted shares;

(k)   trading activities by the trustees or scheme manager.

The *Occupational Pension Schemes (Investment) Regulations 2005 (SI 2005/3378)* contain the following provisions:

(a)   Assets must be invested in the best interests of members and beneficiaries; and in the case of a potential conflict of interest, in the sole interest of members and beneficiaries.

(b)   The powers of investment, or the discretion, must be exercised in a manner calculated to ensure the security, quality, liquidity and profitability of the portfolio as a whole.

(c)   Assets must consist predominantly of investments admitted to trading on regulated markets, and other investments must be kept to a prudent level. There must also be diversification of assets, and special rules apply to derivatives and collective investment schemes.

(d)   The requirements of the *IORPs Directive 2003/41/EC* are adopted in a proportionate and flexible manner, where appropriate using the 'small scheme exemption' which is contained in Article 5. Schemes with fewer than 100 active and deferred members are exempted from much of the requirements of the regulations, but are still required to have regard to the need for diversification on investment rule.

(e)   A triennial review of the statement of investment principles is required. The previous requirements on the statement's contents are largely restated.

(f)   Trustees must consider 'proper advice' on the suitability of a proposed investment, and there are specific requirements in relation to borrowing and a restriction on investment in the 'sponsors' undertaking' to no more than 5% of the portfolio (where a group is concerned, the percentage is no greater than 20%).

Borrowing

5.5   A registered pension scheme may borrow from any source, which opens up such activity to borrowings from members or connected persons. The only stipulations are that all borrowing is contracted at a commercial rate and shall not exceed 50% in total of the net fund value of the scheme at the date of borrowing *(Finance Act 2004, ss 182(2), 184(2))*.

If there are multiple members' arrangements in the scheme, borrowing can be at arrangement level *(Finance Act 2004, s 163(4))*. In the case of a money purchase scheme, the value of any funds which are providing pensions in payment must be deducted from the fund value for the purpose of the 50% test *(Finance Act 2004, s 183(d))*.

Excessive borrowing will be deemed to be a scheme chargeable payment *(Finance Act 2004, ss 183(2), 185(2))* and subject to a scheme sanction charge of 40% *(Finance Act 2004, s 240)*.

Employer loans

5.6   A registered scheme may lend monies to the sponsoring employer or any other party which is unconnected with the member including associated companies *(Finance Act 2004, ss 162, 179)*. The DWP restricts loans to sponsoring employers from large self-administered pension schemes to 5% of the value of the fund *(Occupational Pension Schemes (Investment of Scheme's Resources) Regulations (SI 1992/246), reg 3(1)*, and the *Occupational Pension Schemes (Investment) Regulations 1996 (SI 1996/3127))*:

- no more than 5% of the current market value of the resources of a scheme may at any time be invested in employer-related investments; and

- none of the resources of a scheme may at any time be invested in any employer-related loan.

SSASs in which all the members are trustees may make loans up to 50% of the value of the fund to sponsoring employers *(Retirement Benefits Schemes (Restriction on Discretion to Approve) (Small Self-administered Schemes) (Amendment) Regulations (SI 1998/728))*. The HMRC 50% limit applies from A-Day for all schemes *(Finance Act 2004, s 179(1))*.

THE MAIN RULES UNDER THE FINANCE ACT 2004

5.7   The requirements of the *Finance Act 2004* are as follows:

- employer loans are permitted up to five years' duration;

- loan must be repaid by equal annual instalments;

- if it is not possible for an employer to repay a loan within the agreed period, it may be rolled over once for a maximum period of five years;

- loans must be secured against assets of the borrower of at least equal value, including interest;

- any amounts which exceed 50% of total fund value will be taxed at 40%;

- under the *Pension Schemes (Prescribed Interest Rates for Authorised Employer Loans) Regulations 2005 (SI 2005/3449)* a loan reference rate must be charged;

- the loan reference rate is based on an average of the base rates of a specified group of banks;

- the loan reference rate is 1% more than the reference rate (the high street bank rates);

- the loan reference rate is found on the reference date preceding the start of the period (that is, on 6 April).

Non-permitted loans are treated as unauthorised employer payments and are liable to an unauthorised payments tax charge.

Loans where there is no sponsoring employer

5.8 Where a scheme is not an occupational pension scheme there can be no sponsoring employer. Any loans made by the scheme to an employer who is connected to the member will attract a tax charge on the member.

Pre-A-Day loans to employer

5.9 Pre-A-Day loans may run their course, provided there are no changes to their terms. If a change is made, any amount owing, inclusive of interest, will be subject to the post-A-Day rules.

Employer transactions

5.10 All employer transactions must be made on an arm's-length basis if they are not to be treated as unauthorised payments.

Member transactions

5.11 All member transactions must be conducted on a commercial basis, and member loans are prohibited. A member's business may purchase or sell assets to the member's pension scheme provided this is done on an arm's-length basis. Capital gains tax may be payable when the asset is sold, and it is the responsibility of the member to declare the sale on his self-assessment tax return. HMRC has published a leaflet coded CGT1 which provides further information on this matter.

Liquidity

5.12 It has always been prudent in trust law for trustees to maintain a reasonable level of scheme liquidity. The determination of what is a reasonable level depended very much on the likely calls upon the scheme, for example how near the members were to retirement age, or any potential costs for early retirement or redundancies, or on the scheme winding up.

Under the *Finance Act 2004* the trustees or managers of registered schemes are required to exercise similar prudence. RPSM07101030 contains the following guidance note:

> 'When deciding the scheme's investment policy, the administrators/trustees will need to bear carefully in mind the need to have sufficient liquid funds to pay pension benefits?

> For example, investment in land and buildings may be a good long-term investment when the **members** are many years from retirement but becomes less appropriate as their retirement approaches, particularly where the scheme has only one or two members. Even if the purchase of the member's, widow's/widower's or **dependant's** annuity is deferred, it is appropriate to ensure that the scheme is in a position to buy an annuity or provide benefits in the form of **Alternatively Secured Pension** without becoming involved in a forced sale of property. This is particularly so if the property purchased is an important part of the employer's own commercial premises or even the member's own residential property and thus potentially difficult to realise.'

Member use of assets

5.13   The *Finance Act 2004* does not prevent a member or his family or household from using scheme assets. The disadvantage in doing this is that if the beneficiary has use of the assets he will be taxed on the value of the benefit in the same way as an unauthorised payment charge. This charge will be offset by any amount the member has made towards the asset use, such as payment of rent.

Property rental, whether in respect of properties owned by the sponsoring employer and/or the member, is permitted at commercial rates. If commercial rates are not paid an unauthorised payment charge will be incurred.

The term 'member of family' includes:

- a member's spouse;
- a member's children and their spouses;
- a member's parents;
- a member's dependants.

The term 'members of a household' includes:

- a member's domestic staff;
- a member's guests.

There is a formal requirement to report member use of assets. Reports must be sent in by 17 July following the tax year in which the circumstance arose, and the benefit-in-kind will be calculated on a cash equivalent basis. Further details are contained in **Chapter 7**.

Property

5.14   There are no specific bars to investment in property, subject to IRPS in respect of taxable property (see **Chapter 12**). Although members will be subject to tax charges on any benefit-in-kind, the income could of course be reinvested in the registered pension scheme subject to the lifetime allowance limit. This can be a tax-efficient means of investing in a property. Since 6 April 2004 any disposal of assets whilst retaining the ability to use them has incurred a benefit-in-kind tax charge. However, there are exemptions for spouses who own disposed property and taxpayers who received full commercial values in cash terms for any disposition. Exemptions also extend, in appropriate circumstances, in circumstances where an elderly parent retains some enjoyment in the use of the property of a domestic nature following a part disposal.

HMRC has been concerned about the potential to avoid inheritance tax which had previously been available under home loan schemes whereby the owner of the house disposed of it to a trust and received an IOU in return, which he bequested to his heirs through a further trust. The individual then continued to live in the house. Again, benefit-in-kind charges have been imposed on such individuals since April 2004 and will continue to be so in the future.

Residential property considerations

5.15   The ability to invest in residential property, holiday property and in similar types of property situated abroad caused much excitement in the investment market, with particular regard to SIPPs. However, the introduction of taxable property rules into pensions tax law brought in specific bars for IRPS. This also gave HMRC cause to issue guidance in RPSM07101060:

'Using a registered pension scheme to invest in a buy to let residential property or holiday home or any other type of residential property may have the following consequences:

- The property becomes an asset of the pension fund and there is a requirement to put all rental income into the pension fund so it is locked away and cannot be accessed until authorised benefits are paid.

- If the property is made available to a member of the scheme or members of their family it will give rise to a benefits-in-kind tax charge if a market rent is not paid (even if they choose not to use it).

- Any property bought by the pension fund in most cases will need to be sold before the pension can be drawn, to provide a secured income in retirement.

- Only 25% of the capital in the pension arrangement will be able to be extracted as a lump sum, the remainder will be locked in the pension to be drawn out over the period of retirement.

- Borrowing to fund a property purchase cannot exceed 50% of the value of the pension arrangement.

- Although any rental income or capital gains from the disposal of the property will be tax free in the pension fund when the money is paid as a pension it will be taxable at the members marginal rate of tax. Depending on the rate of tax this may well be higher than the rate that would be paid if the disposal were subject to the CGT regime after the property has been held for 7 years.

- Putting any previously owned property into the pension scheme will trigger any unrealised chargeable gain on the property, and transaction costs such as stamp duty.'

Other property considerations

5.16   A pension scheme may purchase property from and sell property to members. It may also:

- lease property to members, to their families, and to partnerships of which the members and their families are partners;

- own property jointly with members and their families and partnerships of which the members are partners.

Transactions must always be made on commercial terms, or a tax charge may be incurred by the scheme administrator or member or any other person occupying the property (*Finance Act 2004, s 173(5)*). So, a member who occupies a commercial property must pay market value rent (unless it is provided for their employment – such as a caretaker, janitor etc) in order to avoid an unauthorised payment charge of 40%.

If the scheme has a leasehold interest, and the period of the lease is less than 50 years, the property will fall into the category of wasting asset (see **5.24**), and an additional scheme sanction charge of 15% will be incurred by the member. Additionally, the DWP restricts the value of leases to sponsoring employers for large self-administered pension schemes to 5% of the value of the fund. However, the *IORPS Directive* provides some exemptions for schemes with fewer than 100 members.

SHAREHOLDINGS

5.17   A registered scheme may invest in any type of shares, including quoted and unquoted shares. However, this must be restricted to 5% of the net value of the fund in respect of shares purchased by the sponsoring employer. If there is more than one employer, a separate calculation applies to each one, with a ceiling of 20% of the fund. The limits are not relevant to non-occupational pension schemes as there is no limit on share purchase in such cases.

Valuations of quoted securities of a registered pension scheme for benefit calculations or fund valuations are normally done on the 'quarter-up' basis from the non-publicly available Stock Exchange Daily Official List. From A-Day HMRC has permitted two alternative valuation methods, either the bid price or mid price less 1% may be used by the scheme.

NON-INCOME PRODUCING ASSETS

5.18   Subject to the taxable property and tangible moveable asset provisions (see **Chapter 12**), non-income producing assets, such as works of art, may be held by a registered pension scheme if acquired on a proper commercial basis. Transactions may take place without restriction (subject to **5.13**), so schemes may purchase such assets from, and sell to, scheme members. Members may also be able to enjoy the use of the asset itself on a commercial footing. However, if asset is deemed to be a wasting asset (see **5.24**), an unauthorised payment charge of 40% and an additional scheme sanction charge of 15/% will arise on the member.

INHERITANCE TAX ON INVESTMENTS

5.19   *Finance Act 2004, s 203* concerns inheritance tax exemptions and amends the *Inheritance Tax Act 1984*. It effectively continues the exemptions for discretionary schemes which existed prior to A-Day, ensuring that contributions are not taxed as transfers of value.

TRUSTEE TRADING

5.20   Trustees are not prohibited from trading. However, trading should not be so habitual as to bring into question the bona fides of the scheme. This situation did not change significantly under the *Finance Act 2004*. Trading activities will be subject to taxation as receipts fall within the income tax legislation and therefore do not enjoy the exemptions on fund yield and gains. The scheme must return the amount of income received under the self-assessment tax return.

HMRC will not normally give a view on whether an action is deemed to be trading in advance of the transaction being carried out. Trading income of a registered pension scheme must be returned on a Self-Assessment Tax Return. Information on trading can be found in BIM20205.

UNAUTHORISED PAYMENTS

5.21   Unauthorised payments are described in detail, together with the charges which are incurred on such payments, in **Chapters 8** and **14**, as appropriate. The main elements of investment activity which fall within such a category are described under the three sub-headings below.

Value shifting

5.22   Any scheme which transacts with a connected party on less than commercial terms will attract an unauthorised payment charge. The concept of value shifting in the *Finance Act 2004 (Finance Act 2004, s 174)* envisages transactions which increase the value of an asset or decrease the liability of a member or employer without making a payment. The main concern is transactions not made on an arm's-length basis (ie which involve connected parties).

Three categories of connected parties have been identified for the purpose of conducting an arm's-length test. These are:

- *Category A:* transactions between the scheme and the member or sponsoring employer;

- *Category B:* transactions between the scheme and persons connected with members and/or connected employers ('connected' has the meaning given in *ICTA 1988, s 839*);

- *Category C:* transactions between the scheme and a third party which are directly or indirectly for the benefit of the member or sponsoring employer.

It is an HMRC requirement that trustees ensure that they take a sensible, commercial and prudent course and obtain relevant valuations from suitably qualified valuers in such transactions.

Waivers of debt

5.23   Whenever a member debt is waived by a registered scheme it is deemed to be a loan to the member. As such it will be taxed as an unauthorised payment.

Wasting assets

5.24   Any scheme which invests in wasting assets will incur a scheme sanction charge on the scheme administrator. A tax charge will also be made on the member of a scheme if he receives the benefit. Wasting assets are described in the *Taxation of Chargeable Gains Act 1992 (TCGA 1992), s 44,* as assets that have an anticipated life of less than 50 years. Examples of such assets are properties with less than 50-year leases, cars, racehorses, plant and machinery etc.

Chapter 6

Transfers

INTRODUCTION

6.1   The relaxation in the transfer rules under the post 6 April 2006 tax regime has attracted a great deal of attention. There has been a considerable widening in the rules which apply to transfers, much of which has been brought about by the impact of the *EU Directive 2003/41/EC on the Activities and Supervision of Institutions for Occupational Retirement Provision* and a draft EU portability directive. Although the EU is concerned mainly with easing transferability of members' rights between Member States, it has been necessary to free up some of the UK transfer restrictions internally and internationally in order to achieve a level playing field. **Chapter 9** of this book describes the specific application of the new transfer rules where overseas pension schemes are concerned. In this chapter attention is given to transfers to and from UK pension schemes.

PERMITTED TRANSFERS

6.2   There is no longer any prohibition on the types of scheme that can receive transfers from a tax-advantaged pension scheme. Transfers may be made freely between the various forms of occupational and personal schemes that exist in the UK without the same restrictions that applied before 6 April 2006, subject only to scheme rules permitting. The need to certify transfer amounts and lump sums has fallen away, as has the need to seek HMRC approval for certain transfers.

However, if a transfer is made from a registered pension scheme that does not meet the definition of a 'recognised transfer' in s 169 FA 2004, it will be an unauthorised payment and subject to the range of unauthorised payment charges (see **Chapter 14**). A recognised transfer is defined as:

> 'a transfer of sums or assets held for the purposes of, or representing accrued rights under, a registered pension scheme so as to become held for the purposes of, or to represent rights under another registered pension scheme or a qualifying recognised overseas pension scheme in connection with a member of that pension scheme.'

The unauthorised payment charges may be disapplied if the scheme administrator made the transfer in good faith and based on false or incorrect information from the member.

There is no prohibition on a registered pension scheme receiving a transfer from a non-registered scheme.

TRANSFERS BETWEEN REGISTERED PENSION SCHEMES

6.3   A transfer from one **registered pension scheme** to another registered pension scheme is a recognised transfer. No tax charges or sanctions apply to recognised transfers. However, transfers must be made directly between the schemes concerned; funds should not be routed through intermediaries. Where the receiving scheme is an insured scheme but the transfer value is not paid directly to the scheme administrator or **insurance company,** the transferring scheme administrator will be liable to a penalty of up to £3,000.

A recognised transfer from one registered scheme to another is not a benefit crystallisation event and therefore not subject to the lifetime allowance. A recognised transfer from a registered scheme to a qualifying recognised overseas pension scheme (QROPS), however, *is* a benefit crystallisation event, and the transfer value must be tested against the member's lifetime allowance. If the transfer value exceeds the available lifetime allowance, it is subject to a tax charge of 25%.

A recognised transfer is not a contribution, and no tax relief is due in respect of the transfer.

The making of transfer payments has implications when assessing the value of a member's rights against his annual allowance. If benefits are transferred from a defined benefit arrangement, the transfer value is included in the member's closing value at the end of the input period. If a transfer is received by a defined benefit arrangement, the transfer value is excluded from the member's closing value at the end of the input period. In a money purchase arrangement only the contributions paid are tested against the annual allowance, and a transfer should therefore have no effect with regards to the annual allowance.

Transfers may be made in cash, in specie or as a combination, subject only to the rules of the schemes concerned. Sums and assets transferred should represent the full value of the member rights being transferred.

A recognised transfer can be made from a registered scheme to a deferred annuity contract, as the deferred annuity contract is automatically treated as a registered pension scheme. The assignment of an annuity policy which does not provide for immediate payment of benefits is also a recognised transfer.

Partial transfers were not normally permitted under the pre 6 April 2006 tax rules. This is no longer a problem for HMRC under the post 6 April 2006 regime, and partial transfers may now be made in respect of members' uncrystallised rights. This is subject to scheme rules permitting. Pension practices and arrangements, especially money purchase arrangements, may therefore now be designed with this new flexibility in mind.

Note that although a transfer payment may fall within the definition of a recognised transfer, Department for Work and Pensions legislation must still be adhered to where the scheme is used to contract out of the additional state pension.

TRANSFERS FROM REGISTERED PENSION SCHEMES TO NON-REGISTERED SCHEMES

6.4 A transfer from a registered pension scheme to a UK scheme that is not a registered pension scheme is not a recognised transfer. An unauthorised payment charge of 40% of the payment will be levied on the member. A 15% unauthorised payment surcharge will also be levied on the member if the transfer payment (together with any other unauthorised payments in the previous 12 months) exceeds 25% of the member's rights.

The scheme administrator will be liable for a scheme sanction charge of 40% of the payment, although this is reduced to 25% where the member has paid the unauthorised payment charge. If amounts transferred are 25% or more of the funds held in the scheme, HMRC may deregister the scheme, and a 40% deregistration charge would become payable.

Note that the amount transferred is not included in the member's closing value at the end of an input period for the purpose of the annual allowance.

The transfer is not a benefit crystallisation event and will not therefore be taken into account against the member's lifetime allowance.

TRANSFERS FROM NON-REGISTERED SCHEMES TO REGISTERED PENSION SCHEMES

6.5 There is no prohibition on a registered pension scheme receiving a transfer payment from another UK scheme that is not a registered pension scheme (eg an employer-financed retirement benefit scheme).

The transfer payment would not count against the annual allowance, and it would benefit from the tax-advantaged investment environment of a registered scheme. However, it would be subject to the lifetime allowance once it was brought into payment from the registered pension scheme.

Such a transfer payment will not be treated as a contribution, and therefore no tax relief will be available on the payment. It should therefore be questioned whether such a transfer is the best course of action, or whether the benefits from the non-registered scheme may be drawn first and then paid to a registered scheme as a contribution.

A registered pension scheme may receive a transfer from an overseas scheme. Where this is from an recognised overseas pension scheme (see **Chapter 9**), the member may receive an uplift to his lifetime allowance to reflect the value of any rights transferred in that have not benefited from UK tax relief.

LOSS OF PROTECTION

6.6 Members of registered pension schemes who benefit from transitional protection for low retirement ages or tax-free lump sums greater than 25% lose these protections if they transfer their rights to another pension scheme. It is therefore very important to take this into account when considering whether or not to proceed with a transfer.

However, where a member's rights are transferred as part of a block transfer, he may retain his protection for a low retirement age or tax-free lump sum. See **4.20** for further information.

PRE A-DAY RESTRICTIONS

6.7   It is no longer necessary to adhere to restrictions imposed by cash certificates obtained where a transfer was made before 6 April 2006; the post 6 April 2006 tax rules apply instead.

However, where rights have to be valued at 5 April 2006 for protection purposes, such restrictions may still need to be taken into account.

TRANSFER OF RIGHTS IN PAYMENT

6.8   A transfer of pension rights once they had come into payment was not generally possible under the pre 6 April 2006 tax rules. Under the post 6 April 2006 rules a transfer of crystallised rights is possible.

A scheme pension, once it has started to be paid, may be transferred to another arrangement and will be a recognised transfer as long as it takes the same form and is paid at the same level in the receiving arrangement (although reasonable administrative costs relating to the transfer may be deducted). The scheme pension under the receiving arrangement will be treated as if it were still payable under the transferring arrangement. It will not therefore be treated as a benefit crystallisation event (BCE), and any guarantee will run from the original start date.

A lifetime annuity, once it has come into payment, may be transferred from one insurance company to another. The new annuity would not be treated as a BCE, but any annuity protection lump sum death benefit must be calculated by reference to the original annuity.

Where a member or dependant is in receipt of income withdrawal (whether under unsecured pension or alternatively secured pension), he may transfer his income withdrawal fund to another arrangement set up for the purpose of the transfer. A partial transfer is not possible. All the sums and assets relating to his income withdrawal fund must be transferred to the new arrangement, and the receiving scheme must not mix the transferred rights with other rights of the member existing at that time. The administrator of the receiving scheme must be provided with the necessary information relating to review periods etc to enable him to administer the income withdrawal fund as if it were still administered in the ceding arrangement.

MUST A SCHEME RECEIVE A TRANSFER?

6.9   It is not compulsory for the trustees or managers of a scheme to receive an incoming transfer unless its rules so provide. The one exception to this is stakeholder pension schemes which must accept transfers-in at the request of a member.

REPORTING TO HMRC

6.10   The scheme administrator of a registered pension scheme must include in the HMRC event report any transfer to a qualifying recognised overseas pension scheme and any transfer that is an unauthorised payment. Event reports must be received by HMRC by 31 January following the end of the tax year in which the transfer took place.

If a scheme administrator is requested to complete a pension scheme return by HMRC, he would have to report amounts transferred to other pension schemes in the tax year and transfer amounts received from other pension schemes. The scheme return must be received by HMRC by 31 January following the tax year to which it relates.

Chapter 7

Reporting

INTRODUCTION

7.1   The reporting requirements under the post 6 April 2006 pension tax regime have undergone a significant change in many areas. The *Retirement Benefits Schemes (Information Powers) Regulations 1995 (SI 1995/3103)* have been replaced by the *Registered Pension Schemes (Provision of Information) Regulations 2006 (SI 2006/567)*. The new regime reporting service began to be made available on HMRC's Pension Schemes Online from April 2006, and online reporting has been compulsory for a number of events since October 2007.

Penalties are incurred if the information requirements are not met. The normal range of penalties begin at £300, with an additional £60 per day for any continuing failure to comply. However, where fraud or negligence relates to tax returns, transfer payments, statements, declarations and information provision, fines of up to £3,000 per event may be levied.

The main information requirements under the primary legislation (*Finance Act 2004*) are contained in *s 251* under the heading 'General requirements'. This section also empowers HMRC to make regulations requiring persons of a prescribed description to provide information to HMRC. The regulatory making power extends to requirements to give information to other parties as described under the remaining headings in this chapter.

Section 252 states that HMRC may issue notices requiring persons to produce information to HMRC, be available for inspections in respect of any documentation required by HMRC, and provide such other information as it shall deem appropriate.

Any notices issued under *s 252* will specify the compliance period. The period may not end earlier than 30 days beginning with the day on which the notice is given. Both *ss 251* and *252* extend to employer-financed retirement benefit schemes (EFRBS) (see **Chapter 15** for more information). The right to appeal against notices is contained in *s 253* of the Act.

The following sub-headings set out the reporting duties of each party involved with a registered pension scheme and the person to whom information must be given.

EVENT REPORTS

Administrator to HMRC

7.2

- Where scheme rules are changed to:

  (a)   entitle any person to require the making of unauthorised payments; or

  (b)   permit investment other than in policies of insurance.

- A change in scheme rules where the scheme was treated immediately before 6 April 2006 as two or more separate schemes within *s 611 Income and Corporation Taxes Act 1988*.

- Where the legal structure of the scheme changes from one of the following categories to another:

  (a)   a single trust under which all of the assets are held for the benefit of all members of the scheme;

  (b)   an overall trust within which there are individual trusts applying for the benefit of each member;

  (c)   an overall trust within which specific assets are held as, or within, sub-funds for each member;

  (d)   an annuity contract;

  (e)   a body corporate.

- Membership movements – where the number of scheme members falls in a different band at the end of a tax year from that in which it fell at the end of the previous tax year. The bands are:

  0

  1–10

  11–50

  51–10,000

  10,000 plus

  This applies to total membership of a scheme.

- A benefit crystallisation event in relation to a member where:

  (a)   the amount crystallised exceeds the standard lifetime allowance, or exceeds the standard lifetime allowance when taken with other crystallised amounts; and

  (b)   the member relies on an enhanced lifetime allowance or enhanced protection.

- Payment of a lump sum death benefit payment which either alone or together with other lump sum death benefits from the scheme is more than 50% of the standard lifetime allowance.

- Payment of benefits to a member who is under normal minimum pension age (50, or 55 from 6 April 2010) where the member was at that time or within the previous six years:

    (a)   a director or a person connected with a director in relation to the sponsoring employer or an associated company;

    (b)   the sponsoring employer, whether alone or with others; or

    (c)   a person connected with the sponsoring employer.

- A change in the country or territory in which the scheme is established.

- Payment of a lump sum death benefit in respect of a member aged 75 or over.

- Payment of alternatively secured pension, or alternatively secured pension failing to meet the minimum level.

- Payment of pension commencement lump sum which, when added to the crystallised amount, exceeds 25% of the total, and which is more than 7.5%, but less than 25%, of the current standard lifetime allowance.

- Payment of a pension commencement lump sum where the member has primary or enhanced protection and the lump sums exceeds 25% of the standard lifetime allowance.

- Payment of a serious ill-health lump sum to a member who is or was in the previous six years:

    (a)   a director or a person connected with a director of the sponsoring employer or an associated company; or

    (b)   the sponsoring employer, whether alone or with others; or

    (c)   a person connected with the sponsoring employer.

- Suspension of an ill-health pension.

- Transfers to qualifying recognised overseas pension schemes.

- Unauthorised member or employer payments.

- Where a member is able to control scheme assets and that member, whether alone or with others, gains or loses the ability to control the way in which scheme assets are used to provide pension benefits.

- Scheme chargeable payment (income or gains from taxable property (see **12.5**)).

- Payment of a stand-alone lump sum (see **4.22**) greater than 7.5% of the standard lifetime allowance or where the member has primary or enhanced protection and lump sum rights exceeded £375,000 on 5 April 2006.

- Scheme becomes or ceases to be an occupational pension scheme.

- Termination of scheme adminstrator appointment.

- Scheme wind-up (three-month notification period).

Administrator to member

7.3   The scheme administrator must report the following information to scheme members:

- On a benefit crystalisation event, the level of lifetime allowance used up.

- To each member:

    - to whom a pension is being paid, at least once in each tax year; or

    - in respect of whom a benefit crystallisation event has occurred, within three months of that event,

    a statement of the cumulative total percentage of the lifetime allowance crystallised, at the date of statement, by the events in respect of the scheme and any other scheme from which that scheme has received a transfer payment.

- Where a scheme has made an unauthorised payment to a member, before 7 July following the tax year in which the event took place, the following information:

    - the nature of the benefit provided;

    - the amount of the unauthorised payment which is being treated as being made by the provision of the benefit;

    - the date on which the benefit was provided.

- Where the scheme adminstrator makes a payment on account of his liability to pay for the lifetime allowance charge, within three months of the crystallisation event, details of:

    - the chargeable amount on which the charge arises;

    - how the chargeable amount is calculated;

    - the amount of the tax charge; and

    - whether he has accounted for the tax or intends to do so.

Member to administrator

7.4   The member must report to the administrator, if an enhanced lifetime allowance or enhanced protection is to apply under the *Finance Act 2004, s 256(1)*, the reference number given by HMRC under the enhanced lifetime allowance regulations.

Administrator to administrator

7.5   If part or all of a member's pension rights are transferred from one scheme to another (scheme A to scheme B), the administrator of scheme A must provide the administrator of scheme B, within three months of the transfer, a cumulative total percentage of the standard lifetime allowance crystallised by the event in respect of scheme A and any scheme from which that scheme has received directly or indirectly a transfer payment.

Administrator to personal representatives

7.6   On the death of a member the scheme administrator must report to the personal representatives:

- The percentage of the standard lifetime allowance crystallised by, and the amount and date of payment of, a defined benefit or uncrystallised funds lump sum death benefit paid by the scheme in relation to the member (no later than the last day of the period of three months beginning with the day on which the final such payment was made);

- The cumulative total percentage crystallised by benefit crystallisation events in respect of the deceased member under the scheme or any schemes from which assets have been transferred (whether directly or indirectly), in respect of the deceased member's pension rights, but excluding any amount in respect of lump sum death benefit in respect of the deceased member. The information must be provided no later than the last day of the period of two months beginning with the day on which a request is received from the member's personal representatives.

Administrator of annuities in payment – provided to and by administrator, insurance company and annuitant

7.7   If, on the crystallisation of a member's pension rights, an insurance company is provided with funds to provide (whether from secured or unsecured pension) a scheme pension or lifetime annuity, the scheme administrator must, within three months of annuity purchase, provide the insurance company with details of the percentage of the standard lifetime allowance crystallised both before and after such a purchase.

At least annually, the insurance company must provide the annuitant with a statement of the percentage of the standard lifetime allowance crystallised at the date of the statement in respect of the annuity.

Employer company

7.8   If an unauthorised employer payment is made to a company, that company must provide the following information to HMRC:

(a)   details of the scheme that made the payment;

(b)   the nature of the payment;

(c)   the amount of the payment;

(d)   the date on which the payment was made.

The information must be provided to HMRC no later than 31 January following the tax year in which the payment was made.

Insurance company etc to personal representatives on death

7.9   Where an insurance company or similar provider has paid an annuity from the assets of the scheme and the person concerned has died, the provider must, on request, provide the following information to the personal representatives within two months of the request:

(a)   the date the annuity was purchased;

(b)   the amount crystallised as a percentage of the standard lifetime allowance.

Personal representatives to HMRC

7.10   Where a defined benefit or uncrystallised funds lump sum death benefit is paid which, either alone or when aggregated with other similar payments, results in a lifetime allowance charge, the following information must be provided within 13 months of the death of the member, or 30 days from the date the personal representatives became aware of the event giving rise to the charge:

(a)   the name of the scheme and the name and address of the administrator;

(b)   the name of the deceased member;

(c)   the amount and date of the payment; and

(d)   the chargeable amount on which the charge arises.

If a requirement to report arises after expiration of the above period, the information must be provided within 30 months of the death of the member. On the discovery of further information after the expiry of such a period, a report must be made within three months of discovery.

RECORD KEEPING

7.11   The general rule is that all records which are held by administrators, trustees, advisers, employers or directors must be kept for a period of at least six years.

Accounting for tax reports

7.12   The accounting for tax return APSS302, which replaced Forms 1(SF) and 2(SF) in their entirety, must be submitted to HMRC covering:

(a)   lifetime allowance charges,

(b)   tax due on lump sums repaid,

(c)   taxable death benefits,

(d)   taxable refunds of surpluses, and

(e)   de-registration charges.

The return must be made on a quarterly basis and must be provided within 45 days of the relevant quarter end.

Registered pension scheme return

7.13 Under the *Finance Act 2004, s 250* HMRC may give notice to the scheme administrator of a registered scheme that it requires a registered pension scheme return to be completed. The information required by the return is as follows:

- contributions made under the scheme;

- transfers of monies or assets representing accrued rights;

- income and gains from investments or deposits held by the scheme;

- other receipts of the scheme;

- sums and other assets held for the purposes of the scheme;

- the scheme's liabilities:

- provision of benefits by the scheme;

- other expenditure of the scheme;

- membership of the scheme;

- any other matter relating to administration of the scheme.

The normal timescale for submission applies, being 31 January following the relevant tax year (or three months after any notice which is given after 31 October in the relevant tax year, or three months from the completion of the winding up of a scheme which wound up before that date).

Online reporting

7.14 Since October 2007 HMRC have only accepted electronic filing of certain tax returns. This includes the three most important returns of information – the accounting for tax return, the event report and the pension scheme return.

If paper versions of these reports are submitted to HMRC, they will be returned and treated as if they had never been received. It is therefore important for scheme administrators to ensure they can submit these electronically. Electronic returns can be submitted over the internet either by using commercial software developed for the purpose or by using the free web-based online service provided by HMRC. If an electronic return is greater than 23.8 megabytes, it should be sent to HMRC on compact disc.

Not all reports of information come under the mandatory HMRC e-filing protocol. The following table sets out what information must be submitted online and what information may still be supplied in paper format.

Form number	Description	Online or paper
APSS 100	Pension Scheme Tax Registration	Online
APSS 100 (Insert 1)	Supplementary page to Q6	Online
APSS 101	Election to contract out	Paper
APSS 102	Election for Industry-wide money purchase schemes to contract out	Paper
APSS 103	Relief at Source Details	Online or paper
APSS 103A	Relief at Source Details – Specimen Signatures	Paper
APSS 105	Relief at Source Interim Claim	Paper
APSS 106	Relief at Source Annual Claim	Paper
APSS 107	Relief at Source Annual Statistical Return	Paper
APSS 108	Declaration as a Scheme Administrator of a deferred annuity contract scheme	Online
APSS 109	Notification of succession to a split scheme	Paper
APSS 109 (Insert)	Supplementary page for Q3	Paper
APSS 110	Notification of succession to a sub-scheme	Paper
APSS 150	Authorising and De authorising a practitioner	Online or paper
APSS 151	Add Scheme Administrator for second and subsequent notifications of pre-A day Scheme Administrators or for any post-A day Scheme Administrators	Online
APSS 151	Add Scheme Administrator for first notifications of Pre-A day Scheme Administrators	Online or paper
APSS 152	Amend Scheme Details	Online or paper
APSS 153	Change of Scheme Administrator/Practitioner user details	Online or paper
APSS 154	Associate Scheme Administrator to Scheme	Online or paper
APSS 155	Election to vary a Contracting out or Appropriate Scheme Certificate	Paper
APSS 160	Cessation of Scheme Administrator	Online
APSS 161	Pre-register as a Scheme Administrator/ Practitioner	Online or paper
PS 199	Scheme Wind-Up pre-A day	Paper
APSS 200	Protection of Existing Rights	Paper
APSS 201	Enhanced Lifetime Allowance (Pension Credit Rights)	Paper
APSS 202	Enhanced Lifetime Allowance (International)	Paper
APSS 209	Request by Scheme Administrator for Lifetime Allowance Certificate Details	Paper
APSS 250	Qualifying Overseas Pension Schemes	Paper
APSS 251	Qualifying Recognised Overseas Pension Schemes	Paper
APSS 252	Report of Benefit Crystallisation Events	Paper
APSS 252 (Insert)	Supplementary page for relevant migrant members	Paper
APSS 253	Payments in respect of Relevant Members	Paper
APSS 253 (Insert)	Supplementary page for APSS 253	Paper
APSS 254	Election for deemed benefit crystallisation event	Paper

Accounting and auditing requirements

7.15 The following regulations govern the required accounting and auditing actions for registered schemes:

- the *Registered Pension Scheme (Accounting and Assessment) Regulations 2005 (SI 2005/3454)*;

- the *Registered Pension Scheme (Audited Accounts) (Specified Persons) Regulations 2005 (SI 2005/3456)*.

SELF-ASSESSMENT

Pension schemes

7.16 From 6 April 2007 pension schemes will only be issued with a self-assessment tax return (form SA970) if they have previously been liable to tax or if a repayment of tax has been claimed. For most registered pension schemes a self-assessment tax return is therefore no longer necessary.

If a self-assessment return does need to be completed, note that this cannot be done online as the facility does not yet exist. Returns must therefore be made in paper format. As far as self-assessment is generally concerned, the deadline for submission of paper returns is now 31 October (31 January for electronic returns). HMRC has stated it is considering ways to extend the online service but will in the meantime allow more time for filing form SA970 (using powers in s 118 Taxes Management Act 1970). Penalty notices should not be issued where a 2007/08 tax year SA970 return is submitted by 31 January 2009, but it may be advisable to check with HMRC.

The SA970 self-assessment return is not to be confused with the pension scheme return, which may be requested by HMRC in addition.

Members

7.17 Members of registered pension schemes may need to complete self-assessment tax returns if they receive interest on short service refund lump sums (see **4.25**). If they do not receive a notice to make a return, they should inform HMRC of chargeability.

Self-assessment tax returns have now been modified to cover any member liability to the annual allowance charge. Self-assessment should also be used for any unauthorised member payments.

EMPLOYER-FINANCED RETIREMENT BENEFIT SCHEMES (EFRBS)

7.18 The *Employer-Financed Retirement Benefits Schemes (Provision of Information) Regulations 2005 (SI 2005/3453)* state that the term 'responsible person' has the same meaning as in the *Income Tax (Earnings and Pensions) Act 2003, s 399A*.

7.18 *Reporting*

The information requirements run on a year of assessment basis, being a year beginning 6 April in any year and ending the following 5 April. The regulations state that the responsible person is the prescribed person for the purpose of their requirements. The main requirement is that the responsible person must notify HMRC before 31 January following the year of assessment after the coming into existence of the EFRBS.

The responsible person is also responsible for providing details of the relevant benefits which have been paid during the year of assessment (with certain exceptions which are otherwise chargeable to tax). The information required is:

(a)   the name, address and National Insurance number of the recipient of the relevant benefit;

(b)   the nature of the relevant benefit provided;

(c)   the amount of the relevant benefit calculated in accordance with *ITEPA 2003, s 398(2)*.

The information must be provided no later than 7 July following the end of the year of assessment in which the benefit was provided.

Chapter 8

Compliance

INTRODUCTION

8.1   This chapter describes the main requirements for tax compliance in respect of registered pension schemes and individuals. Paragraphs **8.2** to **8.16** contain a general list of charges, the penalties and the de-registration rules which can apply. Paragraphs **8.16** to **8.71** below explore the matter of general compliance with the main UK tax rules in the wider issues of meetings, visits, appeals, mitigation, communication and taxpayers' rights and entitlements.

The incurred tax charges, penalties and sanctions under the post A-Day pensions regime are codified. This is in keeping with the withdrawal of HMRC's discretionary powers in relation to tax-advantaged pension arrangements. The main charge under the current regime is the unauthorised payment tax charge of 40%, which can be imposed (according to circumstances) on the scheme member, the scheme administrator or the employer.

- The annual allowance charge and the lifetime allowance charge are described in **Chapter 10**.

- The charges which relate to taxable property for IRPS are covered by **Chapter 12**.

- The charges which relate to unauthorised payments are covered by **Chapter 14**.

SOURCES OF TAX CHARGES AND PENALTIES

8.2   Traditionally, the tax charges which could apply to approved pensions schemes had relied heavily on the provisions of the *Taxes Management Act 1970*. Whereas this is still an important, and relevant, statute, the *Finance Act 2004* brought in new charges and compliance rules for registered schemes.

The penalties and charges which existed at A-Day are in the main retained beyond that date. The relevant statute, in addition to the *Finance Act 2004*, is therefore the *Taxes Management Act 1970*.

SUBJECT LIST OF TAX CHARGES AND PENALTIES

8.3   The following is a list of tax charges and penalties:

- general charge of unauthorised payments of 40%;

- benefit-in-kind charge;

- charge on deliberately winding up a scheme;

- deregistration of a scheme charge;

- penalties on failures to provide documents or required particulars;

- penalties for failure to provide information;

- penalties for submitting fraudulent or negligent statements;

- charges on liberated pension savings;

- charges on relevant non-UK scheme (RNUKS – see **Chapter 9**);

- charges on false or fraudulent information concerning the lifetime allowance;

- charges on surplus repayments;

- charges on value-shifting transactions;

- charges on withholding information;

- unauthorised payments surcharge;

- scheme sanction charge.

ACCOUNTING FOR TAX RETURN

8.4   Failure by a scheme administrator to make a return may attract a penalty under the *Finance Act 2004, s 260*. The amount of the penalty will depend on the amount of the tax which should have been paid and the number of people who have been omitted from the return. However, where fraud or negligence is concerned additional penalties may be incurred under *s 260(6)*.

ENHANCED PROTECTION

8.5   Where incorrect or false documents or information is provided when seeking enhanced protection from the lifetime allowance, the *Finance Act 2004, s 261* empowers HMRC to impose a penalty of up to 25% of the excess allowance claimed on the individual return. Where HMRC requests evidence of an individual's registration for enhancements, failure to comply may incur a charge of up to £3,000 on the individual concerned (*s 262*).

If additional benefits accrue after A-Day, and a member has claimed enhanced protection, HMRC must be notified. Failure to notify HMRC within 90 days of the recommencement of benefit accrual can incur a penalty on the individual of up to £3,000 under the *Finance Act 2004, s 263*.

GENERAL PENALTIES FOR NON-COMPLIANCE BY REGISTERED SCHEMES

Main principles

8.6   Registered pension schemes have to report unauthorised payments, and deemed unauthorised payments (see **Chapter 14**) to HMRC under events reports (see **Chapter 7**). Event reports must be filed by 31 January following the end of the tax year in which the event occurred.

An incorrect report will result in the scheme administrator incurring a penalty charge not exceeding £3,000. A failure to report will result in the scheme administrator incurring an initial penalty charge of £300, with penalties of £60 a day for continuing non-compliance. The same penalties apply for failures by companies to report an unauthorised payment.

The penalties for failures by individuals to report an unauthorised payment on a tax return, or to declare liability if no return has been issued, or the late submission of a return remain under the self-assessment rules (see **Chapter 7**).

Further details are given in **8.7** to **8.16**.

Fraudulent or negligent statements

8.7   Any individual who makes a fraudulent or negligent claim, representation or order to obtain tax reliefs, repayments or unauthorised payments may attract a penalty of £3,000 under the *Finance Act 2004, s 264(1)*. Any other persons who are implicated in the action may attract penalties of the same amount under *s 264(2)*.

Failure to provide information

8.8   The *Taxes Management Act 1970, s 98*, was amended to extend penalties in circumstances where there has been a failure to provide information, or false information has been provided. Additionally, failure to preserve documents can incur a penalty not exceeding £3,000 under the *Finance Act 2004, s 258(2)*.

Failure to comply with notices

8.9   Failure to comply with notices regarding documents or particulars may incur penalties under the *Finance Act 2004, s 259(1)*. The penalties shall not exceed £300, plus an additional £60 per day for continuing failure. Where a person fraudulently or negligently produces incorrect documents or particulars the penalty shall not exceed £3,000 under *s 259(4)*.

Misdirection of transfer payments

8.10   It is a scheme administrator's duty to ensure that transfers to a registered scheme which invests in insurance policies are made to the appropriate person. Failure to do so can attract a penalty of up to £3,000 under the *Finance Act 2004, s 266.*

Winding-up lump sums

8.11   Any attempt to deliberately wind up the scheme for the purpose of providing lump sums to member's or beneficiaries can attract a penalty on the administrator under the *Finance Act 2004, s 265.* The penalty shall not exceed £3,000 in respect of each member to whom a lump sum has been paid. It is also important to note that the scheme may lose its registration and so suffer a 40% tax charge.

Trust-busting

8.12   Trust-busting is deemed to have occurred normally where tax-free lump sums are paid to scheme member's in excess of the amounts that are permitted under the existing approval terms, and member's often pay 20% to 30% of the amount extracted in the form of commission.

In Pensions Update Number 132, HMRC stated that 'transfers are often arranged with offshore companies and bank accounts to a scheme in the name of a fictitious new employer'. The post A-Day tax regime imposes many charges and penalties on trust-busting, including possible scheme de-registration (see **8.13**).

SCHEME DE-REGISTRATION

8.13   HMRC will only consider giving notice to the scheme administrator under the *Finance Act 2004, s 157,* to de-register a scheme under *s 158,* in extreme circumstances. For example, complex screenings from tax, and schemes which are set up to avoid, reduce or delay the payment of tax which is lawfully due, can bring about loss of registration. In other words, it is the administration of the scheme which counts, and a blatant lack of good faith will be heavily penalised. Specific examples may include:

●   where unauthorised and deemed unauthorised and other payments incur the scheme sanction charge under *s 241*; and

●   the amount exceeds the de-registration threshold in **8.14**.

The de-registration charge under *s 242* is 40% of the value of the scheme immediately before it was de-registered.

The de-registration threshold

8.14   The de-registration threshold is breached when the total percentages of the fund used up by each scheme chargeable payments in any 12-month period is 25% or more.

The percentages of the fund used up by each scheme chargeable payments is calculated as follows:

$$\frac{\text{Scheme chargeable payment}}{\text{Value of scheme at that time}} \times \frac{100}{1}$$

The market value must be applied.

Right to appeal

8.15   A right to appeal against any action or decision by HMRC may be made to the General Commissioners or Special Commissioners within 30 days of the relevant event taking place. An appeal may be made in the following circumstances, where there is a grievance which can be supported by the appellant:

- against failure to register a scheme;

- against de-registration of a scheme;

- against exclusion from a scheme being treated as a recognised overseas pension scheme;

- against notices which call for the release of documents or particulars or other information; or

- in respect of the discharge of the lifetime allowance charge.

Exoneration/discharge from liability

8.16   There may be cases where scheme administrators have been provided with false information by scheme members, for example in connection with the lifetime allowance. Scheme administrators can ask HMRC for a discharge under *Finance Act 2004, s 267* from the lifetime allowance charge if they think that it is fair and reasonable to do so. This may also apply where the unauthorised payment or scheme sanction charges have been incurred.

Appeals (see **8.15**) can be made under the *Finance Act 2004, s 269*, if there is a refusal by HMRC to discharge the scheme administrator. The appeal should be made to the General Commissioners or Special Commissioners within 30 days of HMRC refusing to discharge the said person.

TAX AVOIDANCE SCHEMES

8.17   Tax avoidance schemes must be declared (*Finance Act 2004, ss 306–319*). Mandatory disclosure by promoters of tax avoidance schemes came into effect on 1 August 2004.

The *Finance Act 2004, Pt,7*, relates to general tax avoidance. *Section 306* concerns notifiable arrangements and notifiable proposals under tax avoidance schemes. Such arrangements are those which fall within any description prescribed by the Treasury by regulations. They enable a person to gain a tax advantage by means of the main, or one of the main, benefits of the arrangement. A promoter is described in *s 307* as a person in relation to a notifiable proposal, if, in the course of a trade, profession or business which involves the provision to other persons of services relating to taxation:

- he is to any extent responsible for the design of the proposed arrangements; or

- he makes the notifiable proposal available for implementation by other persons;

- in relation to notifiable arrangements, if he is a promoter in relation to a notifiable proposal which is implemented by those arrangements or if, in the course of a trade, profession or business which involves the provision to other persons of services relating to taxation, he is to any extent responsible for:

  - the design of the arrangements; or

  - the organisation or management of the arrangements.

A person is not to be treated as a promoter by reason of anything done in prescribed circumstances. By way of a relaxation, the Government stated on 24 June 2004 that only those at the heart of the scheme or arrangement, who are capable of meeting its obligations, will be treated as the promoter.

Under *s 308* the promoter must provide information to HMRC within a prescribed period after the date on which he makes a notifiable proposal, or the date on which he first becomes aware of any transaction forming part of the proposed arrangements. Under *s 319* this applies to post-17 March 2004 relevant dates and transactions.

Under s *309* the duty falls on any client who enters into any transaction forming part of any notifiable arrangements in relation to which a promoter is resident outside the UK, and no promoter is resident in the UK. By *s 310* the duty extends to any other person who enters into any transaction forming part of any notifiable arrangements in similar circumstances. *Sections 309* and *310* apply, by virtue of *s 319,* to post-22 April 2004 transactions.

There are comprehensive guidance notes on the HMRC website. The main regulations which apply are described in **8.18** to **8.20**.

Tax Avoidance Schemes (Promoters and Prescribed Circumstances) Regulations 2004 (SI 2004/1865)

8.18 The Regulations concern income tax, corporation tax and capital gains tax. Promoters of tax avoidance schemes must notify HMRC within a prescribed period of the earlier of:

- where a promoter makes schemes available for implementation by others, the date on which he does so; and

- for other promoters, the date on which they first become aware of any transaction forming part of the notifiable arrangements.

Tax Avoidance Schemes (Prescribed Descriptions of Arrangements) Regulations 2006 (SI 2006/1543)

8.19   The Regulations make fresh provision for the disclosure of tax avoidance schemes in relation to income tax, corporation tax and capital gains tax. They replace the *Tax Avoidance Schemes (Prescribed Descriptions of Arrangements) Regulations 2004 (SI 2004/1863,* amended by *SI 2004/3429).* In particular, they prescribe the arrangements:

- which a promoter or (where he is obliged to report them) a user might wish to keep confidential from either HMRC or other promoters;

- for which a promoter might reasonably expect a premium fee;

- where:

    (a)   the tax advantage arises, to more than an incidental degree, from the inclusion of a financial product;

    (b)   a promoter or someone connected with him becomes a party to the financial product;

    (c)   the price of the financial product differs significantly from what might reasonably be expected in the open market.;

- which involve the use of standardised tax products;

- which are made available to more than one individual and are expected to generate losses to enable individuals to reduce their income tax or capital gains tax liability;

- which include a plant or machinery lease.

Tax Avoidance Schemes (Information) (Amendment) Regulations 2006 (SI 2006/1544), as amended

8.20   These Regulations amended *regulation 4* of the *Tax Avoidance Schemes (Information) Regulations 2004 (SI 2004/1864)* by providing that the period within which prescribed arrangements in connection with tax avoidance schemes are to be notified to HMRC under *Finance Act 2004, s 310*, was 30 days from the date of the first transaction which formed part of the arrangements.

Subsequently, the regulations were further amended as follows:

- the *Tax Avoidance Schemes (Information) (Amendment) (No 2) Regulations 2007(SI 2007/3103)* came into force on 20 November 2007 and amended *SI 2004/1864)* by inserting a new *regulation 8B*. The new regulation sets out the period after which a higher rate of penalty under the *Taxes Management Act 1970, s 98C(2B)*, will apply where there is a failure to comply with the obligations under the *Finance Act 2004, s 308*, following an order under the *Finance Act 2004, s 314A* (order to disclose); as follows:

    8B.   For the purposes of section 98C (2B) of the Taxes Management Act 1970 (higher rate of penalty after the making of an order under section 314A (5)) the prescribed period is 10 days beginning with the date on which the order is made;

- the *Tax Avoidance Schemes (Information) (Amendment) Regulations 2008 (SI 2008/1947)* came into force on 1 November 2008 and:

  - prescribed the information to be provided by a promoter to a client under the Finance Act 2004, s 312, or by a client to other parties under s 312A;

  - prescribed the period within which information prescribed under s 312A is to be delivered to the other parties as the period of 30 days beginning with:.

  - the day on which the client first became aware of any transaction forming part of notifiable arrangements or proposed notifiable arrangements; or; if later,

  - the day on which the prescribed information was notified to the client by the promoter under s 312;

  - exempted an employer from the duty to notify under s 312A if an employee of that employer received or expected to receive a tax advantage by reason of employment.

PENALTIES FOR NON-COMPLIANCE

8.21   Under the *Finance Act 2004, s 312,* the promoter had to provide information to the client within 30 days in relation to the arrangements. Penalties would be incurred for non-compliance (*Taxes Management Act 1970, s 98C*). A penalty not exceeding £5,000 would be imposed on a promoter, with penalties of £600 a day for continuing non-compliance. Any person who was a party to the arrangement who failed to comply would be fined £100 per scheme, or £500 or £1,000 if he had previously failed to comply during the preceding period of 36 months on one or more occasion (respectively).

These penalties were subjected to some change:

The *Tax Avoidance Schemes (Penalty) Regulations 2007 (SI 2007/3104)* came into force on 20 November 2007 and:

- increased the penalty following the making of an order under the *Finance Act 2004, s 306A,* so that the daily penalty imposed under the *Taxes Management Act 1970, s 98C (1),* was increased to £5,000;

- increased the penalty following the making of an order under the *Finance Act 2004, s 314A,* so that the penalty imposed under the *Taxes Management Act 1970, s 98C(1)(b),* was increased to £5,000.

DISCLOSURE

8.22   Disclosures must be made on the forms available on the HMRC website, which were published on 28 May 2004. These are form S292 for UK promoters, form S293 for users where there is an overseas promoter and form S294 for users where there is no external promoter. A summary of the arrangement must be provided on the forms, with an explanation of how the tax advantage arises, a description of the transaction and the tax relief involved. There should also be an explanation of the statutory provisions on which the advice has been based.

NON-DISCLOSURE

8.23   It is not necessary to disclose an arrangement if at least one of the following tests is failed:

Premium fee test

Both of the following factors must be present:

- the fee must be chargeable in relation to the tax avoidance element of the arrangements;

- the fee must be attributable to, and contingent upon, obtaining a tax advantage.

Confidentiality test

The criterion is: Is there something about the tax avoidance scheme that the promoter would want to keep confidential?

Off-market terms test

This means that the promoter becomes a party to the financial product, such as being party to a loan, derivative or other financial product. The criterion is: Are the terms offered different from market rates?

The statutory rules are not only very wide, they are almost impossible to understand. The intended meanings of 'avoidance' and 'promoter' in the Act remain unclear, despite the amending regulations which are described above. It is hoped that further clarification will be received at a future date. The rules potentially impact on employment terms, securities, financial products, premium fees and confidentiality testing – which will widely impact on disclosure rules for employers, advisers and others and can involve pension schemes.

HMRC visits and audits

8.24   Audit programmes will be conducted on the basis of random selection and risk assessment. Audits cover various matters including administration, contributions and valuation of assets, investments and benefits-in-kind, scheme payments, the calculation of the lifetime allowance etc. Non-compliance will incur penalties and sanctions, as will false claims for transitional protection and the making of payments that do not comply with existing protection.

Tax inspections, investigations, penalties and mitigation

HMRC and Revenue and Customs Prosecutions Office

8.25   Many matters are common to all investigations and appeals, not only to registered pension schemes. The main compliance concern of the Treasury in recent years has been to block what it considers to be 'unacceptable tax loss'. The following list addresses the main issue of taxation avoidance, and the relevant bodies and statutes concerned with such activity:

- tax avoidance schemes;

- the role of HMRC inspectors and its executive officers;

- the powers of official compliance officers;

- the investigation offices, and their functions;

- the Special Compliance Office;

- the VAT civil evasion procedures;

- the Taxpayers' Charter;

- the relevant appeal procedures and the timescales which apply;

- the role of the Appeal Commissioners as independent bodies from HMRC comprised of either the General Commissioners or the Special Commissioners;

- the effect of the National Audit Office on the Civil Service offices they visit, and the consequential changes to working practices and tightening-up of procedures;

- when it is appropriate to use the internal procedures of government departments in order to have a matter reconsidered, and what those internal procedures are;

- the use of the independent adjudicator;

- the recourse to judicial review;

- the settlement of tax by agreement, following investigations;

- the methods by which penalties and loss may be mitigated;

- the Chancellor's commission of HMRC to look into tax avoidance schemes and tax loss through unacceptable tax-planning devices;

- the penalty regimes which apply to pension scheme trustees and administrators;

- the automatic tax charges which are triggered by certain actions or by unauthorised payments out of approved schemes; and

- the anti-avoidance legislation.

It should be noted that HMRC follows a system of co-ordinated case working, which means that it is likely that HMRC SPSS and the inspectors of taxes will be aware of most of the tax circumstances that affect pension schemes and the activities of their sponsors and members.

Subject to the principle that Treasury Ministers do not intervene in the affairs of individual taxpayers, including matters relating to criminal investigations, the Commissioners of the HMRC and Revenue and Customs Prosecutions Office are responsible for, and accountable to, parliament via Treasury Ministers for:

- anything done in the course of an investigation;

- the quality of legal advice given by HMRC lawyers;

- decisions as to the mix of cases necessary to secure HMRC Public Service Agreements; and

- HMRC policy including the criteria to be used in deciding whether alternatives to prosecution should be applied.

Department of Constitutional Affairs (DCA)

8.26 The Department of Constitutional Affairs (DCA) is responsible for the overall policy governing the way in which HMRC operates and is administered. The DCA issued the following leaflet in order to assist with the making of tax appeals: *Tax Appeals: A guide to appealing against decisions of the Inland Revenue [HMRC] on tax and other matters.*

The leaflet has been replaced and is now available from the General Commissioners' website.

National Audit Office (NAO)

8.27 The National Audit Office (NAO) is the external auditor of government departments. It scrutinises public spending on behalf of Parliament and is totally independent of government. Its work involves auditing the accounts of all central government departments and agencies, as well as a wide range of other public bodies, and it reports to Parliament on the economy, efficiency and effectiveness with which these departments and agencies have used public money.

The NAO is headed by the Comptroller and Auditor General. During the pensions consultative process the Chancellor asked the NAO for a report on the number of people who would be disadvantaged by the new simplified tax system.

Special Compliance Office (SCO) and codes of practice

8.28 The Special Compliance Office (SCO) operates under codes of practice. SCO is the senior investigation arm of HMRC which deals with the most serious cases of fraud and suspected fraud and have the power to make criminal prosecutions. However, the majority of cases are finalised by way of a contract settlement requiring payment of tax, interest and penalties. The penalties are frequently at the heavy end of the spectrum where the maximum penalty is 100% of the tax lost. This can be mitigated if disclosure and co-operation are good – and professional advice is recommended by HMRC if this is to be achieved.

The three categories of SCO investigation, in order of seriousness, are:

- Cases other than suspected serious fraud.

- Cases of suspected serious fraud, where no prosecution is intended – most cases are finalised by contract settlement rather than prosecution.

- Cases of suspected serious fraud, where prosecution is intended.

Receipt of a form COP8 indicates that the SCO suspects that some irregularities have occurred. At this stage it can be possible to negotiate an agreement with the SCO if serious fraud is not involved. This means exploratory meetings and the inspection of relevant documentation. Receipt of a form COP9 means that serious fraud is suspected from the outset. Where this is proven, prosecution may result.

The following relevant codes of practice are available on www.hmrc.gov.uk:

- COP1: 'Putting things right – How to complain';

- COP4: 'Inspection of schemes operated by financial intermediaries';

- COP8: 'Special Compliance Office investigations: Cases other than suspected serious fraud' – it states that HMRC does not conduct investigations with a criminal prosecution in mind but towards a financial recovery of any tax, interest and penalties which are owed;

- COP9: Special Compliance Office Cases of suspected serious fraud – the investigation will be undertaken with or without the tax-payer's voluntary co-operation, and will be conducted with a view to the imposition of a civil penalty for fraudulent conduct, if HMRC's suspicions are confirmed. The investigation is **not** conducted with a view to the taxpayer being prosecuted for tax fraud;

- COP10: 'Information and advice';

- COP11: 'Self-assessment. Local office enquiries';

- COP14: 'Corporation Tax Self assessment Enquiries';

- IR160: 'Enquiries under self-assessment. How settlements are negotiated';

- SA/BK4: 'Self assessment. A general guide to keeping records';

HMRCs website states:

'We are currently updating and merging the information contained within SA/BK4, "Self Assessment – a general guide to keeping records" and SA/BK8, "Self Assessment – your guide". This means these publications are no longer available to download or view. We hope to have the new and improved guidance available very shortly. We apologise for any inconvenience this may cause'

The SFO liaises with other government bodies. For example, it is investigating an independent trustee firm from August 2008, following a referral by The Pensions Regulator. The Regulator had removed authority for 29 schemes from the independent trustee firm.

Complaints against HMRC

8.29 As a first step it's usually best to speak to someone in the relevant tax office. The complaints procedure is:

- The complainant should write to, or ask to speak to, the customer relations or complaints manager for the relevant HMRC office. If the complaint is made in writing, the word 'Complaint' should be written at the top of the letter. Most complaints are resolved within 15 days.

- If the complainant is unhappy with the negotiation, he should request the director with overall responsibility for the office concerned to review the complaint. This can be done in writing, by fax or phone, or HMRC will do it for the complainant if this is preferred.

- If the complainant is still unhappy, he can ask the Adjudicator to look into his complaint.

Additionally, the Independent Police Complaints Commission (IPCC) can deal with complaints that include one of the following serious allegations about the conduct of HMRC staff:

- staff behaviour resulting in death or serious injury;

- serious assault by HMRC staff;

- serious sexual assault by HMRC staff;

- serious corruption;

- criminal offence or behaviour aggravated by discriminatory behaviour.

Serious arrestable offences (such as murder, rape, kidnapping and death by dangerous driving)

The IPCC only has authority for incidents occurring in England and Wales. Where an incident occurred in Scotland or Northern Ireland the local HMRC complaints team should be consulted.

Adjudicator

8.30 Leaflet AO1 is available from the Adjudicator's Office and HMRC. Details are as follows:

The Adjudicators Office
Eight Floor
Euston Tower
286 Euston Road
London
NW1 3US

Telephone: 0300 057 1111 or 020 7667 1832 (Typetalk facilities are available)
Fax: 0300 057 1212
Email: **adjudicators@gtnet.gov.uk**
Website: **www.adjudicatorsoffice.gov.uk**

The Adjudicator will consider complaints provided that the matter:

(a)   cannot be considered by the courts or other tribunals;

(b)   has been fully considered by HMRC or the Valuation Office Agency;

(c)   does not concern departmental policy;

(d)   is not being investigated by the Ombudsman.

The Adjudicator is an impartial referee whose recommendations are independent.

Ombudsman

8.31   If the complainant is unhappy with the response of HMRC or the Adjudicator, or with the handling of a complaint, he can ask a Member of Parliament to refer his case to the Parliamentary Ombudsman. The Ombudsman will accept referrals from a Member of Parliament, but the taxpayer should approach his own Member of Parliament first. Details are as follows:

Office of the Parliamentary Commissioner for Administration
Millbank Tower
Millbank
London
SW1P 4QP
Helpline: 0845 015 4033
Fax: 020 72174160
Email: **pca-enqu@ombudsman.org.uk**
Website: **www.ombudsman.org.uk**

Appeals may be made against a determination by the Ombudsman. Appeals are made to the High Court, and may progress to the Court of Appeal.

A taxpayer can also ask his Member of Parliament to take up his case with HMRC or Treasury Ministers.

COMPENSATION AND COSTS

8.32   Any reasonable costs can be claimed back. HMRC lists the following examples as reasonable costs:

- postage;
- phone calls;
- travelling expenses;
- professional fees; and
- financial charges.

Payments for worry and distress will usually range from £25 to £500. If a complaint was handled badly or took an unreasonable time to be dealt with, additional compensation on top of any reasonable costs will usually range from £25 to £500.

Extra Statutory Concession A19, 'Arrears of tax arising through official error', explains the position in more detail. Various tax charges and National Insurance contributions can be mitigated.

What is judicial review?

8.33 Judicial review progresses through the courts and relates to the *way* in which a public service or official decision was reached (rather than the decision itself). In other words, judicial reviews are a challenge to the way in which a decision has been made, rather than the rights and wrongs of the conclusion reached.

Once leave of the court has been given, a notice is served on the persons concerned. A review may be granted without the HMRC's prior knowledge. The court will not substitute what it thinks is the 'correct' decision.

Inspections and negotiations – the taxpayer

8.34 HMRC will arrange a meeting and invite the taxpayer to attend with his professional adviser. Generally, penalties may be incurred of an amount which does not exceed 100% of an underpaid amount, and additional surcharges may be imposed. Maximum penalties are likely to be imposed in cases of fraud, and lesser penalties imposed in cases of neglect.

Confidentiality

8.35 The taxpayer has a right to a high degree of confidentiality. HMRC is a data controller under the *Data Protection Act 1998*. The taxpayer may refuse to discuss any matter in front of other people, including his business partners, fellow directors and spouse or partner. His adviser may accompany him at all meetings and correspond with HMRC on his behalf.

Meetings

8.36 If the taxpayer decides to attend meetings HMRC will make a written record of the meetings. The taxpayer may ask for a copy of the record; and HMRC may ask the taxpayer to sign a copy of its notes to show that they accurately reflect what was said. Meetings may be held at:

- the office of a professional adviser;
- HMRC's local office or another HMRC office;
- the taxpayer's business premises; or
- the taxpayer's home.

The taxpayer can ask his professional adviser to attend these meetings.

The investigation

8.37   Following a meeting the taxpayer should tell HMRC without delay if he subsequently thinks that he may have provided incorrect or incomplete information, or he wishes to add anything to what he has already said.

Keeping the taxpayer informed

8.38   The taxpayer may request HMRC at any time to explain:

- his legal rights;

- why HMRC has taken a particular action;

- the taxpayer's obligation under the law.

The taxpayer has the right to ask HMRC why it is continuing with an investigation if, for example, he believes that he has provided all the relevant information and explanations and HMRC has had adequate time to investigate the position and bring matters to a close. If the investigation includes an enquiry into a self-assessment tax return, the taxpayer may ask the Appeal Commissioners to consider whether that enquiry should be closed.

Paying tax during enquiries

8.39   HMRC will ask the taxpayer to make a payment on account towards any additional liability it thinks is due pending the conclusion of the investigation. It may make a provisional amendment to the taxpayer's or company's self-assessment before the end of the investigation. The taxpayer has a right to appeal against such assessments or amendments and can ask to postpone payment. If the two sides cannot agree, the taxpayer can ask the Appeal Commissioners to decide how much tax he should pay.

Appeal hearings

8.40   The taxpayer has 30 days to appeal to independent Appeal Commissioners against any self-assessment amendment or assessment. If the two sides cannot agree, they both have the right to ask the Commissioners to hear any appeal.

Concluding the investigation

8.41   If HMRC conclude that it is appropriate to seek a money settlement it will try to reach an agreement with the taxpayer covering the amount of tax and other duties, interest and penalties which it believes are due. If the two sides cannot agree, HMRC may formally determine the tax, interest and penalties, and the taxpayer has a right to have any appeals he makes heard by an independent appeal body.

Where there have been errors or omissions in the taxpayer's accounts or tax returns he will be asked to sign a certificate of full disclosure.

Interest, surcharge and penalties

8.42 Interest will be charged on any tax paid late, and a penalty may be imposed (eg where fraud or negligence applies). When calculating any penalty HMRC will take into account:

- the extent of any voluntary disclosure of irregularities the taxpayer makes;

- the taxpayer's co-operation with the investigation, such as attending meetings and providing information and documents;

- the seriousness of any errors or omissions.

(See **8.56** to **8.58** concerning mitigating charges.)

Leaflet **IR160, Enquiries under Self Assessment. How settlements are negotiated**, explains how HMRC calculates penalties. In some cases, a surcharge may be imposed, in addition to interest and penalties. Leaflet **SA/BK7, Self-assessment: Surcharge for late payment of tax**, explains surcharges.

Contact for enquiries

8.43 SCO is located in a number of different locations in the country. The main contact address for enquiries is:

The Director
HMRC Special Compliance Office
Room 326
New Court
48 Carey Street
London WC2A 2JE

Disclosure

8.44 If the taxpayer states that there are matters that need to be disclosed, he will be invited to provide a disclosure report, the nature of which will depend on the individual circumstances of the case. Areas to be covered in the report will be:

- a brief business history;

- the nature of the irregularities and how they came about;

- the extent of the irregularities;

- steps taken to verify amounts with supporting documentation and any assumptions made; and

- a detailed schedule of the irregularities for each period involved for each tax.

Normally, the disclosure report should be submitted within six months of the opening meeting. HMRC will ask for payments on account towards any tax arrears, both at the initial meeting and throughout the enquiry. Payments on account will reduce any interest charges.

No disclosure

8.45   If the taxpayer does not make a disclosure, HMRC will undertake its own investigation, using statutory information powers (including to third parties) if necessary. If it discovers irregularities it will issue formal assessments and pursue collection of unpaid tax with interest. Any penalties are likely to be significantly higher due to a reduction in the level of mitigation reflecting the fact that the taxpayer did not take the opportunity to disclose the irregularities.

What happens after the meeting?

8.46   HMRC will discuss the disclosure report with the taxpayer and his advisers. It should be signed by the taxpayer as representing a full disclosure of irregularities, and submitted within the agreed timescale. HMRC will ask the taxpayer to certify that this is the case and will not accept the report as his disclosure unless he does so. The taxpayer may be asked for other certified documents such as statements of assets and liabilities, and of bank and other accounts, including debit and credit cards operated. False statements may lead to prosecution.

Once the signed report has been received, HMRC will test the information supplied to satisfy itself that it is correct and complete. In doing so HMRC may need to exercise its legal powers to obtain information. The law may allow it to do this without the taxpayer's knowledge or approval. If HMRC disagrees with or needs to clarify any aspect of the report, it may be necessary to have a further meeting, at which it will make every effort to resolve these issues and reach an agreement with the taxpayer.

Costs

8.47   All personal costs are payable by the taxpayer, including the fees of a solicitor, accountant or other professional adviser. HMRC will close its investigation as soon as it is satisfied that the taxpayer's tax affairs are in order or settled.

Keeping the taxpayer informed

8.48   The taxpayer can ask HMRC at any time to explain:

● his legal rights;

● why HMRC have taken a particular action;

● the taxpayer's obligation under the law.

The taxpayer has the right to ask HMRC why it is continuing with an investigation if, for example, he believes that he has provided all the relevant information and explanations, and HMRC has had adequate time to investigate the position and bring matters to a close.

Providing information

8.49 HMRC will ask for the information and documents that it needs, and allow a reasonable amount of time for any information to be provided.

Reaching an agreement

8.50 Once HMRC has agreed the nature and extent of any irregularities, the procedures for concluding the investigation and paying amounts due are slightly different for direct and indirect taxes, as shown in **8.52** and **8.53**.

Direct taxes

8.51 HMRC will try to reach an agreed figure with the taxpayer covering the amount of tax, interest and penalties due. It will invite the taxpayer to sign a letter offering to pay an agreed sum and, if both parties agree the sum, it will issue a letter of acceptance. This exchange of letters is a legal contract and both parties are bound by its terms.

Indirect taxes

8.52 HMRC will write to the taxpayer informing him of the amount of tax, interest and any penalty due. If the taxpayer agrees, he will be asked to sign and return a copy of the letter. He will then be formally notified of the assessment for tax, interest and any penalty. He will be asked for payment, less any amounts paid on account. Whilst tax subject to interest charges remains unpaid, interest charges will continue to accrue.

If the parties cannot reach agreement

8.53 If the parties cannot reach agreement, HMRC may seek formally to determine the tax, interest and penalties it considers appropriate. The taxpayer has the right to appeal any formal determination of tax or penalty. For direct taxes, appeals are to the Appeals Commissioners; for indirect taxes, appeals are to the VAT and Duties Tribunal.

Calculation of interest and penalties

8.54 Interest will be charged on any tax paid late, and there may be a surcharge. The maximum penalty for both direct and indirect tax is an amount equal to 100% of the tax understated. The level of penalty can be significantly reduced in certain circumstances.

For direct taxes a penalty can be charged for an incorrect tax return if it was delivered fraudulently or negligently, or the taxpayer failed to correct the error within a reasonable time.

For indirect taxes a civil evasion penalty will normally be applied where HMRC identifies irregularities due to dishonest conduct.

Charges can be mitigated in some cases (see **8.56** to **8.58**).

Mitigation

8.55　In some cases it is possible to mitigate penalties. The rules are as shown below.

Direct taxes

8.56　When calculating any penalty HMRC takes into account the following:

- *disclosure* – a reduction of up to 20% (30% for full voluntary disclosure where there was no fear of early discovery by HMRC which reflects the extent of any voluntary disclosure of irregularities the taxpayer makes);

- *co-operation* – a reduction of up to 40%. If the taxpayer supplies information quickly, attends interviews, answers questions honestly and accurately, gives all the relevant facts including full written disclosure and pays tax on account when it becomes possible to estimate the amount due,he will be entitled to the maximum reduction; and

- *seriousness* – a reduction of up to 40%. This reflects the seriousness of the taxpayer's errors or omissions.

8.57　The maximum penalty of 100% tax evaded is reduced by an amount which depends on whether the taxpayer disclosed full details of the true VAT liability, and by the extent of the taxpayer's co-operation during the whole enquiry.

Reductions from the 100% penalty figure will normally be made, to the maximum percentages specified, as follows:

- up to 40% – early and truthful explanation as to why the arrears arose and their true extent; and

- up to 40% – fully embracing and meeting responsibilities under this procedure by, for example, supplying information promptly, including full written disclosure, attending meetings and answering questions.

In most cases, therefore, the maximum reduction obtainable will be 80% of the culpable tax. In exceptional circumstances, however, consideration will be given to a further reduction, for example where the taxpayer made a full and unprompted voluntary disclosure.

Leaflet IR160 concerns negotiating settlements.

Time to pay following settlements

8.58　If a settlement amount is agreed, but the taxpayer cannot pay the full amount immediately, it may be possible to arrange payment by instalments.

HMRC expects a taxpayer to make as large a down payment as possible, and pay the rest, including an amount for extra interest, by agreed instalments over as short a period as possible.

INSPECTION OF SCHEMES INVOLVING FINANCIAL INTERMEDIARIES

What are financial intermediaries?

8.59 Financial intermediaries are individuals or persons who deduct tax and deal with tax reliefs at source; they may include providers of tax-advantaged savings schemes. Form COP4, 'Inspection of Schemes Operated by Financial Intermediaries', explains how investigations are conducted.

Notices

8.60 In normal circumstances at least 14 days' notice of an inspection will be given, and visits may be rearranged or a pre-meeting arranged if there are sound commercial reasons to do so. If the intermediary is aware that there have been incorrect returns made to HMRC or that there has been a failure to retain records which should still be held, it is important that HMRC is informed before the visit takes place. This, and the accommodation of the inspectors during their visit (including familiarising them with internal accounting methods and giving them prompt responses), can have a significant bearing on any later settlement, particularly where penalties may be involved.

Intermediary's entitlement to information

8.61 An intermediary has a right to be appraised of the reasons why a visit is continuing if he believes that all the relevant information has been supplied to the inspection team. Additionally, an intermediary is entitled to know why certain records are required and why any explanation has been questioned. He is also entitled to a description of his rights and duties in law, a description of the powers of the inspectors, and an explanation of how the inspector's proposals and sample cases for inspection were arrived at.

Who and what will be involved?

8.62 Apart from the financial intermediary, the inspectors will almost certainly need to ask the staff some questions, which will usually concern how the internal systems operate and how and where the records are stored.

All records relating to the scheme must be made available, even if these are with an agent, and permission will be requested by the inspectors to discuss these records with the persons who are responsible for their upkeep. It will not be necessary to put all the records in one place; the inspectors will normally access the records at the place where they are kept and select a sample for review.

The inspectors may request further information and explanations as the inspection proceeds. Both parties are required to deal with requests promptly or to inform the other where the required information may be obtained.

Under their code of practice the inspectors will respond as soon as possible to enquiries (normally within 28 days) and will provide within seven days photocopies of records which have been borrowed.

Meetings and reports

8.63 Attendance at subsequent meetings is not compulsory but can be beneficial. After each visit or meeting a report will be sent and advice given by the inspectors on any necessary improvements to systems. A formal report will be sent within 20 days. Queries can be raised by the intermediary, who may agree or disagree with the findings.

Agreement of report

8.64 If tax is deemed to be due, or is deemed to have been underclaimed, the inspectors will endeavour to agree a reasonable amount with the intermediary. An offer will be made to accept a payment on account of any tax which is due, or which it seems likely will be due, in order to avoid interest building up on late payment. Occasionally, an off-set against future repayments may be agreed. Tax under-claimed will be repaid.

Non-agreement of report

8.65 If agreement cannot be reached or information is withheld, the inspectors will raise an assessment on the best of their judgment (a 'BOJ').

APPEALS AND APPEAL COMMISSIONERS

8.66 Appeals against BOJs must be lodged within 30 days of assessment (unless an extension is negotiated with the inspector concerned) and should normally be supported by an indication of how long it will take to obtain outstanding information or to provide a declaration of the income which is considered to be taxable. An offer to pay an amount within 30 days of the agreement as the inspector shall agree should have the effect of deferring a hearing before the Appeal Commissioners; otherwise the matter will proceed to appeal.

If the intermediary calls for a hearing to be held before the Appeal Commissioners the inspectors may only delay that hearing if there is good reason to do so. If no progress is made towards settlement of the appeal the inspectors may themselves call for the appeal hearing.

The Commissioners will decide on the correct figures for determining the assessment at the hearing. It is important to note that the Commissioners may well decide on a higher amount than the first settlement figure which was offered.

Normally 28 days' notice of a hearing will be given. An explanation must be given to the clerk to the Commissioners if attendance is not possible. If this is not done, or a deferral of the hearing is refused, it is likely that the tax will be determined in the absence of the party concerned.

The Appeal Commissioners usually permit a representative and witnesses to attend a hearing. However, if the representative is not a professional person they may refuse, and they will in any event normally expect the person who wishes to be represented to attend.

Contesting a decision by the Appeal Commissioners

8.67   Tax will need to be paid even if the decision is contested through the courts.

Decisions by the General Commissioners may be contested by either party in writing to the clerk to the Commissioners within 30 days of the decision being reached. The request should be for the case to go before the High Court. In Scotland the appropriate court is the Court of Session, and in Northern Ireland it is the Court of Appeal. The nominal statutory fee should be enclosed. It may be necessary that the point of law on which the case is to be stated be identified. The clerk will have 56 days to prepare a draft of the case; the appellant will have a further 56-day period in which to make any representations, plus a further 28 days for final representations. The draft must be sent to the court within 30 days if the case is to proceed.

Either party may contest decisions by the Special Commissioners by written notice sent direct to the court within 56 days. The grounds of appeal must be stated and the Inspector of Taxes and the Special Commissioners must be sent copies.

Interest and penalties

8.68   Interest will be charged and penalties may be raised on a failure to pay tax or make returns, or on reclaiming too much tax. Appeals may be made against the charges to the Appeal Commissioners. Following settlement, a visit and assistance will be offered in order to put things on a proper footing for the future.

LANDMARK TAX CASES

8.69   In the much-quoted case of *W T Ramsay v IRC* [1982] AC 300, a circular and self-cancelling scheme was set up. It was a complicated scheme which involved the making of very long-term loans by the taxpayer to interrelated companies purely for the purpose of tax avoidance as the taxpayer had no prospect of making a profit. Artificial losses were created thus avoiding corporation tax and capital gains tax by means of the manipulation of loans.

The *Ramsay* case was referred to in *R v CIR ex parte Roux Waterside Inn Limited* (1997) STI 527 which was ruled to have involved a deliberate ploy to have a scheme's approval withdrawn or lapsed following the receipt of a transfer value. In order to gain a tax advantage for the receiving scheme, overseas trustees were appointed. The ploy was countered by the Revenue's disapproval of the scheme from which the transfer had been received.

In the House of Lords case of *MacNiven (HMIT) v Westmoreland Investment Limited* [2000] UKHL 6, the *Ramsay* case was not felt to be applicable. *MacNiven* involved a property investment company owned by a large pension scheme. The company was financed by loans from the scheme. It was unsuccessful in business, and it was liquidated with few assets and owing a large debt to the scheme. The debt included over £40 million in outstanding arrears of interest.

The scheme proceeded to lend money to the company to assist it in paying the outstanding interest, and with a view to making the company more attractive to prospective purchasers. The loans were found to have been made for proper business reasons under the *Income and Corporation Taxes Act 1988 (ICTA 1988), s 338*, and it was ruled that the interest paid was real interest for tax-deduction purposes.

The case of *Venables and others v Hornby (Inspector of Taxes)* [2003] UKHL 65, [2003] All ER (D) 86 (Dec) concerned a person who had stepped down from a position as an executive director to one of a non-executive director. The Revenue maintained that such an action did not constitute 'retirement'. It lost this case in the House of Lords. However, the case gave some useful pointers as to what was likely to be deemed a genuine early retirement. The new flexibilities for drawdown of income, whilst still in service for many schemes under the post-A-Day tax regime, have rendered the case less relevant for the future.

The circumstances were as follows:

(a)   Mr Venables was a member of an SSAS, who retired (partly due to ill-health) at age 53, having been employed as an executive director in the development and construction industry.

(b)   He continued in the company as an unpaid non-executive director with a normal retirement age of 60.

(c)   The Revenue assessed the scheme lump sum under *ICTA 1988, s 600* and made a determination under the *Income Tax (Employments) Regulations 1993 (SI 1993/744), reg 49* in respect of the basic rate of tax that should have been deducted under Schedule E (now under *ITEPA*) by the trustees (both of which were appealed against).

(d)   The appellants elected to be heard by the Special Commissioners, meaning that the decision would be published publicly.

(e)   The trust deed took precedence over the rules, and did not refer specifically to ill-health early retirement from age 50 (only to retirement in normal health).

(f)   The Schedule E assessment and the determination were confirmed, due to the making of an unauthorised payment in the nature of a failure under (e) above.

It is of significant interest that the Special Commissioners:

(i)   considered the Revenue's meaning of 'retirement' to be fallacious; and

(ii)   drew attention to the potentially serious effect on a person's final remuneration for pension and lump sum purposes in postponing retirement due to the meaning of 'employee' in *ICTA 1988, s 612*. The inspectors said that to read such a meaning into *s 612* 'would produce an anomaly which would discourage early retirement in any but the most absolute and legalistic basis, and would constitute a widening of the tax charge for which the wording of *section 600* provides no clear warrant'.

CITIZEN'S CHARTER/TAXPAYER'S CHARTER

8.70   The Citizens Charter sets out the quality and standards of service that people are entitled to receive when dealing with public bodies. In HMRC, the Citizens Charter requirements that have a bearing on everyday work are contained in the Taxpayers Charter. HMRC staff are required, when dealing with the public, to:

• be helpful, courteous and considerate;

• have a polite and professional manner;

• be fair and impartial;

• give clear, honest and accurate explanations when needed;

• have regard to confidentiality; and

• handle matters promptly.

Their aims are to:

• secure the payment, returns and/or information with the minimum amount of friction;

• perform their duties efficiently in accordance with the law and official instructions; and (in appropriate cases)

• educate taxpayers in their responsibilities and try to secure an improved performance and attitude for the future. There is clear evidence, especially in PAYE cases, that a prompt and tactful approach does lead to greater co-operation and awareness.

Chapter 9

Overseas considerations

INTRODUCTION

9.1   As explained in **6.1**, the relaxation in the transfer rules under the post A-Day tax regime has widened the scope to make transfers to and from registered schemes considerably. The *EU Directive 2003/41/EC*, and other pending changes in the EU (see **9.9** to **9.11**), had a significant influence on the revisions to UK pensions legislation. In this chapter attention is given to overseas considerations in general, including transfers to and from overseas pension schemes.

The main tax changes were contained in the *Finance Act 2004*, the regulations made thereunder and subsequent Finance Acts. Additionally, the *Pensions Act 2004* and subsequent legislation addressed the issue of international mobility of labour in connection with scheme membership and sponsorship. The interplay between the UK tax laws for overseas schemes, the UK pension laws for membership, transfers and the investment of such schemes and the related EU legislation are key factors for consideration when designing tax-efficient overseas pension provision. Accordingly, some detail is provided on such matters in this chapter.

Many of the changes and relaxations relating to overseas matters will be of particular interest to high earners, who are more likely to be investors overseas, members of overseas schemes and/or the internationally mobile.

Also, there has long been a dearth of providers of international schemes for the main workforces involved in multinational companies. Some companies do have long-established schemes in different jurisdictions, for example the motor industry and the oil industry. However, the different tax rules within various jurisdictions have made international benefit provision problematical to say the least. The UK tax authorities have developed complicated laws with regard to international benefit provision over the years, in an attempt to deal with such situations, and there has been a minefield of transitional arrangements and grandfathering rules in order to make provision for such employees. Refreshingly, the new regime enables many of these obstacles to be swept aside within EU Member States and other acceptable overseas pension benefit providers, ensuring the protection of members' benefits and widening the availability of tax reliefs.

UK TAX RULES DEVELOPMENT

9.2   The following regulations which affect overseas schemes have been made:

114

- the *Pension Schemes (Categories of Country and Requirements for Overseas Pension Schemes and Recognised Overseas Pension Schemes) Regulations 2006 (SI 2006/206).*

These regulations prescribe the requirements which must be met by a scheme in order to qualify as an overseas pension scheme under the *Finance Act 2004*. The regulations have been amended. Details are given in **9.18** and **9.19**.

- the *Pensions Schemes (Application of UK Provisions to Relevant Non-UK Schemes) Regulations 2006 (SI 2006/207).*

These regulations explain the method of calculation of tax on a payment made by a relevant non-UK scheme (RNUK) in respect of a payment which is referable to a member's UK tax-relieved funds. They also contain provisions for HMRC to mitigate the charge to tax in appropriate circumstances (see **9.33** to **9.35**).

- the *Pension Schemes (Information Requirements – Qualifying Overseas Pension Schemes, Qualifying Recognised Overseas Pension Schemes and Corresponding Relief) Regulations 2006 (SI 2006/208).*

These regulations describe the information which must be sent to HMRC for a qualifying overseas pension scheme and a qualifying recognised overseas pension scheme to be recognised as such. They also describe the information which must be sent to HMRC in respect of an individual's contributions, and the 30-day rule which applies to the provision of information following the issue of a notice by HMRC. Details are given in **9.22** and **9.23**.

- the *Pension Schemes (Relevant Migrant Members) Regulations 2006 (SI 2006/212).*

These regulations describe the application of migrant member relief for a member of an overseas pension scheme (an individual is a relevant migrant member if he meets the requirements of the *Finance Act 2004, Sch 33*). The regulations have been amended. Details are given in **9.12** to **9.15**.

- the *Registered Pension Schemes and Overseas Pension Schemes (Electronic Communication of Returns and Information) Regulations 2006 (SI 2006/570).*

These regulations describe the electronic reporting and tax return rules for UK and overseas schemes.

OTHER UK LEGISLATIVE DEVELOPMENTS

Investment regulations

9.3   *The Occupational Pension Schemes (Investment) Regulations 2005 (SI 2005/3378).*

These Regulations revoked the *Occupational Pension Schemes (Investment) Regulations 1996 (SI 1996/3127)*, and supplemented the changes to the *Pensions Act 1995* which were made by the *Pensions Act 2004*. The

Regulations were primarily for the purpose of bringing in UK legislation to accord with the EU Directive 2003/41/EC. The most important parts of the Directive which were taken into consideration were:

- Art 12 (to which the *Pensions Act 1995, s 35,* refers), concerning the need for a written statement of investment policy principles;

- Art 18, concerning the need for a prudent person approach to be applied as the underlying principle for capital investment;

- various investment restrictions and requirements for sole and multiple employer schemes.

A summary of the main provisions is given below:

- Scheme assets must always be invested in the best interests of the members and beneficiaries.

- Assets must mainly consist of investments trading on regulated markets.

- Alternative investments must be kept at a prudent level.

- There must be diversity in the investment of assets (and special rules apply to derivatives and collective investment schemes).

- The investment powers and discretions under the scheme must ensure the security, quality, liquidity and profitability of the portfolio in its entirety.

- A statement of investment principles is required, and must be subjected to a triennial review.

- Trustees must always consider proper advice when advising on the suitability of a proposed investment.

- Specific requirements apply to borrowing, and there is a restriction in investment in the sponsors undertaking to no more than 5% of the portfolio (20% where a group is concerned).

- The small scheme exemptions which already existed for SSASs in the UK (under the *Pensions Act 1995* and the regulatory rules) were retained, and the exemptions under *Art 5* of the *Pensions Directive* for schemes with fewer than 100 active or deferred members were adopted.

It is noteworthy that the exemptions for small schemes do not include the need for diversity of investments.

On the matter of underfunded schemes, the ECJ ruled on 25 January 2007 that the UK government had failed to meet EU standards for protecting workers from losing their pensions if their employer went bankrupt. The case concerned the collapse of Allied Steel and Wire in 2002 which adversely affected 12,000 staff in Cardiff, Sheerness and Belfast. The ECJ said workers will have to take their claim for compensation from the Government to the British courts. The parliamentary ombudsman had said that the Government was guilty of maladministration and that workers should be compensated, but ministers had refused to accept the ruling. However, at a High Court case in

February, four people who lost company pensions won against the Government after the court ruled that the government was wrong to reject completely the ombudsman's report into collapsed pension schemes. Since that ruling, the Government has pledged more monies to the Financial Assistance Scheme.

Trust and Retirement Benefits Regulations

9.4   The *Occupational Pension Schemes (Trust and Retirement Benefits Exemption) Regulations 2005 (SI 2005/2360)* prescribe the description of schemes which are exempt from:

- the requirement in *s 252(2) Pensions Act 2004*, that trustees or managers of an occupational pension scheme with its main administration in the UK must not accept funding payments unless the scheme is established under irrevocable trust;

- the requirement in *s 255(1)* of the Act, that an occupational pension scheme with its main administration in the UK must be limited to retirement-benefit activities.

The effect is:

- *s 252(2)* transposes *Article 8* of the *EU Pensions Directive* on the activities and supervision of IORPs (*Article 8* requires legal separation of the assets of an occupational pension scheme and those of a sponsoring employer);

- *s 255(1)* transposes *Article 7* of the *Directive* (*Article 7* requires that occupational pension schemes are limited to retirement-benefit activities).

Pensions Acts

9.5   The *Pensions Act 2004* (like the *Finance Act 2004* – see **2.17**) paved the way for wider membership of schemes. The *Act* set out the conditions that apply for a UK scheme to accept contributions from employers in other EU Member States and for UK employers to make contributions to an occupational pension scheme established in another EU Member State. In addition, the regulations in **9.6** and **9.7** were made.

Cross-border provision

9.6   The *Occupational Pension Schemes (Cross-border Activities) Regulations 2005 (SI 2005/3381)* make provisions in connection with the carrying-out by the Pensions Regulator of its functions in relation to cross-border activity within the EU by occupational pension schemes and their trustees or managers, or by European pensions institutions. Minor amendments were made by the *Occupational Pension Schemes (Cross-border Activities) (Amendment) Regulations 2006 (SI 2006/925)*.

9.6 *Overseas considerations*

The provisions under the Regulations concern:

- the meaning of 'European employer' and 'host Member State' under the *Pensions Act 2004, Pt 7*;

- the information to be supplied to the Regulator when the trustees or managers of an occupational pension scheme make an application to the Regulator for a general authorisation to accept contributions from European employers;

- the conditions which must be met by an applicant for general authorisation before the Regulator may grant the application;

- the criteria to be applied by the Regulator in reaching any decision as to the revocation of a general authorisation;

- the information to be supplied to the Regulator when the trustees or managers of an occupational pension scheme make an application to the Regulator for approval in relation to a particular European employer;

- the conditions which must be met by an applicant for approval before the Regulator may grant an approval;

- the revocation of approvals and the criteria to be applied by the Regulator in reaching any decision as to the revocation of an approval;

- the modification of certain provisions of pensions legislation in their application to European members of occupational pension schemes which carry out cross-border activity;

- the circumstances in which the Regulator may issue a ring-fencing notice, and what such a notice may require of the trustees or managers of an occupational pension scheme;

- the requirements of the law relating to occupational pension schemes to be notified by the Regulator to the competent authorities of other Member States and complied with by European pensions institutions which accept contributions from UK employers;

- the manner of applying to the Regulator for authorisation or approval.

From 30 December 2005, pension schemes located in one EU Member State needed to apply for authorisation and approval to accept contributions from employers that employ members who are subject to the social and labour law of another EU Member State. UK schemes need authorisation and approval from the Pensions Regulator to operate cross-border within the EU.

The Regulator's website contains guidance on these matters and states:

'This guidance sets out the application process for authorisation and approval.

As a trustee of an occupational pension scheme you need to decide whether you have to apply to the Pensions Regulator for authorisation and approval for your scheme to operate as an EU cross-border scheme. (References to trustees in this guidance include scheme managers where there are no scheme trustees.)

If you are an employer sponsoring an occupational pension scheme, you need to consider whether your scheme is operating as a cross-border scheme, and if it is likely to operate as an EU cross-border scheme in future.'

A flowchart to help decision-making was placed on the website on 7 December 2006. Revised guidance was put in place to accommodate the accession of Bulgaria and Romania to the EU in January 2007.

The DWP published its response to consultation from 10 October 2007 to 4 December 2007 on 15 April 2008 on the success of the cross-border regulations (Directive 2003/41C). The response covers EU and EEA states.

Contracting-out

9.7   The *Protected Rights (Transfer Payment) (Amendment) Regulations 2005 (SI 2005/2906)* amended the *Protected Rights (Transfer Payment) Regulations 1996 (SI 1996/1461)*. The Regulations include among the schemes that may give effect to a members protected rights by making a transfer payment to an appropriate personal pension scheme or an occupational pension scheme, the money purchase part of a mixed benefit contracted-out scheme and a scheme which has ceased to be the money purchase part of a mixed benefit contracted-out scheme.

Additionally, provision is made for transfer payments to be made to a money purchase contracted-out scheme or the money purchase part of a mixed benefit contracted-out scheme, and for transfers to be made without a member's consent.

The transfer of contracted-out rights was simplified under the *Contracting-out, Protected Rights and Safeguarded Rights (Transfer Payment) Amendment Regulations 2005 (SI 2005/55)*. The requirement that the member must have permanently emigrated before a transfer of contracted-out or safeguarded pension rights is made to an overseas pension scheme has been removed.

The *Pensions Act 2007* triggered further changes:

- The transfer of contracted-out rights was further simplified by *the Personal and Occupational Pension Schemes (Amendment) Regulations 2008 (SI 2008/1979)*. The Regulations permit SIPPS to accept protected rights from 1 October 2008 if they are contracted-out. Additionally, *reg 2* amended *reg 12(11)* of the 1996 Regulations which applies where the member of a pension scheme dies before effect is given to that member's protected rights. The amendment removed the provision which allowed payment of such a pension to or for someone who was not the spouse, civil partner or child of the member.

- Contracting-out will be abolished for future accrual under defined contribution occupational pension schemes and personal pension schemes from a date to be determined. The timing of the abolition is intended to tie in with the uprating of basic state pension by 2012.

- Guaranteed minimum pensions accrued under contracted-out salary-related occupational pension schemes may be converted into ordinary scheme pension, at the trustees' discretion and with the employer's consent. The post conversion benefit must have at least equal actuarial value as pre-conversion rights.

EU PENSIONS DIRECTIVE AND DRAFT PORTABILITY DIRECTIVE

EU Pensions Directive

9.8 Below is a summary of the main aims of the *EU Directive 2003/41/EC*:

- to establish a framework for IORPs;

- to permit Member States to decide on their own investment rules, subject to permitting investment up to 70% in shares and corporate bonds and at least 30% in currencies other than the currency of their future pension liabilities;

- to restrict portfolio self-investment in the sponsoring undertaking to 5% of the portfolio value (under the *EU Investment Services Directive*, this can be disapplied for schemes with fewer than 100 members);

- to achieve a high level of protection for future pensioners and beneficiaries, under prescribed rules of operation;

- to permit freedom to develop effective investment programmes and policy within prudent guidelines ('prudent person principle');

- to achieve greater investment security and diversity;

- to improve investment management, and the choice of managers approved by the Member State;

- to ensure that schemes have effective liquidity on a needs basis;

- to rationalise tax problems encountered in differing states by pension schemes and arrangements;

- to allow flexibility in scheme design, whether by advance funding or pay-as-you-go schemes;

- to remove obstacles to effective management of pensions schemes across one Member State to another (in compliance with the principle of a single integrated financial market, so avoiding an unnecessary multiplicity of managers around the EU);

- to control administration costs;

- to simplify or remove current restrictions and obstacles to integration;

- to ensure prudent calculation of benefits which are covered by sufficient assets;

- to enable Member States to give supervisory powers to relevant authorities to monitor and supervise their IORPs to the required standard;

- to achieve mutual recognition of Member States' supervisory regimes to enable cross-border management ('home country control' principle);

- to permit a 'host' Member State (where the sponsoring employer is located) to be able to request a 'home' Member State (where the fund is located) to apply quantative rules to assets held by cross-border schemes, provided the host Member State applies the same, or stricter, rules to its domestic funds – quantative rules concern unlisted assets, assets issued by the sponsoring company and assets held in a different denomination from that in which the scheme liabilities are expressed;

- to allow Member States to permit a fund to offer survivor benefits and disability cover, particularly if requested by the employer and employee(s);

- to preserve any existing right to receive a lump sum without restrictions; and

- to give members rights to be informed about transfer rights on a change of employment.

Portability Directive

9.9   The draft EU Portability Directive issued in October 2005 and the issue gave rise to much animated debate in the EU. The UK government sought exemptions for schemes in wind-up and to enable a reduction in transfer values for underfunded schemes. The intent remains that the Directive applies to all work-related pension schemes, both funded and unfunded. However, pension rights existing before the Directive came into force (which was no later than 1 July 2008) are excluded. This also applies to self-employed workers.

The Directive was accepted by MEPs in its first reading and it guaranteed a maximum vesting period of five years, after which workers are entitled to a pension under any supplementary pension arrangement offered by employers. Companies are not compelled to offer a supplementary pension, and pension funds are not required to make rights portable. However, people leaving a company remain entitled to any supplementary pension benefits they accrued, and they are protected against inflation

EU warning on tax discrimination

9.10   The EC issued formal notices on Germany and Estonia on 1 February 2008 requesting information in the different tax treatment of foreign pension funds in respect of dividends and interest. Those counties give full or partial tax exemption for their home schemes, but foreign schemes have to pay the full tax. Similar letters were sent to the Czech Republic, Denmark, Spain, Lithuania, the Netherlands, Poland, Portugal, Slovenia, Sweden, Italy and Finland in spring and summer 2007.

The ECJ has already ruled against Denmark and Belgium in perceived cases of tax discrimination and is clearly taking an active interest in member-state compliance.

In November 2007 the ECJ said that it was illegal for the Dutch Government to tax dividends paid to foreign investors that domestic investors received tax-free. The case was brought by Amurta, a Portuguese company that lost 25% of its dividend payments from its investment in Retailbox, a Dutch company. Retailbox's Dutch investors were not charged the tax.

MIGRANT MEMBER RELIEF

9.11   The main effect of migrant member relief is that it replaces, and extends beyond, corresponding relief. It is available for a migrant member who is a member of a qualifying overseas pension scheme. The individual's domicile does not have to be taken into account and it does not matter where the scheme is established. Nevertheless, the scheme does have to be regulated in its country of origin and it must provide certain information to HMRC in respect of the member. Transitional protection applies for any individual's who are already enjoying corresponding relief who may be adversely affected by the change. The general effect is to widen the number of people who may benefit from tax reliefs under the new regime considerably.

In order to understand how migrant member relief works it is necessary to be familiar with the terms which are used in the legislation. The main terms are as follows:

Relevant migrant member

9.12   This is a member who belongs to an overseas pension scheme, who was not resident in the UK when he joined the scheme and who was a member of the overseas scheme at the beginning of his residence in the UK when he began to pay contributions. The member must also have received tax relief in respect of his contributions in his previous country of residence, or received tax reliefs on contributions paid to the scheme in the country of residence at any time in the previous 10 years. The *Finance Act 2004, Sch 33* contains the main provisions.

Qualifying for migrant member relief

9.13   In order to be entitled to tax relief on contributions made to a qualifying overseas pension scheme the member must have relevant UK earnings which are tax chargeable for the year in question, be resident in the UK when those contributions are made and have notified the scheme manager of his intention to claim relief. Under the *Finance Act 2004, s 188*, employers may receive relief on their contributions to qualifying overseas pension schemes if employees are entitled to migrant member relief. The *Finance Act 2004, ss 196(2)–(6)* and *200* contain the main provisions.

Qualifying overseas pension

9.14   In order to secure a scheme's status as a qualifying overseas pension scheme, the scheme manager must:

- notify HMRC of the schemes status and provide any required evidence;

- undertake to inform HMRC if the scheme ceases to hold that status; and

- undertake to HMRC to comply with any prescribed benefit crystallisation information requirements which may be necessary.

HMRC has the right to exclude an overseas pension scheme from being treated as a qualifying scheme if it fails to meet such requirements.

Migrant member relief will be available where an individual:

- is resident in the UK but was not resident in the UK at the time they joined a qualifying overseas pension scheme;

- comes to the UK as a member of that scheme, and remains a member of the overseas scheme;

- notifies the scheme manager that he intends to claim migrant member relief (UK tax relief against UK earnings on contributions paid to the overseas scheme);

- has earnings chargeable in the UK;

- was eligible for tax relief on contributions to the overseas scheme in the country in which they were resident immediate before coming to the UK, or meets such other conditions as may be prescribed by regulations (currently, draft regulations extend to schemes which confer tax exemption on the benefits payable, but not on the contributions paid).

The scheme must either be EEC registered, or one that generally corresponds with a UK scheme, and must:

- notify HMRC that it is an overseas pension scheme, providing supporting evidence if required;

- undertake to notify HMRC if it stops being an overseas pension scheme;

- undertake to provide HMRC with certain information in accordance with regulations; and

- notify any member claiming migrant member relief that it has undertaken to comply with the information requirements.

Employers may claim a deduction for contributions paid to a qualifying overseas pension scheme in respect of employees who are eligible for migrant member relief.

The *Registered Pension Schemes (Extension of Migrant Member Relief) Regulations 2006 SI 2006/1957* extended eligibility for migrant member relief to cases where a person was not resident in the UK at the time they joined a scheme other than where:

- a member's rights have been subject to one or more block transfers;

- a series of block transfers have occurred; and

- the scheme to which the member originally belonged is closed to new accruals for existing members and a further scheme for members of that scheme is set up.

HMRC's leaflet IR20

9.15 HMRC's publication IR20 provides guidance on tax reliefs for residents and non-residents. As the publication is to be updated in order to reflect recent developments it is only available online on a temporary basis. This booklet has been updated and is temporarily available online only. The revised guidance has been promised by the end of 2008. There is, however, an additional HMRC FAQ online entitled 'Taxation of income arising from a non-UK resident trust' dated 15 April 2008.

The *Finance Act, s 91, Sch 29, para 18,* provides for regulations to be made for the granting of inheritance tax relief from A-Day on savings in relevant schemes. The schemes which will benefit are largely QROPS, *s 615(3)* schemes and schemes which provide a pension for life. The draft regulations have been published.

QROPS

9.16 In order to be treated as a qualifying overseas pension scheme, a scheme must comply with one of the two methods under the *Pension Schemes (Categories of Country and Requirements for Overseas Pension Schemes and Recognised Overseas Pension Schemes) Regulations 2006 (SI 2006/206).*

To be a recognised overseas pension scheme, the scheme manager must:

- have notified HMRC that the scheme is a recognised overseas pension scheme if required;

- have informed HMRC of the name of the country or territory in which the scheme is established. If this is not an EU Member State, Norway, Liechtenstein, Iceland or a country or territory with which the UK has a Double Taxation Agreement which contains exchange of information and non-discrimination provisions (see RPSM14101046), the scheme manager must also provide evidence that the scheme fulfils the requirement set out at the third bullet point in RPSM14101040;

- have undertaken to notify HMRC if the scheme ceases to be a recognised overseas pension scheme;and

- have undertaken to provide HMRC with certain information on making payments in respect of certain scheme members (see RPSM14101070).

A scheme may be excluded from being a qualifying recognised overseas pension scheme (QROPS – an overseas scheme which may receive transfers from UK registered schemes without tax charge) if HMRC decides that there has been a significant failure to comply with any information requirements. A failure will be significant if a substantial amount of information has not been provided or if the failure to provide information is likely to result in serious prejudice to the assessment or collection of tax. The methods of qualifying are described in **9.18** and **19.19**

First method of qualifying

9.17   In the country or territory in which the scheme is established, there must be a body which regulates that type of scheme and the scheme itself. The scheme must be recognised for tax purposes in its home state by meeting the following primary conditions below and one of conditions A and B.

Primary condition 1

The scheme is open to persons resident in the country or territory in which it is established.

Primary condition 2

The scheme is established in a country or territory where there is a system of taxation of personal income under which tax relief is available in respect of pensions, and:

(1)   tax relief (including the grant of an exemption) is not available to the member on contributions made to the scheme by the individual or, if the individual is an employee, by their employer, in respect of earnings to which benefits under the scheme relate; or

(2)   all or most of the benefits paid by the scheme to members who are not in serious ill-health are subject to taxation;

(3)   see final paragraph below.

Condition A

The scheme is approved or recognised by, or registered with, the relevant tax authorities as a pension scheme in the country or territory in which it is established.

Condition B

If no system exists for the approval or recognition by, or registration with, relevant tax authorities of pension schemes in the country or territory in which it is established, it must be resident there; and its rules must provide that:

●   at least 70% of a member's UK tax-relieved scheme funds will be designated by the scheme manager for the purpose of providing the member with an income for life; and

●   the pension benefits payable to the member under the scheme (and any lump sum associated with those benefits) must be payable no earlier than normal pension age under the *Finance Act 2004*.

The above was amended by the *Pension Schemes (Categories of Country and Requirements for Overseas Pension Schemes and Recognised Overseas*

Pension Schemes) (Amendment) Regulations 2007 (SI 2007/160) with effect from 1 July 2007. The amendment concerned Primary condition 2. The regulations amended this condition to provide a third way of satisfying it, namely that the scheme is liable to taxation on its income and gains and must also be of a kind specified in the Schedule to the Regulations. This amendment was necessary as Australia has introduced a new way of taxing pensions which will be introduced on 1 July 2007.

Second method of qualifying

9.18   A scheme established (outside the UK) by an international organisation for the purpose of providing benefits for, or in respect of, past service as an employee of the organisation must satisfy the requirements below:

- the scheme rules must provide that at least 70% of a member's UK tax-relieved scheme funds will be designated by the scheme manager for the purpose of providing the member with an income for life; and

- the pension benefits payable to the member under the scheme (and any lump sum associated with those benefits) under the scheme must be payable no earlier than normal pension age under *Finance Act 2004*.

To be a recognised overseas scheme, a scheme must either be established in another EEA State, or in a country or territory with which the UK has a double taxation agreement providing for the exchange of information between the fiscal authorities of the UK and the overseas country or territory and for non-discrimination between UK Nationals and nationals of the overseas country or territory. If it is not established in such a country or territory a scheme may nonetheless be recognised if the rules of the scheme provide that:

- at least 70% of the sums transferred will be designated by the scheme manager for the purpose of providing the member with an income for life;

- the pension benefits (and any lump sum associated with those benefits) payable to the member under the scheme, to the extent that they relate to the transfer, are payable no earlier than normal pension age under *Finance Act 2004*;

- the scheme is open to persons resident in the country or territory in which it is established.

HMRC web-guidance on QROPS

9.19   HMRC has provided the following guidance on its website in the form of answers to frequently asked questions:

'An individual whose UK tax-relieved rights have been transferred to a QROPS could be liable to an unauthorised payments charge unless when a payment is made to or in respect of the individual by the QROPS he/she is not resident for purposes in the UK and has neither been UK resident in that UK tax year nor in any of the previous five tax years'.

'Under regulation 3(3) of SI 2006/208, a QROPS will not have to report to HMRC a payment (or a deemed payment) if the member is not tax resident in the UK when the payment is made and has neither been UK resident in that tax year nor in any of the previous five tax years"."An unauthorised payments charge would arise on the member and a scheme sanction charge would arise on the UK scheme if a transfer were made from a UK registered pension scheme to a non-QROPS whenever it was made. There would not be a charge on the overseas pension scheme'.

QROPS status will not apply:

'if HMRC decides that there has been a significant failure to comply with any information requirements, and that it is inappropriate that transfers from **registered pension** schemes to the recognised overseas pension scheme should be **recognised transfers**. A failure will be significant if a substantial amount of information has not been provided or if the failure to provide information is likely to result in serious prejudice to the assessment or collection of tax'.

Where a transfer was originally received by a QROPS and then subsequently transferred to a non-QROPS:

'The individual would be liable to an unauthorised payments charge unless when the subsequent transfer was made he/she was not resident for tax purposes in the UK and had neither been UK resident in that UK tax year nor in any of the previous five tax years'.

Employer contributions

9.20 Employer contributions to a QROPS are allowable under the normal rules of Sch D for corporation tax purposes. Non-relevant migrant members employers may deduct contributions from profits liable to tax once the relevant benefits are paid out.

The amount of an employer's contribution which has the benefit of tax relief in the UK does not affect the calculation of the proportion of the fund that is subject to UK tax rules. Regulations may deem certain payments to be authorised payments and will also ensure those payments are subject to the authorised payments tax regime for registered pension schemes.

Employers making payments into approved occupational pension schemes will obtain tax relief only on the cash contributions made, not the amount shown in the company accounts.

REPORTING REQUIREMENTS

9.21 The *Pension Schemes (Information Requirements – Qualifying Overseas Pension Schemes, Qualifying Recognised Overseas Pension Schemes and Corresponding Relief) Regulations 2006 (SI 2006/208)* require reports to be made by QROPS administrators or managers of certain events. The relevant form is APSS253. If filed incorrectly through fraud or negligence, then a penalty up to £3,000 may be levied. Late filing may result in a £300 fine with

£60 per for each continuing day of late submission. Reports can be made throughout the year – HMRC will store information on-line for up to 22 months before submission. Nil returns are not required.

Reportable events

9.22

Payments to members	
Relevant member payments	
Has the scheme made or been deemed to make a relevant member payment (see **9.26**)?	Reports are required The information must be sent to HMRC by 31 January following the end of the tax year in which each payment is made.
Reporting payments to HMRC *Form APSS253*	The relevant information to be reported to HMRC is: Name & address of member their date of birth their National Insurance number (if known)~ Date, amount and nature (pension, lump sum, transfer, annuity purchase) of the payment the name of the QROPS; and the country or territory under the law of which that scheme is established and regulated.
Relevant migrant members and corresponding members Has a BCE event taken place?	The information must be sent to HMRC by 31 January following the end of the tax year in which each payment is made. BCEs must be reported to HMRC
Reporting BCEs to HMRC	The relevant information to be reported to HMRC is: Name and address of member where there has been a BCE in the Tax Year Date, amount and nature of the BCE. The information must be sent to HMRC by 31 January following the end of the tax year in which each payment is made.

Administrator's or manager's undertaking to HMRC

9.23   RPSM14101050 explains that the scheme manager of a recognised overseas pension scheme/QROPS must have undertaken to comply with the information requirements. Reports are required in respect of payments out of members' funds which relate to transfers from UK registered schemes or to migrant members. Member payment provisions only not apply in relation to a payment made to or in respect of a relieved member or transfer member of a relevant non-UK scheme (RNUK) if he:

● is resident in the UK when the payment is made (or treated as made); or

● although not resident in the UK at that time, has been resident in the UK earlier in the tax year in which the payment is made (or treated as made) or in any of the five tax years immediately preceding that tax year.

With effect from 6 April 2008, any day where an individual is present in the UK at midnight will be counted as a day of presence in the UK for residence test purposes.

A payment includes a transfer from the scheme. Guidance on deemed payments is provided in RPSM09100170. Broadly speaking, a member will have a relevant transfer fund within the scheme if they have transferred sums or assets into it that relate to UK tax-relieved contributions. That includes transfers from registered pension schemes and certain transfers from non-UK schemes that are not registered pension schemes. Further details are provided at RPSM13102170.

The manager of a QROPS that receives a transfer from another overseas pension scheme will need to check whether or not the transferring member has a UK tax-relieved fund (see RPSM13102150) or a relevant transfer fund in the transferring scheme in order to establish if HMRC will have to be provided with information about payments made in respect of the individual. It would be reasonable for the scheme manager to ask the individual to declare whether or not the transferred funds include any amounts that have received UK tax relief or have originated in a UK registered pension scheme.

Information must be sent to:

Pension Schemes Services
HM Revenue & Customs
Yorke House
Castle Meadow Road
Nottingham NG2 1BG

The scheme manager can use the APSS 253 form to provide notification.

Where a non-pension payment such as a lump sum or a transfer is made, the scheme manager must provide the information to HMRC by 31 January following the end of the tax year in which each payment is made. Where a pension payment is made, the scheme manager must provide the information by 31 January following the end of the tax year in which the first payment is made, but it is only necessary to do this in respect of the first such payment to any individual.

TRANSFERS

Reporting transfer payments

9.24   The administrator must report to HMRC any transfer from their scheme to a QROPS using the online Event Report (see **9.23**). The required information is:

- the name of the member;

- their address;

- their date of birth;

- their National Insurance number (if known);

- the amount of the sums or assets transferred;

- the date of the transfer;

- the name of the QROPS; and

- the country or territory under the law of which that scheme is established and regulated.

The provisions under which a scheme manager is treated as making a payment are in the *Finance Act 2004, ss 172–174A, para 2A of Sch 28 and para 3A of Sch 29*. Guidance on those deemed payments is provided in RPSM09100170.

Additionally, the following main information on transfers is given RPSM:

BCE, member payment and inheritance tax

9.25   RPSM14101060 states:

'Tax relief

The transfer is not a contribution so no UK tax relief is due in respect of it. The contributions to the transferring scheme would have received tax relief when originally made to that scheme, and the transfer is merely re-locating the pension rights represented by those contributions to a different pension scheme.

Annual allowance

The transfer is treated in the same way as a transfer from a **registered pension scheme** to another registered pension scheme. See RPSM14101010 (of relevance only to the transferring registered pension scheme).

Lifetime Allowance

The transfer is a **benefit crystallisation event** for the purpose of the member's **lifetime allowance**. The amount crystallised is the amount of the transfer. The taking of benefits relating to the transferred amount from a **qualifying recognised overseas pension scheme** is not a benefit crystallisation event for the purposes of the individual's lifetime allowance.

If the transfer results in the member's lifetime allowance being exceeded, the rate of tax chargeable is 25%. The 55% rate cannot apply, even though the payment in effect is a "lump sum", because it is not being paid "to the individual", so does not fall within the 55% rate charging provision.

Member payment charge

Any future payment from the overseas scheme, relating to a **recognised transfer,** which is a type of payment which would not have been authorised from a UK registered scheme will give rise to a member payment charge under Schedule 34 Finance Act 2004 on a resident or recently resident individual (for more details see RPSM13102110).

Inheritance tax

When a member transfers from one pension scheme (here a UK registered scheme) to another (here a QROPS) then he has the right to determine the basis upon which the new death benefits under the transferee scheme are to be paid. That "right" is property and an asset of the member's estate in terms of s272IHTA. So when he exercises that right by electing to have the death benefits paid on discretionary trusts outside his estate then there is a loss to his estate in terms of s3(1)IHTA . That loss and the consequent chargeable transfer is largely dependent on the member's state of health and life expectancy at the time of the transfer. If in normal health then the value will be nominal – he would be expected to survive to take his full retirement benefits at which time the death benefits would lapse. If in ill health then the value could be substantive given the short period of time before a purchaser in the hypothetical open market would expect the death benefits to be paid out.

In the light of section 188(5) FA2004 which applies for Schedule 36 FA purposes the transfer payment is not a "contribution" after 5 April 2006 in terms of paragraph 56(2) of schedule 36. It follows that the transitional relieving provisions under paragraphs 56–58 of Schedule 36 will apply i.e. there is full grandfathering of the IHT exemption for the pre-6 April 2006 fund on a transfer to a QROPS [but see **9.16**].'

Transfer of rights to the payment of unsecured pension or ASP

9.26   It is possible within the tax rules on authorised payments for an **unsecured pension** or an ASP (whether payable to the **member** or a **dependant**) to be transferred to a QROPS. This also applies where entitlement to an unsecured or ASP exists but no payments of pension were actually being drawn under the transferring scheme. All the sums and assets transferred become must be held in an arrangement in the receiving scheme under which no other sums or assets are held at that time. In effect, it has to be dedicated for the purpose of the transfer.

For unsecured pension, the sums and assets transferred are treated as if they are remaining held in the unsecured pension fund of the transferring scheme. So no BCE 1 is regarded as arising at the transfer, and no entitlement to a pension commencement lump sum arises. The unsecured pension fund conditions relating to:

- unsecured pension year;
- five-year reference period;
- basis amount for unsecured pension year; and
- nominated date

(see RPSM09102010 onwards) are all continued in the same way under the receiving scheme as if no transfer had taken place. This ensures that the income limits of the unsecured pension and the operation of future reviews of the limits are not changed as for ASP, no BCE or entitlement to a pension commencement lump sum would arise in any event on the commencement of entitlement to these pensions under the original **registered scheme**. So, for the specific purposes of the tax rules, the sums and assets transferred are treated as if they are remaining held in the pension fund of the transferring scheme.

The unsecured or ASP conditions relating to:

- unsecured or ASP pension year;
- review periods;
- basis amount for unsecured or ASP pension year; and
- nominated date

are all continued in the same way under the receiving scheme as if no transfer had taken place. This ensures that the income limits of the unsecured or ASP and the operation of future reviews of the limits are not changed as a result of the transfer.

Transfers of pensions in payment, or rights where there is already an entitlement to benefits

9.27 RPSM14106060 states:

9.28

'Transfers of pensions in payment, or rights where there is already an entitlement to benefits: Additional provisions

Where a transfer takes place of already crystallised rights to a QROPS, BCE 8 will occur. As a BCE 1 for an unsecured pension or a BCE 2 for a scheme pension will have applied at the original entitlement to benefits, overlap provisions will apply. This will have the effect that the amount crystallised (or an appropriate proportion) under the original BCE 1 or 2 will be deducted from the amount crystallised under the BCE 8 occurring on transfer.

Unlike for a transfer of crystallised rights from a registered pension scheme to another registered pension scheme, where no further BCE occurs, a transfer to a QROPS will produce a second BCE and so a further test against the LTA.

Following the transfer to the QROPS, the receiving scheme will be required to provide benefits on a like for like basis as preceding the transfer. So the transfer of a scheme pension in payment, for example, should be continued in that form, and the conditions as set out in RPSM14106030 onwards should be followed. If any of those conditions are not met the member of the receiving scheme will be liable to an unauthorised payments charge by virtue of Schedule 34 (see RPSM13102020 onwards). That will be the case, in particular, if a lump sum is paid, the scheme pension is increased or the income withdrawal is speeded up.'

9.29   RPSM14106010 states:

'It is possible within the tax rules on authorised payments to make a transfer from a **registered pension scheme** relating to a pension which is already in payment, or in the case of an unsecured or **alternatively secured pension fund**, where an entitlement to benefits has already arisen.

A pension in payment under a registered pension scheme, is capable of being transferred to another registered pension scheme or a **qualifying recognised overseas pension scheme** and being regarded as a **recognised transfer**. This applies to any of the following

- member's **scheme pension**
- member's **unsecured pension**
- member's **alternatively secured pension**
- dependant's **scheme pension**
- **dependant's unsecured pension** or
- **dependant's alternatively secured pension**.

If the provision of benefits derived from the transfer meet certain conditions, then the benefits paid from the transfer in the receiving registered pension scheme are capable of being within the pension rules and being authorised payments. Any failure to meet the conditions will result in the amount transferred being regarded as an unauthorised payment.'

TAX CHARGES, PENALTIES AND SANCTIONS

9.30   High levels of charges and surcharges can be incurred where payments are not regarded as authorised payments. These charges are known as 'member payment charges', and are described in the *Finance Act 2004, Sch 34*. They apply to payments made out of a registered scheme to a scheme which is, or is deemed to be, a RNUK.

A RNUK is a scheme under which:

- migrant member relief has been given;

- double taxation relief was received prior to A-Day;

- members have been exempted, under the *Income Tax (Earnings and Pensions) Act 2003, s 307,* from tax on pensions or death benefits at any time after A-Day whilst the scheme was an overseas pension scheme;

- there has been a relevant transfer from a UK registered scheme after A-Day whilst the scheme was a QROPS.

Member payment charges

9.31   Member payment charges include:

- the unauthorised payments charge;

- the unauthorised payments surcharge;

- a short service refund lump sum charge;

- a special lump sum death benefits charge;

- charges on trivial commutation, winding-up lump sums and lump sum death benefits.

Under the *Pensions Schemes (Application of UK Provisions to Relevant Non-UK Schemes) Regulations 2006 (SI 2006/207)* there are two methods to calculate the charge: the first is to calculate the member's tax relieved fund which is held under a RNUK; the second is to compute the amount of the member's relevant transfer fund under a RNUK.

When the charge is incurred

9.32   A member will be subject to the charge if he was resident in the UK at the time the transfer was made or had been so in any of the preceding five years. The rate of tax payable is normally 40%. It is possible in some circumstances to mitigate the charge, if there is good reason to do so. The regulations relating to mitigation are:

- the *Registered Pension Schemes (Discharge of Liabilities under Sections 267 and 268 of the Finance Act 2004) Regulations 2005 (SI 2005/3452)*;

- the *Pensions Schemes (Application of UK provisions to Relevant Non-UK schemes) Regulations 2006 (SI 2006/207)*.

Annual allowance and lifetime allowance charges

9.33   The *Finance Act 2004, Sch 34, paras 8–1* provide formulae for calculating how the annual allowance charge applies to currently relieved members of current relieved RNUK schemes.

The *Finance Act 2004, Sch 34, paras 13–19* describe how the lifetime allowance charge applies in similar circumstances.

Section 615 Schemes

9.34   *Income and Corporation Taxes Act 1988, s 615,* schemes may continue in existence under the provisions of *Chapter 6, ss 245(5)* and *249(3)* of the *Finance Act 2004.* Additionally, a wider class of overseas scheme is referred to in the *Income Tax (Earnings and Pensions) Act 2003, ss 647–654,* which repeal overlapping provisions in *s 615.* If such schemes cease, assets can be transferred into UK registered schemes.

RPSM – international pages

9.35   A considerable amount of information appears in the RPSM's international pages. The links cover a range of matters, including the following main issues:

- General principles of international enhancement.

- International enhancement/non-residence factor:
  - non-residence after 5 April 2006
  - active membership period
  - relevant overseas individual
  - who is not a relevant overseas individual?
  - pension scheme arrangements
  - notifications procedure
  - example of notifying HMRC
  - separate notifications needed
  - example of separate notifications
  - notification and hybrid arrangements
  - after HMRC notified
  - benefit payment
  - cash balance arrangement
  - example for a cash balance arrangement
  - cash balance arrangement: primary protection
  - other money purchase arrangement
  - example for other money purchase arrangement
  - defined benefits arrangement
  - example 1 for a defined benefits arrangement
  - example 2 for a defined benefits arrangement
  - non residence factor for defined benefit arrangements
  - hybrid arrangement

- Recognised overseas scheme transfer factor
  - post 5 April 2005 transfers
  - not a relevant overseas individual
  - benefit payment
  - what happens after HMRC has been notified?
- International enhancement/recognised overseas scheme transfer factor:
  - how to calculate the factor
  - examples of how to calculate the factor
  - the relevant relievable amount
  - cash balance arrangement relevant relievable amount
  - example of relevant relievable amount for a cash balance arrangement
  - other money purchase arrangement relevant relievable amount
  - example of other money purchase arrangement relevant relievable amount
  - defined benefits arrangement relevant relievable amount
  - example 1 of defined benefits arrangement relevant relievable amount
  - example 2 of defined benefits arrangement relevant relievable amount
  - hybrid arrangement relevant relievable amount.

RESIDENCE AND DOMICILE – NON-RESIDENT TRUSTS

9.36 HMRC has published a Question and Answer guide on its website concerning residence and domicile issues that arise in connection with non-resident trusts, as follows:

'Contents

Gains of offshore trustees that are realised before 6 April 2008 will not be taxed on non-domiciled beneficiaries. So does that mean that gains realised prior to 6 April 2008 will not produce a tax charge under section 87 TCGA if matched to capital payments made to a non domiciled beneficiary after 5 April 2008?

Capital payments made to non domiciled beneficiaries before 6 April 2008 will not be taxed. So does this mean that capital payments made to the UK before 6 April 2008 will not produce a tax charge under section 87 TCGA when matched to gains realised by the offshore trustees after 5 April 2008?

Can you confirm that any accrued but unrealised trust gain which relates to a period prior to 6 April 2008 will not be taxed under the new rules on a non domiciled beneficiary? Will that be delivered by some form of rebasing?

Will the remittance basis be extended to section 87 TCGA 1992?

Will Capital Gains accruing but unrealised in a period before 6 April 2008 on assets held by companies which are wholly owned by foreign trusts be taxed on non domiciled settlors or beneficiaries?

Will Offshore Income Gains (OIGs) realised by foreign trusts and taxed under sections 720–730 ITA 2007 by virtue of section 762(5) ICTA 1988 be taxed on a UK resident but non domiciled settlor on the arising basis if the settlor is a remittance basis user?

Will a settlor of a non-resident trust who is a remittance basis user be subject to tax on gains realised by the trust after 5 April 2008?

Does it make any difference if the assets in the non-resident trust or underlying non-resident company owned by the trust are UK situated?

When is an election for rebasing likely to be advantageous for me?

How will rebasing operate when property is appointed from one non-UK resident trust to another?

What if a trust is UK resident on 6 April 2008 but then emigrates?

Example 4 in the supplementary document (Residence and domicile: aligning the Capital Gains Tax treatment for non-UK resident trusts) published at 2008 Budget doesn't seem to work

As a non-UK domiciled settlor of a non-UK resident trust, will I have to pay any tax on income arising to the trustees of the trust?

Gains of offshore trustees that are realised before 6 April 2008 will not be taxed on non-domiciled beneficiaries. So does that mean that gains realised prior to 6 April 2008 will not produce a tax charge under section 87 TCGA if matched to capital payments made to a non domiciled beneficiary after 5 April 2008?

Yes, so long as the beneficiary remains domiciled outside the UK it does not matter that he/she has not made a claim for the remittance basis to apply at the time of the capital payment, provided that such payment is matched to pre 6 April 2008 gains. By pre 6 April 2008 gains we mean gains that were actually realised before 6 April 2008 or, if a rebasing election has been made, those gains which represent the pre 6 April 2008 element. However, if the capital payment made on or after 6 April 2008 is matched under Last In First Out rules (LIFO) to gains realised on or after 6 April 2008 (or the post 5 April element of such gains where a rebasing election has been made), then the payment will be taxable (on a remittance basis if the beneficiary is a remittance basis user and otherwise on an arising basis)

Capital payments made to non domiciled beneficiaries before 6 April 2008 will not be taxed. So does this mean that capital payments made to the UK before 6 April 2008 will not produce a tax charge under section 87 TCGA when matched to gains realised by the offshore trustees after 5 April 2008?

Yes so long as the non domicile is still not domiciled in the UK under general law in the year of charge. It will not be necessary for the beneficiary to be a remittance basis user if post 5 April gains are matched to capital payments made prior to 6 April 2008. There are however special rules to deal with matching of post 5 April 2008 trust gains to capital payments made between 12 March and 5 April 2008 inclusive.

Can you confirm that any accrued but unrealised trust gain which relates to a period prior to 6 April 2008 will not be taxed under the new rules on a non domiciled beneficiary? Will that be delivered by some form of rebasing?

It will be possible for trustees of any non-UK resident trust to elect that trust assets are deemed to have been rebased at market value on 6 April 2008. The election once made will be irrevocable. The rebasing will be in respect of both assets at the trust level and assets owned by companies whose gains are apportionable to the trust under section 13 TCGA 1992. Any gains representing the pre 6 April 2008 element will not be taxed if matched to a capital payment made before or after 6 April 2008 irrespective of whether the non domiciled beneficiary is a remittance basis user in the year of charge. However, if a rebasing election is not made, then any gains realised on or after 6 April 2008 will be taxed if matched to a capital payment made on or after 6 April 2008 even if part of that gain accrued prior to 6 April 2008. The remittance basis would apply if the capital payment was made offshore to a remittance basis user.

Will the remittance basis be extended to section 87 TCGA 1992?

Yes.

Will Capital Gains accruing but unrealised in a period before 6 April 2008 on assets held by companies which are wholly owned by foreign trusts be taxed on non domiciled settlors or beneficiaries?

No, not if the non-resident trust elects to rebase its assets and the gains are matched to a capital payment made before or after 6 April 2008 to a non domiciled beneficiary.

Will Offshore Income Gains (OIGs) realised by foreign trusts and taxed under sections 720–730 ITA 2007 by virtue of section 762(5) ICTA 1988 be taxed on a UK resident but non domiciled settlor on the arising basis if the settlor is a remittance basis user?

No, the legislation will be amended so that the remittance basis applies to settlors who are remittance basis users. However, there are some changes made to the way in which OIGs which are unmatched to capital payments at the end of the tax year in which they are realised will be taxed. They will generally be taken out of the section 87 OIG pool and go into the transfer of assets pool.

Will a settlor of a non-resident trust who is a remittance basis user be subject to tax on gains realised by the trust after 5 April 2008?

Non domiciled settlors, whether or not they are remittance basis users, will not be subject to tax under section 86 TCGA 1992. They will be taxed on benefits or capital payments from the trust. The remittance basis will apply where the settlor is a remittance basis user.

Does it make any difference if the assets in the non-resident trust or underlying non-resident company owned by the trust are UK situated?

There is no difference in the Capital Gains Tax treatment of UK situated vs foreign situated assets when these are owned by a non-resident trust or underlying non-resident company. However, as under current law, any UK source income produced by the trust or company will be taxed on the UK resident settlor or transferor on an arising basis irrespective of whether he has received any benefit if he has power to enjoy such income at the date it arises.

Different rules will apply to gains realised by a non-resident company owned by the remittance basis user directly rather than in a trust.

When is an election for rebasing likely to be advantageous for me?

The decision as to whether to opt for rebasing can only be made by the trustees of a trust which is non-UK resident at 6 April 2008, and will depend on a number of different factors such as the level of unrealised gains within the structure and the tax status of those who receive capital payments. It is not up to the beneficiary or settlor. The decision will have no impact on UK domiciled beneficiaries or settlors, because the date of actual disposal of the asset and the method of computing the gains remains the same. The rebasing simply means that trustees will need to keep a record of the pre 6 April 2008 element of any gain realised on a disposal to work out whether a capital payment made to a non domiciled beneficiary on or after 6 April 2008 is taxable. To the extent that pre 6 April 2008 gains are matched to post 5 April capital payments they are not taxable.

The time limits for making an election do not start to run until the trust makes a capital payment to a UK resident beneficiary or it transfers property to another trust on or after 6 April 2008, whichever is the earlier date.

How will rebasing operate when property is appointed from one non-UK resident trust to another?

In applying the allocation rules to transfers between settlements, the transferor trust gains carried across will be treated as having accrued to the transferee trust in the year in which they in fact accrued to the transferor trust. Those gains that have been matched with capital payments out of the transferor trust in the year of transfer or previous years will be left out of account. Gains carried across will be allocated to a capital payment from the transferee trust on a LIFO basis. Gains on such assets will be governed by whether or not the transferor trust has made a rebasing election.

If the transferor settlement has made a rebasing election by the time of the transfer to the transferee settlement, then pre and post April 2008 gains which are deemed to have accrued on the actual disposal of an asset go across pro rata.

If the transferor settlement has not made a rebasing election by the 31 January following the year of the transfer, then even if no capital payment has yet been made, the right to rebase is lost in relation to the transferred assets and any assets retained in the transferor trust.

However, note that any transfers between settlements made prior to 6 April 2008 will not trigger a time limit on rebasing and any assets moving over to the transferee settlement as a result of a transfer made prior to 6 April 2008 will not be affected by any subsequent election for rebasing made by the transferor trust. If the asset appointed over to the transferee settlement before 6 April 2008 includes shares in a company within section 13 TCGA 1992, then the transferee settlement may wish to elect for rebasing in its own right. Transferee settlements which receive property on or after 6 April 2008 cannot elect for rebasing in relation to the transferred assets – the decision is solely that of the transferor settlement.

Example

Trust 1 – £300,000 gains made

Capital payment made of £10,000 to a remittance basis user.

Election for rebasing made: 90 per cent (£270,000) of gains relate to the period pre 6 April 2008 and 10 per cent (£30,000) post 5 April 2008.

The capital payment is matched only to post 5 April 2008 gains and taxed on remittance basis. £290,000 gain carried forward (£270,000 pre 6 April and £20,000 post 5 April 2008). So now 6.90 per cent is post 5 April 2008 gain and 93.10 per cent is pre 6 April 2008 gain.

Trust 1 appoints cash to Trust 2 of £2.5m at a time when Trust 1 is worth £20m (ie 12.5 per cent of fund). £36,250 gains are transferred to Trust 2 (12.5 per cent of £290,000). 93.1 per cent of these are relate to the period pre 6 April 2008 and 6.9 per cent after.

Trust pool in Trust 1 reduced to £253,750 (93.1 per cent pre 6 April and 6.9 per cent post 5 April 2008).

What if a trust is UK resident on 6 April 2008 but then emigrates?

A rebasing election cannot be made in these circumstances. It must be non-UK resident at 6 April 2008 even if it is UK resident by the time any election is made.

Example 4 in the supplementary document (Residence and domicile: aligning the Capital Gains Tax treatment for non-UK resident trusts) published at 2008 Budget doesn't seem to work.

There was an error in example 4 of the supplementary document (Residence and domicile: aligning the Capital Gains Tax treatment for non-UK resident trusts) published at 2008. The correct example demonstrating how the new allocation rules is set out below:

Example 4 – allocation rules – LIFO – rebasing election made

Three beneficiaries:

A: remittance basis user

B: non-UK resident (domicile irrelevant)

C: UK resident and UK domiciled.

Trust gains carried forward as at 5 April 2008 – £2.5m

2008–09 Gains £2m (£1.9m pre 2008 element and £100,000 post 6 April 2008 element).

Gains pool now £4.5m of which £4.4m relates to pre 6 April 2008.

2009–10 Capital payment to A of £50,000

£50,000 of post 5 April gains are attributed to A and taxed on a remittance basis. (LIFO)

Pool is £4.45m (£4.4 pre April 2008 and £50,000 post April 2008)

2010–11 Capital payment to B of £5m

Gains of £4.45m attributed to B and not taxed. Unmatched capital payment to B of £0.55m to carry forward

2011–12 Gains £1.1m realised (£1m pre 6 April 2008 element and £100,000 post 5 April 2008 element).

Capital payments of £1m (£500,000 to each of A and C). Under LIFO rules these are matched with 2011–12 trust gains before the unmatched capital payment to B from the previous year.

Post 5 April 2008 gains attributed first pro rata. C pays tax at 18 per cent on £50,000; A pays tax on £50,000 on remittance basis.

£900,000 pre April 2008 gains attributed pro rata to A and C. A not taxed on remaining £450,000. C pays tax on £450,000 gain at 18 per cent

The remaining £100,000 trust gains (all post 5 April 2008) are then matched with £100,000 of the unmatched capital payments from 2010–11 to B. The £100,000 gains attributed to B are not taxed.

There are unmatched capital payments to B of £0.45m to carry forward.

As a non-UK domiciled settlor of a non-UK resident trust, will I have to pay any tax on income arising to the trustees of the trust?

The rules on taxing income arising to the trustees of a trust are not being changed. Where income arises to the trustees of a non-UK resident trust then, if the settlor is resident in the UK, the settlor will be chargeable to tax on the income. If the settlor claims, or is entitled to, the remittance basis, then the income will not be chargeable to tax unless it is remitted to the UK. Otherwise, the income will be taxable on the settlor on the arising basis in the tax year in which it arises to the trustees.'

Part Two
Main considerations for high earners

Chapter 10

Tax relievable allowances and tax charges

INTRODUCTION

10.1   The post 6 April 2006 tax regime introduced the concept of maximum tax-relievable pension input amounts, and maximum tax-relievable lifetime entitlements to pension rights. In both cases the allowances, which are referred to in the legislation as the 'annual allowance' and 'lifetime allowance', are aggregated for testing the new limits.

The methods of calculating the annual allowance and the lifetime allowance vary according to the nature of the scheme concerned and how it is funded. Tax charges will be incurred where the allowances are exceeded. The charges are referred to in the legislation as the 'annual allowance charge' and the 'lifetime allowance charge'.

The new allowances effectively replace the old limits on contributions which could be made into schemes by employers and employees and the limits which were placed on benefits (dependent on the tax regimes which applied) prior to 6 April 2006.

The great majority of members of registered pension schemes will never come into contact with either the annual allowance or the lifetime allowance. However, for senior executives and high net worth individuals these constraints might well present a problem for them at some point in their careers. This chapter looks at the allowances, the way the allowances are tested and the tax charges that are levied if the allowances are exceeded.

ANNUAL ALLOWANCE

10.2   The annual allowance covers the increase in a member's uncrystallised pension rights during the year. The legislation defines the amount which is paid into registered schemes, together with additional entitlements accrued, as the 'pension input amount'. The maximum level of the annual allowance increases in each year. The amounts have been set for each year up to the tax year

2010/2011 (see **10.28**). As from the year 2010/2011 the allowances will increase on a five-yearly review basis. They will not be decreased in any year.

The regulation of the allowance will take place through the self-assessment procedure. Any excess will be subject to the annual allowance charge, and any excess tax which has been deducted by the scheme may be returned to the member.

The following do not count towards the annual allowance:

- transfers between registered schemes and recognised and regulated overseas schemes (see **Chapters 6** and **9**);

- input amounts in an input period where benefits are vested in full;

- contributions by a member which exceed the member's earnings and so do not qualify for tax relief;

- additional voluntary contributions which are paid for the purpose of securing added years;

- input amounts in an input period where the individual has died.

Testing against the annual allowance

10.3   An annual allowance applies to each tax year. To see if the annual allowance is exceeded in any tax year, it is necessary to aggregate the total pension input amounts during the input period of each pension arrangement of the individual ending in the tax year concerned.

PENSION INPUT AMOUNT

10.4   For money purchase schemes the pension input amount is calculated by reference to the contributions paid in during the input period.

For defined benefit schemes the input amount is based on the increased capital value of the member's pension rights over the input period.

It is fair to say that this is not the most straightforward part of the new simplified tax regime. However, it is integral to the removal of many of the tests which were required under the earlier tax regimes involving benefits and actuarial valuations. The provision for pensions in the United Kingdom is moving steadily towards money purchase schemes and arrangements, for which the calculation of the **pension input amount** is relatively simple.

The four different types of scheme or arrangement for calculating the pension input amount may be summarised as:

- defined benefit arrangements;

- cash balance arrangements;

- other money purchase arrangements;

- hybrid arrangements.

The methods of calculation are given under the appropriate headings below.

DEFINED BENEFIT ARRANGEMENTS

10.5   Contributions which are made to a defined benefit arrangement are calculated to fund the member's scale benefit entitlements. Such an arrangement is one which provides all benefits in the form of defined benefits (meaning benefits other than money purchase benefits).

The **pension input amount** is the amount of any increase in the value of the individual's rights under the **arrangement** as a whole during the **pension input period** of the arrangement that ends in the tax year. The value of the individual's rights under the arrangement at the beginning of the pension input period and the value of those rights at the end of the pension input period must be compared. An increase will be identified if:

- the value of the individual's rights under the arrangement at the beginning of the pension input period (the 'opening value') is less than

- the value of the individual's rights under the arrangement at the end of the pension input period (the 'closing value').

A member's rights may not only increase as a result of the accrual of an extra year's pensionable service and pensionable pay; there may have also been an augmentation of his benefit entitlement under the scheme.

Opening value

10.6   A factor of 10:1 is used in determining the opening value. This is based on the amount of the pension which would have been payable if the member had become entitled to payment of it at the beginning of the **pension input period**, plus the amount of the lump sum to which the individual would have been entitled (otherwise than by commutation of pension) at the same time. In valuing the pension, it should be assumed that any actuarial reduction for early payment of the pension is ignored and that ill health is not a factor (the 'valuation assumptions'). The opening value is calculated according to the following formula (*Finance Act 2004, s 234(4)*):

'The opening value of the individual's rights under the arrangement is

$(10 \times PB) + LSB$

where

PB is the annual rate of the pension which would, on the valuation assumptions (see *section 277*), be payable to the individual under the arrangement if the individual became entitled to payment of it at the beginning of the pension input period, and

LSB is the amount of the lump sum to which the individual would, on the valuation assumptions, be entitled under the arrangement (otherwise than by commutation of pension).'

Closing value

10.7   The closing value is calculated according to the following formula (*Finance Act 2004, s 234(5)*):

'The closing value of the individual's rights under the arrangement is

$(10 \times PE) + LSE$

where

PE is the annual rate of the pension which would, on the valuation assumptions, be payable to the individual under the arrangement if the individual became entitled to payment of it at the end of the pension input period, and

LSE is the amount of the lump sum to which the individual would, on the valuation assumptions, be entitled under the arrangement (otherwise than by commutation of pension) if the individual became entitled to the payment.'

A factor of 10:1 is used in determining the closing value. This is based on the amount of the pension which would have been payable if the member had become entitled to payment of it at the end of the **pension input period**, plus the amount of the lump sum to which the individual would have been entitled (otherwise than by commutation of pension) at the same time. In valuing the pension, it should be assumed that any actuarial reduction for early payment of the pension is ignored and that ill health is not a factor.

Effect of divorce, transfer (etc) on amount to be calculated

10.8   Under the *Finance Act 2004, s 236(3), (6), (7)* and *(9)* the following considerations must be taken into account:

- any pension debit in the **pension input period** should be added back;

- any pension credit in the **pension input period** should be deducted;

- where there has been a transfer to a registered scheme, or a qualifying recognised overseas pension scheme, during the **pension input period** the aggregate amount transferred together with the market value of the assets is to be added;

- where there has been a transfer-in from a registered scheme, or recognised overseas pension scheme, during the **pension input period** the amount transferred together with the market value of the assets should be deducted;

- benefits that crystallised in the pension input period should be added, except where the member has become entitled to the whole benefit or died in the period;

- minimum payments under the *Pension Schemes Act 1993, s 8* or the *Pension Schemes (Northern Ireland) Act 1993, s 4* are to be deducted.

Effect on deferred benefit

10.9   Where an individual's defined benefit pension ceases to accrue during the whole of a **pension input period** (for example, the entitlement is only to a deferred pension) the amount of the opening value of the individual's rights is increased by the greatest of the following amounts:

- 5%;

- the percentage by which RPI for the month in which the pension input period ends is higher than it was for the month in which it began; and

- the percentage to which regulations made by HMRC refer (basically this allows for revaluation required by contracting-out and preservation legislation).

The relevant HMRC regulations are the *Registered Pension Schemes (Uprating Percentages for Defined Benefits Arrangements and Enhanced Protection Limits) Regulations 2006 (SI 2006/130).*

Example – defined benefit arrangement

10.10   RPSM06103070 contains the following example:

'On 6 April 2006 Mark has completed 10 years pensionable service in a scheme where pension benefit accrues on a n/60th accrual rate. His pensionable salary for that year is £45,000. Accordingly his pensionable entitlement on that date is £7,500. (10 × 1/60th × £45,000). A lump sum is available only by commutation of pension.

By 6 April 2007 Mark's pensionable salary had risen to £50,000. Accordingly his pensionable entitlement on that date is £9,167 (11 × 1/60th × £50,000).

The increase in Mark's pension rights under this arrangement is therefore £16,670 ((£9,167 × 10) – £7,500 × 10)). Mark has no other rights under this or any other registered pension scheme, so his total pension input amount is also £16,670, which is within the **annual allowance** and so Mark has no **annual allowance charge** to pay.'

Cash balance arrangements

10.11   Under a cash balance arrangement the **pension input amount** is the amount of the increase in the value of an individual's rights in the pension input period that ends in the tax year. It is measured by reference to the 'opening value' and the 'closing value'.

Opening value

10.12   The opening value is based on the amount which would be available for the provision of benefits to or in respect of the individual on the assumption that the individual became entitled to the benefits at the beginning of the pension input period. This is uprated in the same manner as shown in **10.9** above, subject to any specific regulations which may be made for cash balance arrangements. It is assumed that the rights under the arrangement are not affected by any scheme provision to discount pension rights by an actuarial reduction for early payment, and that any calculation of rights for ill health under the scheme provisions are ignored.

Closing value

10.13   The closing value is the amount which would be available for the provision of benefits to or in respect of the individual on the assumption that the individual became entitled to the benefits at the end of the pension input period. It is assumed that the rights under the arrangement are not affected by any scheme provision to discount pension rights by an actuarial reduction for early payment, and that any calculation of rights for ill health under the scheme provisions are ignored. The provisions of **10.8** above shall also apply.

The RPSM glossary explains that, although cash balance arrangements are money purchase benefits, the amount that is available to provide those benefits is not calculated purely by reference to payments made under the arrangement by or on behalf of the member. It states that 'This means that, in a cash balance arrangement, the capital amount available to provide benefits (the member's "pot") will not derive wholly from any actual contributions (or credits or transfers) made year on year'.

The RPSM also describes the special provisions for employer contributions paid during the period 6 April 2006 to 7 July 2006. These provisions are contained in the *Finance Act 2004, s 227(7)* and *Sch 26, para 48.* Where an employer, before 8 July 2006, makes contributions to discharge previously unfunded contractual obligations incurred by them before 6 April 2006, the amount of the '**relevant consolidated contribution**' should be subtracted from the closing value.

Example – cash balance arrangement

10.14   RPSM06101070 contains the following example:

'Patricia's **pension input period** ends on 31 March 2008. Her opening value on 1 April 2007 was £100,000 and her closing value on 31 March 2008 was £220,000. During the pension input period she received a **pension credit** of £15,000. The increase in the retail price index from April 2007 to March 2008 is 4.8%

So Patricia's benefits have increased by:

Closing value	
£220,000 – £15,000	£205,000
Opening value	
£100,000 × 105%	£105,000
Increase	£100,000

As the **annual allowance** for the period 6 April 2007 to 5 April 2008 is £225,000, Patricia will not be taxed on the increase of £100,000.'

OTHER MONEY PURCHASE ARRANGEMENTS

10.15   In a money purchase arrangement the opening value of the member's rights is deducted from the closing value. The **pension input amount** is accordingly:

- any tax relievable pension contributions paid by or on behalf of the individual under the arrangement; and

- contributions paid in respect of the individual under the arrangement by an employer of the individual,

during the pension input period that ends in the tax year.

Contributions do not include contracted-out rights known as minimum payments that are made under the *PSA 1993, s 8* or the *Pension Schemes (Northern Ireland) Act 1993, s 4*. The special provisions for employer contributions paid during the period 6 April 2006 to 7 July 2006 described under **10.13** above also apply.

Contributions made by employers on an unallocated basis

10.16   The *Finance Act 2004, s 233(3)* states that it is only at the time the contribution is subsequently allocated to an individual member that the contribution counts for **annual allowance** purposes in respect of that member.

Example – money purchase arrangement

10.17   RPSM06102050 contains the following example:

'Alec is a member of a scheme with 3 other members and his pension input period ends on 30 September. During the **pension input period** of 1 October 2007 to 30 September 2008 his employer made a total contribution of £1,000,000 into the scheme. £800,000 was allocated pro rata to each member but Alec's share (25%) of the remaining £200,000 was not allocated to him until 1 October 2008. Alec had made personal contributions of £100,000 into the scheme during the same period.

In a previous year the employer had made a contribution of £300,000 into the scheme and this had remained unallocated. On 1 August 2008 £150,000 of this was allocated to Alec's fund.

So during the pension input period Alec's benefits had increased by:

Alec's contributions	£100,000
Employer's contribution	£200,000 (1/4 share of £800,000)
Previous employer contribution now allocated to Alec	£150,000
Total	£450,000

As the **annual allowance** for the period 6 April 2008 to 5 April 2009 is £235,000, Alec will be taxed on the excess of £215,000. The **annual allowance charge** will therefore be £86,000 (40% × £215,000).

The following year Alec makes a personal contribution of £15,000 and his employer makes a contribution of £25,000 to Alec's fund. So during this pension input period Alec's benefits have increased by:

Alec's contribution	£15,000
Employer's contribution	£25,000
Previous employer contribution now allocated to Alec	£50,000
Total	£90,000

As the annual allowance for the period 6 April 2009 to 5 April 2010 is £245,000, Alec will not be liable to an annual allowance charge.'

Note from this example that it is not possible to transfer unused annual allowance from another tax year.

Hybrid arrangement

10.18   A **hybrid arrangement** is one where the benefits are calculated as one of two or three alternatives, for example an arrangement under which benefits are provided on a **defined benefit** basis and on a **money purchase** basis. The **pension input amount** must be calculated on the basis that the pension will be provided by each of the types of benefit that may be payable, using the greater or greatest of these amounts as the final figure.

So, the pension input amount is the greater or greatest of such of input amounts **A**, **B** and **C** as are relevant input amounts:

A is what the pension input amount would be under the *Finance Act 2004, ss 230–232* if the benefits provided to or in respect of the individual under the arrangement were cash balance benefits.

B is what the pension input amount would be under *s 233* if the benefits provided to or in respect of the individual under the arrangement were other money purchase benefits.

C is what the pension input amount would be under *ss 234–236* if the benefits provided to or in respect of the individual under the arrangement were defined benefits.

Example of pension input amount – more than one arrangement

10.19   The RPSM also contains the following example for the method of calculation of the pension input amount where there is more than one arrangement:

'*RPSM06105020: Calculating the pension input amount where the individual has two other money purchase arrangements and a defined benefit arrangement:*

Patricia is a member of three **registered pension schemes,** under each of which she has one **arrangement** and wants to calculate whether she will face an **annual allowance charge** for the tax year ending 5 April 2007. Her details are as follows:

Arrangement	Type	Pension input period
1	Other Money purchase arrangement	6 April 2006 to 6 April 2007
2	Other Money purchase arrangement	1 January 2007 to 1 January 2008
3	Defined benefit arrangement	6 April 2006 to 31 March 2007 (a nominated date by the scheme administrator)

Arrangement 1

Patricia's arrangement received a relievable pension contribution of £200,000 from her employer on 5 April 2007 and a further £50,000 on 30 April 2007. These were the only contributions made between 6 April 2006 and 5 April 2008.

Arrangement 2

Patricia made a relievable pension contribution of £50,000 on 5 April 2007. This was the only contribution made between 6 April 2006 and 5 April 2008.

Arrangement 3

The arrangement provides benefits on a strict 60th basis. She had 25 years pensionable service on 6 April 2006 with earnings of £250,000. These had increased to £300,000 by 31 March 2007 and remained at £300,000 on 31 March 2008.

Arrangement 1, as the **pension input period** is from 6 April 2006 to 6 April 2007 neither of the sums will count towards the **annual allowance test** for the tax year 2006–2007 as the **pension input period** ends after the end of the tax year. Arrangement 2, although £50,000 was paid on the same date as the employer's first contribution to arrangement 1 the pension input period for this arrangement is 1 January 2007 to 1 January 2008. This means the impact of this contribution will affect Patricia in the following tax year. Therefore there is no **pension input amount** to arise from this arrangement in relation to the tax year 2006–2007.

Arrangement 3, the pension input period is 6 April 2006 to 31 March 2007. In accordance with the criteria as set out in RPSM06103020, her pensionable entitlement on that date is £104,166.67. (25 × 1/60th × £250,000) and so her opening value before adjustment is £1,041,667.

By 31 March 2007 her pensionable entitlement is £130,000 (26 × 1/60th × £300,000) and so her closing value is £1,300,000

Patricia's pension input amount in respect of this arrangement is therefore £258,333 (£1,300,000 – £1,041,667).

So the **total pension input amount** is £258,333 (£258,333 from arrangement 3). As the annual allowance for the tax year 2006–2007 is £215,000 Patricia will be taxed on the excess of £43,333. The annual allowance charge will be £17,333.20 (40% × £43,333).

The following year Patricia is again making the same calculation for the tax year ending 5 April 2008.

Arrangement 1, as the pension input period is from 6 April 2007 to 6 April 2008 the contributions of £200,000 and £50,000 will count as a pension input amounts.

Arrangement 2, although £50,000 was paid in the tax year ended 5 April 2007 the pension input period for this arrangement is 1 January 2007 to 1 January 2008. This means the impact of this contribution will affect Patricia in the tax year ended 5 April 2008. Therefore a pension input amount of £50,000 will arise from this arrangement.

Arrangement 3, the pension input period is 1 April 2007 to 31 March 2008. In accordance with the criteria as set out in RPSM06103020, her pensionable entitlement on that date is £130,000 (26 × 1/60th × £300,000).

On 1 April 2008 her pensionable entitlement is £135,000 (27 × 1/60th × £300,000) and so her closing value is £1,350,000.

Therefore in this case there is an 'increase' of accrued rights of £5,000 and so there is a pension input amount of £50,000 (£5,000 × 10).

In these circumstances the total pension input amount is £350,000 (£250,000 from arrangement 1, £50,000 from arrangement 2 and £50,000 from arrangement 3).

As the annual allowance for the tax year 2007–2008 is £225,000, there will be an annual allowance charge on the excess of £125,000. The annual allowance charge will be £50,000 (40% × £125,000).'

PENSION INPUT PERIOD

10.20   The first pension input period will commence on the day a member begins to accrue pension rights under the scheme or at the time a contribution is first paid in the case of a money purchase arrangement. By default, the end of the first input period is the anniversary of its commencement, although this can be changed by nominating an earlier date.

Each subsequent input period ends on the anniversary of the end of the previous input period, although this date can be brought forward by nomination as long as it remains in its original tax year. The choice of end date may be, by way of example, the end of the scheme accounting period or the end of the tax year.

Different input periods may apply to members under the same scheme.

The aggregate of all pension input amounts paid in that tax year must be the amount which is tested against the annual allowance. Any excess will be subject to the annual allowance charge.

ANNUAL ALLOWANCE CHARGE

10.21   The annual allowance charge is a freestanding charge which is set at a rate of 40%. The charge is imposed on any excess over the annual allowance of pension input amounts during input periods of each arrangement relating to the individual ending in the tax year concerned. It is the member who is liable to pay the charge and who has a duty to notify HMRC if he has not been issued with a personal tax return for the year concerned. As the charge relates solely to the input to registered UK pension schemes it will be incurred whatever the residence or domicile of the administrator or member.

As the annual charge is freestanding, it is not permitted to set off the charge against general tax repayments, or to allocate it from one year to another year (for example, if the pension input amount for a defined benefit scheme is in the negative for any year), nor is it permissible to set off the charge against other tax allowances or any losses. It should be noted that the excessive amount is not treated as pension income (or any other income) for the purposes of UK bilateral double taxation conventions.

LIFETIME ALLOWANCE

10.22   Benefits must be tested against the lifetime allowance on the occurrence of various benefit crystallisation events (see **4.44**). The amount of the lifetime allowance rises each year. Allowances for the five years to 2010/11 are shown in **10.29**. The allowances for subsequent five-year periods will be set by the government.

There are two possible methods of protecting large accrued rights as at A-Day. The protection methods are available under the transitional arrangements for the protection of benefits and accrued rights, and they are referred to in the *Finance Act 2004* as 'primary protection' and 'enhanced protection'. The two forms of protection are described in detail in Chapter 11.

Testing against the lifetime allowance

10.23   The aggregate pensions saving in tax-advantaged schemes over a member's lifetime must be taken into consideration for the purpose of testing against the lifetime allowance. However, this does not include any dependants' pensions; these are not subject to the lifetime allowance.

The method of testing against the lifetime allowance is not as complex as that for the annual allowance. Nevertheless, it does still depend on the nature of schemes and arrangements under which the member's pension entitlements have accrued.

The amount crystallised by each benefit crystallisation event is described in **4.44–4.45**. Broadly speaking, however, the amounts to be tested against the lifetime allowance can be summarised as follows:

- *Defined benefit schemes*: Pensions must be valued on a factor of 20:1. If the pension increases under the relevant scheme exceed the retail prices index, or a fixed 5% per annum, or aggregate survivors' benefits exceed the member's pensions, a special factor can be agreed with HMRC. Where separate lump sums are payable under a scheme (that is, cash sums which do not derive from a pension commutation) these amounts shall be added on after the calculation has been made.

- *Pensions in payment on A-Day*: Where a pension has already come in to payment as at A-Day, a factor of 25:1 must be applied to the pension in order to determine its capital value. Where an unsecured pension is in payment from a money purchase scheme at A-Day the maximum drawdown level as at 5 April 2006 must be used even if the actual drawdown amount being taken is less than the maximum. The valuation of pre A-Day rights only needs to be taken into account if a benefit crystallisation event occurs in relation to the member after A-Day.

- *Money purchase schemes in general*: These shall be measured as the market value of the sums and assets held under the arrangement in respect of the member.

In addition to the exemption for dependants' pensions, the following exemptions apply:

- partnership retirement annuities, but excluding other retirement annuities;

- transfers to other registered pension schemes;

- discretionary augmentations given across the board to pensions in payment (these do not have to be tested against the lifetime allowance if there at least 50 pensioners under the scheme and the increase applies to a class of at least 20 pensioner members).

RESPONSIBILITY OF SCHEME ADMINISTRATOR ON BENEFIT CRYSTALLISATION EVENT

10.24   The scheme administrator has three responsibilities before, at and after the time when a benefit crystallisation event (BCE) occurs in a member's lifetime:

(a)   establishing whether a chargeable amount arises at the BCE;

(b)   accounting to HMRC for the lifetime allowance charge due on any chargeable amount that arises at the BCE (on a quarterly basis); and

(c)   providing the member after the BCE with a statement confirming the total level of the member's lifetime allowance that has been used up under the scheme, and if a chargeable amount arose at the BCE, a notice confirming:

- the level of chargeable amount that arose at the BCE;

- the lifetime allowance charge due; and

- whether or not they have accounted for the due charge, or intend to do so in due course.

There is no laid down regulatory method for establishing the available allowance at a BCE; schemes can adopt the method which best suits their design and operation.

RPSM11100030 states:

'When calculating the percentage of the standard lifetime allowance being used up at any BCE the **scheme administrator** need only be concerned with the benefits currently being tested under their particular scheme. They do not require specific details of any other benefits the member may have (which in turn avoids the need to obtain details of other rights when the individual joins the scheme). However, in order to calculate whether the member has enough available lifetime allowance to cover the amount crystallising at that BCE (and whether or not a lifetime allowance charge is due) the scheme administrator may well require details from the member of the previous percentages of the 'standard lifetime allowance' they have used up under other registered pension schemes at earlier BCEs.'

Lifetime allowance charge

10.25   Where the lifetime allowance has been exceeded on a benefit crystallisation event, the lifetime allowance charge becomes payable on the chargeable amount. The rate of the charge on the excess over the lifetime allowance is 25% if a pension is taken. If a lump sum is taken, the rate will be 55%. The charge is intended to negate the tax reliefs which the relevant funds will have attracted over time, both on the contributions and the fund growth. The scheme administrator may deduct the charge, and the member should normally declare the payment in his tax return and offset the tax deducted.

The liability for the charge falls jointly and severally on the member and the administrator, or on the recipient in the case of a lump sum death benefit. The charge is payable regardless of the residency or domicile of the administrator or member. Any withholding tax accounted for by the scheme may be offset against the member's liability. The administrator may reclaim any excessive tax which has been paid and repay it to the member.

The scheme administrator may apply to HMRC to be absolved of liability to pay the charge where the administrator acted in good faith and concluded that no charge was due. If the charge arises on the payment of certain lump sum death benefits following the death of the individual, the recipient is liable for the charge (not the member's **personal representatives** or the scheme administrator making the payment). However, the member's personal representatives are responsible for establishing whether a chargeable amount arises following the payment of such a lump sum death benefit, and both the member's personal representatives and the scheme administrator have a duty to report to HMRC.

A formula is provided in the *Finance Act 2004, s 218* for the purpose of calculating the lifetime allowance at the benefit crystallisation date where one or more lifetime allowance enhancement factors apply. The formula is:

$$SLA + (SLA \times LAEF)$$

where:

- SLA is the standard lifetime allowance at that date; and

- LAEF is the lifetime allowance enhancement factor which operates at that date with regard to the event and the member.

Lifetime allowance charge paid by scheme administrator

10.26   If the member does not pay the lifetime allowance charge, or suffer a reduction in rights to pay for it, but the scheme administrator instead pays the charge (a 'scheme-funded tax payment'), the charge must be grossed up as if it were part of the member's rights. RPSM11105220 explains this further:

'The amount that actually crystallises through a **BCE** over and above the member's available **lifetime allowance** is referred to as the basic amount of the **chargeable amount**.

This basic amount will be made up of either a lump-sum amount or retained amount (or a combination of the two) depending on the events taking place. From this breakdown the level of **lifetime allowance charge** due can be identified (see RPSM11105210).

For BCEs other than those dealing with the entitlement to a scheme pension the actual lifetime allowance charge paid by the **scheme administrator** is referred to in the legislation as a "scheme-funded tax payment", and is added on to the basic amount to form part of the chargeable amount. This is because, for these BCEs, the amount crystallised is the net amount after tax (so the net lump sum paid by the scheme, the net amount being designated to provide an **unsecured pension fund** etc.). Adding the tax paid by the scheme administrator ensures that the taxable amount is the gross amount before tax.

Where a scheme-funded tax payment needs to be added to the basic amount to form the chargeable amount, the scheme administrator will want to ensure that the tax they pay, which forms the scheme-funded tax payment, is the same amount that will be due on the gross chargeable amount.

For example, if a member with no available lifetime allowance has £100,000 in a **money purchase arrangement** and wishes to use it to provide a **lifetime annuity**, the scheme administrator is likely to use £75,000 to purchase the annuity and pay £25,000 to HMRC to cover the lifetime allowance charge due. This will mean that the basic amount is the £75,000 crystallising through BCE 4, the scheme-funded tax payment is £25,000 and the chargeable amount is £100,000. The tax due on the chargeable amount is £25,000, the same amount that the scheme administrator has paid.

If the scheme administrator allowed the full £100,000 to be used to purchase a lifetime annuity, and to fund the tax out of the scheme's own resources, then the amount crystallising through BCE 4 would be £100,000. The scheme administrator would need to pay £33,333 of lifetime allowance charge to HMRC as a scheme-funded tax payment – so the chargeable amount would be £133,333 and the charge due (and already paid) would be £33,333.'

RPSM worked examples

10.27   The following examples show methods of testing against the lifetime allowance on successive events:

'RPSM11100030: How the lifetime allowance is measured:

When a member becomes entitled to draw benefits from a **registered pension scheme,** they use up a proportion or percentage of their **lifetime allowance**. That is how the lifetime allowance test works, by reference to percentages of the individual's lifetime allowance used up in particular circumstances.

There is no measure for lifetime allowance purposes of any benefits held by the individual until entitlement to those benefits arises. The exceptions to this rule are where the member reaches age 75 without having taken benefits, or where the member transfers to a certain sort of overseas scheme. In these cases any undrawn entitlement is tested for lifetime allowance purposes at that time.

The circumstances where a lifetime allowance test occurs are referred to in the legislation as **benefit crystallisation** events (BCEs). At each **BCE** a capital value is attributed to the benefits that crystallise. This capital value (the amount crystallising) is converted into a percentage of the **standard lifetime allowance** for the tax year the BCE occurred in. That percentage is then measured against the member's available lifetime allowance at the point of testing.

The percentage of the member's lifetime allowance being used up as a consequence a BCE is added to any percentage used up previously by the member, whether under the same scheme or a different registered pension scheme. Where the total of these percentages exceeds the individual's lifetime allowance the excess (or the **chargeable amount**) is subject to a specific tax charge (the **lifetime allowance charge**).

Example

Mike crystallises benefits with a capital value of £150,000. The standard lifetime allowance at that point is £1.5 million, so the percentage used up is 10%. If Mike had not crystallised any other benefits previously, he will have 90% of his lifetime allowance still available for the next BCE.

The same process occurs when Mike crystallises benefits at a future date.

This time Mike crystallises a further £500,000 when the standard lifetime allowance is £2 million. So Mike has used up a further 25% of the standard lifetime allowance. In total Mike has used up 35% (10% + 25%) of his lifetime allowance.

The percentage of the standard lifetime allowance used up at a particular BCE in a particular tax year remains constant year by year even though the standard lifetime allowance is increased in subsequent tax years. So the 10% of the standard lifetime allowance used up in the example above when the standard lifetime allowance is £1.5 million remains constant at 10% in the later year when the allowance has risen to £2 million. This process ensures that the original crystallisation amount of £150,000 maintains a fixed percentage, despite subsequent increases to the lifetime allowance.

RPSM11100040 explains the logic behind this process in more detail, and the example in RPSM11100090 illustrates this principle.

When calculating the percentage of the standard lifetime allowance being used up at any BCE the **scheme administrator** need only be concerned with the benefits currently being tested under their particular scheme. They do not require specific details of any other benefits the member may have (which in turn avoids the need to obtain details of other rights when the individual joins the scheme). However, in order to calculate whether the member has enough available lifetime allowance to cover the amount crystallising at that BCE (and whether or not a lifetime allowance charge is due) the scheme administrator may well require details from the member of the previous percentages of the 'standard lifetime allowance' they have used up under other registered pension schemes at earlier BCEs.

RPSM11103000 onwards explains in more detail the lifetime allowance testing process and the responsibilities imposed under the tax rules on each party.

RPSM11100090: Lifetime allowance: basic principles: worked example:

On 9 October 2006, Judy decides to draw some of her benefits from a **registered pension scheme**. She wants to take the maximum lump sum and use the residual funds to purchase a **lifetime annuity**. The **scheme administrator** calculates the capital crystallised value of the level of benefits she wants to draw as being £750,000.

The scheme administrator writes to Judy telling her how much will crystallise for **lifetime allowance** purposes and the percentage of the current **standard lifetime allowance** this will represent (50% of the standard life time allowance for the 2006/07 tax year). They ask Judy to provide a statement within 1 month confirming the level of lifetime allowance she anticipates being available on the anticipated BCE date, and to say whether or not she anticipates any other BCE occurring either on or before that date under another scheme. They also ask her whether she is entitled to an enhanced lifetime allowance and, if so, to provide evidence of the certificate confirming the exact level of enhancement, as provided by HMRC.

Judy has not drawn any pension benefits from any other source previously and is subject to the standard lifetime allowance. She provides the requested statement confirming she has not used up any lifetime allowance previously and does not anticipate another BCE occurring either by or on the proposed date of the BCE.

The scheme administrator is satisfied that there is no **chargeable amount** and pays the benefits in full. They send Judy a statement verifying that she has used up 50% of the standard lifetime allowance at the BCE. Judy keeps this for future reference.

In the 2010/11 tax year Judy decides to draw the rest of her benefits under the scheme. The scheme administrator calculates the capital crystallised value of these remaining benefits as £180,000. The standard lifetime allowance is now £1.8 million so this second tranche of pension benefits represents 10% of the standard lifetime allowance at that time.

The scheme administrator writes to Judy outlining the above and asking her again about her anticipated available lifetime allowance at the time she wants to draw benefits. Judy still has 50% of her lifetime allowance available.

The new tranche of benefits will take Judy up to 60% of her lifetime allowance (50% plus 10%), so again there is no chargeable amount on this BCE. Judy declares to the scheme administrator that she has 50% of the standard lifetime allowance available at that time.

Benefits are paid out by the scheme administrator.

The scheme administrator sends a statement to Judy telling her she has now in aggregate used up 60% of her lifetime allowance (the standard lifetime allowance) through the scheme. Again, this certificate helps Judy keep track of the lifetime allowance she has used up, and evidence this fact where necessary.

RPSM11105250: Example of the breakdown of a chargeable amount into the lump sum amount and the retained amount:

Matthew has already used up 100% of his **lifetime allowance**. He still holds £300,000 **uncrystallised funds** in a **money purchase arrangement**. Matthew decides to draw these benefits on 3 October 2010.

Matthew tells the **scheme administrator** that he has no available lifetime allowance, so the scheme administrator knows that any amount crystallising will be a **chargeable amount**.

The scheme rules give Matthew the option of drawing some or all the chargeable amount as a **lifetime allowance excess lump sum** or as an authorised pension benefit. Matthew chooses to draw two thirds of the chargeable amount as a lump sum, and use the remaining amount to generate an **unsecured pension**. A **pension commencement lump sum** may not be paid as his lifetime allowance has already been fully used.

Before making the payments the scheme administrator calculates the **lifetime allowance charge** due on the chargeable amount.

Two **BCE**s occur: the payment of the lifetime allowance excess lump sum (BCE 6) and the designation of funds to provide unsecured pension (BCE 1).

The amount potentially crystallising on the payment of a lifetime allowance excess lump sum (through BCE 6) is £200,000. But the lump sum will be reduced by the scheme administrator to reflect the lifetime allowance charge due on this sum. The lump sum attracts a lifetime allowance charge at the rate of 55% so the lifetime allowance charge due on this part of the chargeable amount is £110,000. The net lifetime allowance excess lump sum paid to Matthew by the scheme is £90,000 (£200,000 – £110,000).

The amount crystallising through BCE 6, plus the lifetime allowance charge paid by the scheme administrator in relation to this payment (a scheme-funded tax payment), represent the lump sum amount of the chargeable amount. The lump sum amount is the £90,000 crystallising through BCE 6 on the payment of the (net) lifetime allowance lump sum, plus the £110,000 scheme-funded tax payment paid by the scheme in respect of the lump sum amount. The £90,000 crystallising through BCE 6 forms part of the basic amount, but the scheme-funded tax payment of £110,000 does not.

The amount crystallising on the designation of funds to provide unsecured pension (through BCE 1), plus the scheme-funded tax payment paid by the scheme administrator in relation to this designation represents the retained amount of the chargeable amount. This sum attracts a lifetime allowance charge at the rate of 25%.

The scheme administrator will fund the lifetime allowance charge due on the designation of uncrystallised funds to provide an unsecured pension direct from those funds. The lifetime allowance charge due on this part of the chargeable amount will be £25,000 (25% of £100,000). So only £75,000 of the £100,000 uncrystallised funds being crystallised is designated to provide an unsecured pension (with the other £25,000 being used to fund the charge due).

The retained amount is the £75,000 crystallising through BCE 1 on the designation of funds to provide an unsecured pension, plus the £25,000 scheme-funded tax payment paid by the scheme in respect of the retained amount. The £75,000 crystallising through BCE 1 forms part of the basic amount, but the scheme-funded tax payment of £25,000 does not.

The total lifetime allowance charge paid is therefore £135,000 (£110,000 + £25,000).

The unsecured pension paid from the unsecured pension fund is still taxable as pension income on Matthew through PAYE.'

ANNUAL ALLOWANCE RATES

10.28

2006/2007	£215,000
2007/2008	£225,000
2008/2009	£235,000
2009/2010	£245,000
2010/2011	£255,000

LIFETIME ALLOWANCE RATES

10.29

2006/2007	£1,500,000
2007/2008	£1,600,000
2008/2009	£1,650,000
2009/2010	£1,750,000
2010/2011	£1,800,000

Chapter 11

Transitional protection

INTRODUCTION

11.1   The pension tax regime which was introduced by the *Finance Act 2004* on 6 April 2006 ('A-Day') differs from the introduction of previous tax regimes in one very important aspect: it is retrospective. The introduction of previous pension tax regimes permitted those already accruing benefits in their particular occupational scheme to continue to do so on the same tax terms in the future, while new employees had to be pensioned under the new tax terms. Not only did this lead to inequalities in the employment context, but it also gave rise to a complicated system of tax controls with each new layer of legislation or HMRC discretionary practice.

The *Finance Act 2004* ensures that no future benefits will accrue on historical tax terms, but without a system of protection for accrued rights many would have been faced with controversial tax bills whenever they came to retire. As one of the main goals of the *Finance Act 2004* is simplification, the method of protecting members' accrued rights also had to be simple. Two methods were devised to try and achieve this: 'enhanced protection' and 'primary protection'.

Member protection

11.2   The effect of enhanced protection is to ensure that scheme members are able to protect their accrued rights and avoid the new lifetime and annual allowance charges completely. Certain conditions must be met in order to achieve and retain enhanced protection. The most important of these is that no further relevant benefit accrual, as defined, has occurred in respect of the individual concerned. What is meant by relevant benefit accrual is covered in depth later in this chapter.

Primary protection, on the other hand, allows further benefit to accrue after A-Day. It provides a simple protection on accrued rights by offering an uplift to an individual's lifetime allowance in the form of a lifetime allowance enhancement factor based on the amount of pension rights already accrued at 5 April 2006. However, further benefit accrual is likely to attract a lifetime allowance charge as it is almost by definition above the protected amount.

Scheme members with large pension rights adversely affected by the new regime have a relatively short period of time – until 5 April 2009 – to notify HMRC that they will be relying on one or both of the protections. However, because of the restriction of benefit accrual under enhanced protection, many of those affected will find that they needed to take decisions about enhanced protection before or shortly after A-Day.

Scheme protection

11.3   At the same time it was recognised that references to pre 6 April 2006 HMRC limits had been incorporated into the rules of tax-approved pension schemes. Removing the effect of HMRC limits overnight could have increased the rights of a number of members unintentionally, thereby exposing pension schemes and their sponsors to additional costs. A set of transitional regulations therefore imposed some of the pre 6 April 2006 HMRC limits on schemes that had been tax-approved on 5 April 2006. These limits can be disapplied by a resolution of the trustees of the scheme and are due in any event to fall away on 6 April 2011.

Furthermore, if members had a right to benefits that did not meet the form of the new authorised payments, the payment of such benefits would bring unauthorised payment charges to both the member and the scheme. In this case the regulations override trustees' obligations to pay the benefits and instead grant them the discretion to make the payment.

This chapter looks at the two forms of member protection, primary and enhanced protection, and at the scheme protection that applies until 5 April 2011.

RPSM examples

11.4   Throughout this chapter extensive use is made of the examples published by HMRC in its Registered Pensions Schemes Manual (RPSM). Specific HMRC examples referred to in the text below can be found in Chapter 3 of the RPSM, but they are also reproduced at the end of this chapter for ease of reference.

VALUING PRE-A-DAY RIGHTS FOR PROTECTION

11.5   Whether primary or enhanced protection is chosen, or both, it will be necessary to value the rights that have accrued at 5 April 2006. In the case of primary protection this is necessary because an amount no greater than the maximum pension under the applicable pre-A-Day regime can be protected. In the case of enhanced protection, the amount of benefit above the appropriate pre-A-Day limit (if any) must be surrendered. Rights are valued in the same manner for both these purposes, but note that there are some extra easements when calculating pre-A-Day limits. Note also that the value of benefits is not based on one of the traditional actuarial methods, e.g. transfer value, but on the standard HMRC valuation factor.

Rights not yet in payment

11.6   The valuation of rights which have not yet come into payment depends on the type of arrangement from which they derive (money purchase, cash balance, defined benefit or hybrid).

Money purchase arrangements

11.7 For money purchase arrangements, which includes both personal pensions and occupational defined contribution schemes, the value of a member's uncrystallised rights is the sum of any cash held under the scheme and the market value of the other assets held to provide the member's benefits on 5 April 2006.

Note that, where primary protection applies, it may be possible to recalculate the value of rights as at 5 April 2006 in a case where compensation for poor performance of an investment owned by the scheme was paid between 6 April 2006 and 5 April 2009. *Regulations 9, 10* and *11* of the *Taxation of Pension Schemes (Transitional Provisions) Order 2006 (SI 2006/572)* apply.

Cash balance arrangements

11.8 For a cash balance scheme, the value of a member's uncrystallised rights is the amount that would be available for the provision of immediate benefit if the member had been entitled to receive it on 5 April 2006. For this purpose it is assumed that the member is in good physical and mental health and has reached either age 60, or, if a different age was specified in the rules at 10 December 2003 as the minimum age at which benefits could be paid without reduction, that age.

Defined benefit arrangements

11.9 For a defined benefit arrangement, the value of a member's uncrystallised rights is calculated by the formula:

$$(RVF \times ARP) + LS$$

where:

RVF is the relevant valuation factor (ie 20)

ARP is the annual rate of pension to which the member would be entitled if he acquired an actual rather than a prospective right to receive it on 5 April 2006

LS is the amount of lump sum the member would have received otherwise than by commutation (ie only applicable for schemes that provide separate pension and lump sum).

As for cash balance arrangements, it is assumed that the member is in good physical and mental health and has reached either age 60, or, if a different age was specified in the rules at 10 December 2003 as the minimum age at which benefits could be paid without reduction, that age.

Hybrid arrangements

11.10 In a hybrid arrangement the value of uncrystallised rights is simply calculated on whichever of the bases produces the highest result.

HMRC limits

11.11   The value of uncrystallised rights must be restricted to comply with pre A-Day HMRC limits where those rights derive from one of the following occupational pension schemes:

(a)   a retirement benefit scheme approved for the purpose of the *Income and Corporation Taxes Act 1988 (ICTA 1988), Ch I, Pt XIV*;

(b)   a scheme formerly approved under *ICTA 1970, s 208*;

(c)   a relevant statutory scheme as defined in *ICTA 1988, s 611A* or a pension scheme treated by HMRC as such; or

(d)   a deferred annuity contract securing benefits under any of the three types of scheme above.

The restriction is expressed by the formula:

$20 \times MPP$

where

> MPP is the maximum permitted pension that could be paid to the individual on 5 April 2006 under the arrangement without giving HMRC grounds for withdrawing tax approval. See **Appendix 1** for the main features of the pre A-Day tax approval regime.

In arriving at MPP it is assumed that the member is in good physical and mental health and has reached either age 60, or, if a different age was specified in the rules at 10 December 2003 as the minimum age at which benefits could be paid without reduction, that age. For a member still in service on 5 April 2006, it is assumed that he left employment on that date.

As an example, if a member of a defined benefit scheme was subject to the pre '87 regime, was still in service on 5 April 2006, had 30 years potential service to his normal retirement date and had 20 years service accrued to 5 April 2006, his HMRC maximum permitted pension at 5 April 2006 would be calculated as:

The higher of:

(a) $20/60 \times$ final remuneration, and

(b) $20/30 \times (40/60 \times$ final remuneration – retained benefits)

In this case the member has more than 10 years service to his normal retirement date, and, as the pre '87 regime applies, he can therefore count on the uplifted 60ths scale, which gives him a maximum pension ('**P**') of 40/60. Retained benefits must then be deducted, if necessary, and the result multiplied by **N/NS**, where **N** is service accrued, in this case, to 5 April 2006, and **NS** is potential service to normal retirement date (20 years and 30 years respectively in this example). (See para 7.47 of the Practice Notes IR12 (2001).)

Retained benefits do not have to be taken into account if the member's P60 earnings from pensionable employment did not exceed £50,000 in the 2004/05 tax year, even for controlling directors. If pensionable service did not continue for the whole of the 2004/05 tax year, a pro rata calculation applies. If pensionable service ceased before 6 April 2004, retained benefits do not have to be taken into account if P60 earnings in the last complete tax year before date of leaving did not exceed £25,000. These easements were introduced by Update 159 (now incorporated into paragraph 7.6a of the Practice Notes) and are applicable on and from 5 April 2006. See also paragraph 16.55a of the Practice Notes on the valuation of money purchase benefits. Retained benefits may also be ignored under the other administrative easements described in paragraphs 7.5–7.7 of the Practice Notes.

A copy of the Practice Notes IR12 (2001) is retained by HMRC on its website at:

www.hmrc.gov.uk/pensionschemes/ir12.pdf

Note that HMRC limits are subject to the requirements of the preservation legislation. This means that it will not always be possible to restrict **MPP** to the **N/60** or **N/NS × (P–RB)** formulae above. This is an especially important consideration for members of occupational money purchase pension schemes. For example, the maximum permitted pension for a member of such a scheme approved after 1991 would be the pension he could have received if he had retired on ill health grounds at the date of leaving, ie using potential service up to his normal retirement date.

In an occupational money purchase pension scheme the calculation of **MPP** should be carried out on the appropriate preservation basis depending on when the scheme was approved. The appropriate preservation basis will be the version of HMRC's limits calculation that was set out in the Practice Notes at the time of approval. The three versions for this calculation appear in RPSM03101551, RPSM03101560 and RPSM03101570 and are reproduced at the end of this chapter.

Under primary protection where the value of uncrystallised rights is greater than **20 × MPP**, note that the excess **over 20 × MPP** is not lost, nor does it have to be surrendered (as it would for enhanced protection). **20 × MPP** is simply the maximum value that can be taken into account when calculating the lifetime allowance enhancement factor. The excess rights remain in the scheme, but would obviously be more likely to be subject to a Lifetime Allowance Charge.

Rights in payment

11.12 Where rights have come into payment, they are valued as 25 times the annual rate of pension that is being paid. Note that any lump sum already paid is not taken into account; this is already catered for by multiplying the pension in payment by 25 instead of 20. There is no need to test pensions in payment against HMRC pre A-Day limits as this will already have been done when the benefits were brought into payment.

Where the rights in payment are in the form of income drawdown, they are valued as 25 times the maximum annual rate of drawdown that could have been received on 5 April 2006. For this purpose it is not necessary to obtain a new drawdown valuation as at 5 April 2006; the maximum rate established at the last review is sufficient. See the two examples in RPSM03101040.

Lump sum rights

11.13   The method of valuing lump sum rights on 5 April 2006 is expressed by the formula:

$$(\tfrac{1}{4} \times VCPR) + VULSR$$

where:

VCPR is the value of relevant crystallised pension rights

VULSR is the value of relevant uncrystallised lump sum rights

VCPR is calculated as 25 times the annual rate at which any existing pension (or the sum if more than one) is currently payable on 5 April 2006 from one or more of the following arrangements:

(a)   a retirement benefit scheme approved under *ICTA 1988, Ch I, Pt XIV*;

(b)   a scheme formerly approved under *ICTA 1970, s 208*;

(c)   a relevant statutory scheme;

(d)   a *s 32* policy;

(e)   a parliamentary pension fund;

(f)   a retirement annuity contract (also known as a *s 226* annuity);

(g)   a personal pension scheme approved under *ICTA 1988, Ch IV, Pt XIV*; or

(h)   a right to make income withdrawals under *ICTA 1988, s 634A*.

The calculation of **VCPR** in this way differs from the actual lump sum that would have been paid, but is done in the interest of simplicity.

Any dependant's pension paid as a result of the death of another person is not to be taken into account for **VCPR**.

For the purpose of **VCPR**, if an individual is taking income drawdown it is valued as 25 times the maximum annual rate that could be taken.

VULSR is calculated as if the member had become entitled on 5 April 2006 to the present payment of any lump sum payable under the rules of any of the arrangements mentioned in (a) to (g) above. For this purpose it is assumed that the member is in good physical and mental health and has reached either age 60 or, if a different age was specified in the rules at 10 December 2003 as the minimum age at which benefits could be paid without reduction, that age.

The exception is that a lump sum from a retirement annuity contract will be limited to 25% of the funds held for the purpose of the arrangement on 5 April 2006, even though a lump sum percentage higher than 25% could have been paid.

For members of occupational pension schemes the value of the lump sum is restricted by reference to the HMRC limits which applied before A-Day. For a member still in service on 5 April 2006, it is assumed that he left employment on that date. As an example, if a member was subject to the pre-1987 regime, was still in service on 5 April 2006, had 30 years' potential service to his normal retirement date and had 20 years' service accrued to 5 April 2006, his HMRC maximum lump sum at 5 April 2006 would be calculated as the higher of:

(a) $3/80 \times 20 \times$ final remuneration; and

(b) $20/30 \times (120/80 \times$ final remuneration – lump sum retained benefits).

In this case the member has more than 20 years' service to his normal retirement date, and, as the pre-1987 regime applies, he can therefore count on the uplifted 80ths scale, which gives him a maximum lump sum of 120/80. Lump sum retained benefits must then be deducted, if necessary, and the result multiplied by **N/NS**, where **N** is service accrued, in this case to 5 April 2006, and **NS** is potential service to normal retirement date (20 years and 30 years respectively in this example).

Retained benefits do not have to be taken into account if the member's P60 earnings from pensionable employment did not exceed £50,000 in the 2004/05 tax year, even for controlling directors. If pensionable service did not continue for the whole of the 2004/05 tax year, a pro rata calculation applies. If pensionable service ceased before 6 April 2004, retained benefits do not have to be taken into account if P60 earnings in the last complete tax year before date of leaving did not exceed £25,000. Retained benefits may also be ignored in the usual circumstances set out in the Practice Notes IR12 (2001). Note that consideration of retained benefits is only necessary for pre-1987 members. Lump sum retained benefits do not need to be considered for 1987–1989 regime members or for post-1989 regime members.

If lump sum rights are valued at more than £375,000 they may be included in the notification to HMRC to rely on primary and/or enhanced protection.

PRIMARY PROTECTION

Method of protection

11.14   Primary protection is achieved by working out an uplift to be applied in individual cases to the standard lifetime allowance, called a lifetime allowance enhancement factor, and registering the details with HMRC. The enhancement factor will be the percentage by which the value of rights on 5 April 2006 exceeds £1,500,000 and is expressed in the following formula:

(RR – SLA)/SLA

where:

RR is the value of pension rights on 5 April 2006

SLA is the standard lifetime allowance for the 2006/07 tax year (£1,500,000)

For example, if the value of an individual's total pension rights on 5 April 2006 was £1,830,000, his lifetime allowance enhancement factor would be 0.22, calculated as:

$$(1,830,000 - 1,500,000)/1,500,000 = 0.22$$

This means that he would be entitled to a personal lifetime allowance 22% greater than the standard lifetime allowance at the time he takes benefits.

When calculating a lifetime allowance enhancement factor, the factor should be rounded up to two decimal places. When advising a member of the percentage of lifetime allowance used by any benefit crystallisation event, this should be rounded down to two decimal places. Further information is provided in RPSM11100040.

Note that Articles 9, 10 and 11 of the *Taxation of Pension Schemes (Transitional Provisions) Order 2006 (SI 2006/572)* provide transitional protection for individuals who qualify for primary protection but whose pre-commencement rights may have been undervalued on 5 April 2006 due to the poor performance of investments held by the scheme. If the scheme receives compensation in respect of the poor performance on or after 6 April 2006, this compensation becomes potentially chargeable to the lifetime allowance charge. *Article 9* sets out the conditions which the individual needs to satisfy to qualify for the transitional protection. *Article 10* modifies the valuation of uncrystallised rights. The compensation payment must be made between 6 April 2006 and 5 April 2009.

Primary protection is only available if the amount of an individual's relevant pension rights exceeds £1,500,000 on 5 April 2006 and he has notified HMRC of his intention to rely on primary protection before 6 April 2009.

For pension rights to be relevant, they must derive from one or more of the following arrangements:

(a)   a retirement benefit scheme approved under, *ICTA 1988, Ch I, Pt XIV*;

(b)   a scheme formerly approved under *ICTA 1970, s 208*;

(c)   a relevant statutory scheme;

(d)   a *s 32* policy;

(e)   a parliamentary pension fund;

(f)   a retirement annuity contract (also known as a *s 226 annuity*); or

(g)   a personal pension scheme approved under *ICTA 1988, Ch IV, Pt XIV*.

Rights built up in a funded or unfunded unapproved retirement benefit scheme (FURBS or UURBS) do not count as relevant pension rights, nor does any entitlement to a pension which arises upon the death of another.

The value of uncrystallised relevant pension rights must not exceed the maximum approvable limit by reference to the appropriate tax regime applicable to each of an individual's occupational pension scheme rights on 5 April 2006. If the valuation of uncrystallised relevant pension rights *does* exceed the value of the maximum permitted pension, the excess is not lost, nor does it have to be surrendered, but it cannot be taken into account in working out the lifetime allowance enhancement factor.

If primary protection applies and an individual's pension rights are decreased by a pension debit as a result of pension sharing on divorce, the lifetime allowance enhancement factor needs to be recalculated by reference to the value of rights that remain after the pension debit is deducted. If this reduces the value of rights below £1,500,000 then primary protection is lost and the individual will be subject to the standard £1,500,000 lifetime allowance.

Registration for protection

11.15   The *Registered Pension Schemes (Enhanced Lifetime Allowance) Regulations 2006 (SI 2006/131)* set down the procedural and administrative requirements for notification, certification and compliance for those wishing to rely on primary and/or enhanced protection.

Notification of a member's intention to rely on primary protection must be made by him on the appropriate form to reach HMRC by 5 April 2009. The current version of the form of notification is APSS200, with accompanying notes.

The notification must be signed and dated by the individual. Only in exceptional circumstances may someone other than the individual sign the notification form. Where someone is incapable by reason of mental disorder or physical disability, then a person having responsibility for managing the individual's affairs, or having power of attorney, may sign on the individual's behalf. Where an individual has died, his personal representatives have the power to complete the notification form and otherwise do whatever the individual could have done in regards to notification.

Notification of intention to rely on enhanced protection can be made on the same form, and there is also a section for notifying HMRC of lump sum entitlements greater than £375,000 on 5 April 2006.

Where HMRC receive a notification form and it contains no obvious errors or omissions, they must issue a certificate. Where they receive a notification and it *does* contain obvious errors or omissions, they must return the form to the individual.

The individual to whom a protection certificate is issued must preserve it until no further benefit crystallisation event can occur. Each certificate must have a unique reference number.

Where HMRC have issued a protection certificate they may instigate a review of any information given in connection with the certificate within a period of twelve months from the date on which the notification was given to them. Even where the twelve month period has passed, HMRC may still instigate a review at any time if they have reason to believe that any information in connection with the notification was, or has become, incorrect. Individuals must keep records relating to the protection notification for at least six years.

Pension benefits

11.16   The amount of a benefit crystallised at a benefit crystallisation event is usually tested against the standard lifetime allowance at the time of crystallisation (see **4.44**). Under primary protection the crystallised amount is tested against an individual's personal lifetime allowance, ie the standard lifetime allowance as increased by his lifetime allowance enhancement factor.

If the standard lifetime allowance is £1,800,000, an individual has an enhancement factor of 0.22, and crystallises benefits valued at £2,100,000, he would still escape the lifetime allowance charge as illustrated by the following:

> personal lifetime allowance = $1,800,000 \times 1.22 = £2,196,000$, which is greater than the crystallised amount of £2,100,000.

If an individual vests benefits at different times, the application of the personal lifetime allowance is operated in the same way as the standard lifetime allowance. See the example in RPSM03102030 at the end of this chapter.

Lump sum benefits greater than £375,000

11.17   Where an individual has applied for primary protection and has registered lump sum rights at 5 April 2006 which are greater than £375,000, the normal rules for calculating pension commencement lump sums (see **4.12**) at a benefit crystallisation event do not apply. Instead, the pension commencement lump sum is calculated as the amount registered at A-Day increased by the rise in the standard lifetime allowance between A-Day and the year in which benefits are vested.

For example, if lump sum rights of £400,000 were registered at A-Day, and in the year of vesting, eg 2010/11, the standard lifetime allowance had increased to £1,800,000, the maximum lump sum that could be paid would be:

> $£400,000 \times 1,800,000/1,500,000 = £480,000$

Note that the sum registered at A-Day relates to the aggregate of all lump sum rights an individual may have under several pension arrangements. If lump sums are taken from two different schemes at two different times, the protected lump sum amount will have to be adjusted to take account of the first lump sum paid. This is done by increasing the first lump sum in line with increases in the standard lifetime allowance, and then deducting it from the increased protected lump sum amount at the second payment date.

In the example above, if a £200,000 lump sum had been paid in the 2007/08 tax year when the standard lifetime allowance was £1,600,000, then the maximum lump sum that could be paid on vesting in 2010/11 would be:

> $(£400,000 \times 1,800,000/1,500,000) - (£200,000 \times 1,800,000/1,600,000)$
> $= £255,000$

With lump sum protection under primary protection it may be possible to transfer protected lump sum allowance from one scheme to another, and even commute the benefits entirely from one scheme if this would still be within the protected lump sum allowance. This of course would be subject to scheme rules permitting such commutation. See the example given in RPSM03105160 at the end of this chapter.

The amount of lump sum payable tax-free must not exceed the amount of lifetime allowance available. It is therefore very important to take great care over the timing of different lump sum payments to ensure that valuable tax-free lump sum rights are still within the lifetime allowance available. If an individual uses up too much of his personal lifetime allowance by vesting benefits in pension form first of all, he may find that there is insufficient lifetime allowance left to cover all of a protected lump sum being vested later on. The examples in RPSM03105170 and RPSM03105180 reproduced at the end of this chapter illustrate the danger of this.

Death benefits

Normal protection

11.18 Payment of a defined benefit lump sum death benefit and an uncrystallised funds lump sum death benefit (see **4.37** and **4.38**) are tested against an individual's lifetime allowance. If the lump sum exceeds the available lifetime allowance, it is subject to the 55% charge. Excess amounts over the available lifetime allowance will not be subject to a lifetime allowance charge if they are paid in the form of dependants' pensions.

Under primary protection a lump sum death benefit is tested against the deceased's personal lifetime allowance (ie as increased by the application of the lifetime allowance enhancement factor) instead of the standard lifetime allowance.

Protected life cover

11.19 An increased form of protection is available if lump sum death benefits, payable in respect of death on 5 April 2006, were greater than the sum of an individual's crystallised and uncrystallised pension rights. In such a case a higher lifetime allowance enhancement factor can be claimed by the deceased's beneficiaries in the event of death post A-Day. The higher lifetime allowance enhancement factor is based on the value of lump sum death benefit rights instead of pension rights. For protected life cover to apply, all the following conditions must be met:

(a) Primary protection applied immediately before the member's death.

(b) Either a defined benefit lump sum death benefit (see **4.37**) or an uncrystallised funds lump sum death benefit (see **4.38**) is paid.

(c) The recipients inform HMRC of their intention to rely on protected life cover.

(d) The value of lump sum death benefits under all approved pension arrangements relating to the member on 5 April 2006 is greater than the value of his crystallised and uncrystallised pension rights on the same date.

(e)   If the lump sum death benefits had been paid on 5 April 2006, they would not have exceeded HMRC limits. If they exceeded HMRC limits on 5 April 2006, only the amount up to HMRC limits can be used for protected life cover.

(f)   The member had been employed by the same or a connected employer continuously from 5 April 2006 to the date of his death.

(g)   The member's employer participated in the scheme on 5 April 2006.

(h)   The member had not started to receive payment of benefits under the pension scheme before his death.

There are further conditions where the death benefits are insured and the scheme is not an occupational scheme with at least 20 members on 5 April 2006. In this case protected life cover is only available if:

(a)   A sum is paid under the insurance policy when the member actually died, and

(b)   The terms of the policy have not been varied significantly between 5 April 2006 and the date of death.

Care must therefore be taken when rebroking life assurance policies held by small schemes, as rebroking would be a significant variation.

ENHANCED PROTECTION

Method of protection

11.20   As long as an individual retains enhanced protection he will have no liability for the lifetime allowance charge at any benefit crystallisation event. It will also not be possible for him to receive payment of a lifetime allowance excess lump sum.

While enhanced protection is in place, an individual will not be subject to any annual allowance charge.

Two conditions must exist for enhanced protection to apply. The first is that an individual must have given notice to HMRC of his intention to rely on it. The second is that the valuation of his uncrystallised rights derived from all occupational pension schemes on 5 April 2006 does not exceed an amount calculated as $20 \times$ **MPP**, where **MPP** is the maximum permitted pension that would be allowed by reference to the appropriate tax regime in force before 6 April 2006.

For an explanation of **MPP** and information on the valuation of uncrystallised rights on 5 April 2006, please refer to 'Valuing pre A-Day rights for protection' in **11.5** above.

Surrender of relevant excess

11.21   If an individual's uncrystallised occupational pension scheme rights on 5 April 2006 exceed $20 \times$ **MPP**, then the excess has to be surrendered if enhanced protection is to be relied on. This is addressed by the *Registered*

Pension Schemes (Surrender of Relevant Excess) Regulations 2006 (SI 2006/211), which were laid on 2 February 2006.

These regulations modify the rules of a pension scheme so as to allow members to be able to surrender those rights in excess of **20 × MPP**. At the same time the provisions of the *Occupational Pension Schemes (Assignment, Forfeiture, Bankruptcy etc) Regulations 1997 (SI 1997/785)* were amended so that such a surrender does not fall foul of the inalienability requirements of the Pensions Act 1995.

Paragraph 38 of *Schedule 10* to the *Finance Act 2005* inserts a new section into the *Finance Act 2004, s 172A*, which provides that where a member surrenders any benefit to which he has a prospective entitlement, it is to be treated as an unauthorised payment. The *Registered Pension Schemes (Surrender of Relevant Excess) Regulations 2006 (SI 2006/211)* exempts the surrender of relevant excess from *s 172A, Finance Act 2004* as long as the following conditions are met:

(a)   The value of rights surrendered is determined in accordance with *s 212, Finance Act 2004* (ie the usual method of valuing uncrystallised rights), and

(b)   The surrendered rights do not include:

- A surrender in respect of a pension sharing order,

- A surrender in exchange for additional dependant's benefit,

- A surrender for the purpose of transferring rights to another arrangement under the pension scheme relating to the member or a dependant,

- A surrender which constitutes an assignment of benefits, or

- Rights to prospective entitlement which an individual has as a dependant of another individual.

Any surrender of rights greater than the relevant excess will be an unauthorised payment in accordance with *s 172A, Finance Act 2004*.

Note that it is not necessary to surrender rights in the pension scheme in which the excess arose. Rights may be surrendered from any one or more other schemes in order to come within the enhanced protection requirements.

There is no requirement to make a payment to a member in return for any rights surrendered; the value of rights surrendered may be distributed elsewhere within the pension scheme. However, where a payment is made to a member in respect of the surrender, such a payment will most likely be an unauthorised member payment and subject to the unauthorised payments charges. If the payment includes a return of surplus additional voluntary contributions, some of the unauthorised payments charges might be mitigated depending on particular circumstances.

The value of rights surrendered could alternatively be paid to a sponsoring employer if it meets the requirements of the *Registered Pension Schemes (Authorised Surplus Payments) Regulations 2006 (SI 2006/574)*.

Registration for protection

11.22 Notification of a member's intention to rely on enhanced protection must be made by him on the appropriate form, to reach HMRC by 5 April 2009. However, because an application for enhanced protection involves making certain decisions about the accrual of benefit beyond A-Day, most people will not be able to wait until 2009 and will need to have considered their position before A-Day. The *Registered Pension Schemes (Enhanced Lifetime Allowance) Regulations 2006 (SI 2006/131)* apply.

Notification of intention to rely on primary protection can be made at the same time as a notification for enhanced protection provided an individual's rights are valued at more than £1,500,000 on 5 April 2006. In fact, an individual with A-Day rights greater than £1,500,000 who registers for enhanced protection would be well advised to register for primary protection as well. If enhanced protection is ever lost, then at least primary protection would provide a fallback position. The notification form will also include a section for notifying HMRC of lump sum entitlements greater than £375,000 on 5 April 2006. Records relating to the protection notification must be kept for at least six years.

If the form is completed by someone else on the individual's behalf, the individual must still sign the form unless he is physically or mentally incapable of doing so. An individual's personal representative may also sign the form if the individual has died. Once HMRC has processed the form it will issue a certificate giving details of the enhanced protection.

Pension benefits

11.23 Since there is no liability for a lifetime allowance charge, the payment of a member's pension benefits may proceed, subject only to income tax and the scheme administrator receiving appropriate notice of the member's enhanced protection status.

Payment of lump sum benefits greater than £375,000

11.24 Where an individual has applied for enhanced protection and has registered lump sum rights at 5 April 2006 which are greater than £375,000, the normal rules for calculating pension commencement lump sums (see **4.12**) do not apply. Instead, the pension commencement lump sum is calculated as the same percentage of rights being crystallised at the vesting date as the percentage arrived at by dividing uncrystallised lump sum rights at A-Day by the value of uncrystallised rights at A-Day and multiplying by 100. This is best demonstrated by an example:

At A-Day

If the value of uncrystallised lump sum rights on 5 April 2006 = £400,000

and the value of uncrystallised rights on 5 April 2006 = £2,000,000 then the lump sum percentage on 5 April 2006 = (£400,000/£2,000,000) × 100 = 20%

At retirement

If the value of rights crystallised at retirement = £2,400,000

then the maximum lump sum at retirement = 20% × £2,400,000 = £480,000

If an individual had more than one pension arrangement, the maximum lump sum that could be taken from each arrangement would be limited by the percentage derived from the total uncrystallised lump sum rights at A-Day divided by the total uncrystallised rights and multiplied by 100. This means that if one arrangement paid a lump sum less than this percentage, the excess could not be taken from another arrangement. See the example in RPSM03105210 reproduced at the end of this chapter.

Death benefits

Normal protection

11.25 The application of enhanced protection to lump sum death benefits depends on whether the arrangement is a money purchase arrangement or a defined benefit arrangement.

In the case of a money purchase arrangement an uncrystallised funds lump sum death benefit may be paid equal to the accumulated value of the assets in a member's pension fund at the date of death, and enhanced protection would not be lost. The situation becomes complicated, however, if an insured lump sum is payable.

If the proceeds of a life assurance policy would form part of the member's overall fund and the scheme rules simply provide for a death benefit calculated as a return of fund, as opposed to a defined benefit (eg 4 × salary), then the total fund including the life policy proceeds could be paid as a lump sum without jeopardising enhanced protection.

However, the payment of tax-relievable life assurance premiums in respect of a money purchase arrangement would normally constitute relevant benefit accrual (see **11.29**). Enhanced protection would therefore be lost unless the conditions for protected life cover (see **11.26** below) are satisfied. Note also that HMRC stated in Simplification Newsletter No 8 (published on 23 December 2005) that if such premiums were paid out of the existing assets of a member's scheme, this would not jeopardise enhanced protection.

In the case of a defined benefit arrangement a lump sum may be paid to the extent of the usual appropriate limit (see **11.29**) without jeopardising enhanced protection. If a lump sum is paid that is greater than the usual appropriate limit, this is relevant benefit accrual and would normally cause the loss of enhanced protection. The exception to this is if protected life cover applies (see **11.27**), in which case a higher appropriate limit may be relied on.

If any benefit is paid in the form of dependants' pensions, enhanced protection would not be lost as this does not constitute a benefit crystallisation event.

Protected life cover – money purchase arrangements

11.26 Premiums paid to a life assurance policy under a money purchase arrangement do not count as relevant benefit accrual (see **11.29**) where the following conditions are met:

(a) The contribution is only used for the payment of premiums under an insurance policy on the life of the member.

(b) The policy is issued, or issued in respect of insurances made, before 6 April 2006.

(c) There is no right to surrender any rights under the policy.

(d) The terms of the policy must not be varied significantly in the period between 6 April 2006 and the member's death so as to increase the benefit or extend the cover term.

(e) No benefits may be paid under the policy except by reason of the member's death.

Rebroking a life assurance policy would therefore seem to cause the loss of enhanced protection, as premiums to the new policy would not be able to benefit from this protection. There are exemptions, however, where a new scheme is set up to comply with age discrimination legislation or to comply with the Pensions Act 2004 prohibition on life assurance only categories in occupational pension schemes.

Protected life cover – defined benefit arrangements

11.27 A higher appropriate limit may be claimed by beneficiaries on the death of a member with enhanced protection. For a higher appropriate limit to apply, the following conditions must be met:

(a) Either a defined benefit lump sum death benefit (see **4.37**) or an uncrystallised funds lump sum death benefit (see **4.38**) is paid.

(b) The recipients inform HMRC of their intention to rely on protected life cover.

(c) If the lump sum death benefits had been paid on 5 April 2006, they would not have exceeded HMRC limits. If they exceeded HMRC limits on 5 April 2006, only the amount up to HMRC limits can be used for the appropriate limit.

(d) The member had been employed by the same or a connected employer continuously from 5 April 2006 to the date of his death.

(e) The member's employer participated in the scheme on 5 April 2006.

(f) The member had not started to receive payment of benefits under the pension scheme before his death.

There are further conditions where the death benefits are insured and the scheme is not an occupational scheme with at least 20 members on 5 April 2006. In this case a higher appropriate limit is only available if:

(a)   A sum is paid under the insurance policy when the member actually died, and

(b)   The terms of the policy have not been varied significantly between 5 April 2006 and the date of death.

Care must therefore be taken when rebroking life assurance policies held by small schemes, as rebroking would be a significant variation.

The new appropriate limit is calculated as the aggregate of the maximum amounts that could have been paid, if the member had died on 5 April 2006, as lump sum death benefits from the defined benefit arrangement in question together with lump sum death benefits from any other defined benefit arrangement relating to the same employment. Note the requirement to take into account only so much of these benefits as would not have prejudiced HMRC approval at 5 April 2006. If this is higher than the appropriate limit that would otherwise have applied, it may be relied on instead. The revised appropriate limit may be increased in the same ways applicable to the appropriate limit normally (see **11.29**) including salary growth.

HMRC would consider a group life assurance scheme to be a defined benefit scheme only where the rules of the scheme determine the lump sum death benefit to be paid. If the rules of the scheme do not specify a certain benefit but simply provide for the lump sum death benefit payable to be the proceeds of an insurance policy (even if the policy provides a defined benefit), HMRC have stated they would consider this to be a money purchase scheme. Given that contributions to a money purchase arrangement may constitute relevant benefit accrual, it may be necessary to determine whether a group life scheme is money purchase or defined benefit in nature. If the scheme is not a defined benefit scheme (contributions to a defined benefit arrangement do not constitute relevant benefit accrual), it will be important to ensure that the conditions in **11.26** continue to be met.

Loss of enhanced protection

11.28   Loss of enhanced protection may be occasioned by any of the following:

1.   Relevant benefit accrual (see **11.29**).

2.   Impermissible transfer (see **11.30**).

3.   Transfer that is not a permitted transfer (see **11.31**).

4.   Creating a new arrangement under a registered pension scheme other than:

    (a)   To receive a permitted transfer,

    (b)   As part of an exercise to comply with age discrimination legislation, or

    (c)   As part of an exercise to comply with the *Pensions Act 2004* prohibition on life assurance only categories.

RELEVANT BENEFIT ACCRUAL

11.29   For enhanced protection to remain valid there must be no relevant benefit accrual on or after A-Day. If relevant benefit accrual occurs, enhanced protection will be lost at the time relevant benefit accrual occurs.

Relevant benefit accrual occurs under a money purchase arrangement (but not a cash balance arrangement) if a contribution is paid which is:

(a)   a tax relievable contribution paid by or on behalf of the individual;

(b)   a contribution in respect of the individual by his employer;

(c)   any other contribution which becomes held for the benefit of the individual.

See **11.26** for an exemption for premiums in respect of protected life cover.

Relevant benefit accrual occurs under a cash balance or defined benefit arrangement if, at the time a benefit is paid, or upon a permitted transfer to a money purchase arrangement, the crystallised value of the benefit exceeds the appropriate limit. The appropriate limit is the higher of (1) and (2) below.

(1)   the value of an individual's rights on 5 April 2006 increased to the date of payment by the highest of:

5% compound;

the increase in the Retail Prices Index;

an increase specified in statutory order (relating to contracting-out and preservation legislation);

(2)   the benefit derived by using pensionable service to 5 April 2006, the scheme's accrual rate, and the amount of pensionable earnings at the actual date of payment, which may be some time after A-Day.

See **11.27** for calculation of the appropriate limit in the case of protected life cover.

There are some restrictions on the earnings that can be used under option (2). The elements included in earnings must be the same elements that were pensionable prior to A-Day.

If the member was subject to the post-1989 regime on 5 April 2006, his earnings are limited to the highest earnings in any consecutive 12-month period in the three years before retirement, or 7.5% of the standard lifetime allowance if that is lower.

If the member was not subject to the post-1989 regime on 5 April 2006, his earnings are similarly calculated as the highest earnings in any consecutive 12-month period in the three years before retirement, but if they exceed 7.5% of the standard lifetime allowance they must be restricted to a three-year average, or to 7.5% of the standard lifetime allowance, whichever is greater.

This means that it is feasible for defined benefits to continue to accrue post-A-Day under enhanced protection as long as the eventual amount crystallised on retirement does not exceed the appropriate limit set out above. This allows for modest pay rises to the date of retirement, but, more importantly, it allows for normal accrual to continue and for early retirement to be taken where the early retirement reduction factor takes the value of the actual benefit paid under the appropriate limit. See the examples in RPSM03104590, RPSM03104600 and RPSM03104610 reproduced at the end of this chapter which illustrate when benefit accrual in a defined benefit arrangement would and would not occasion the loss of enhanced protection.

Impermissible transfers

11.30   An impermissible transfer covers the following actions:

- Conversion of a defined benefit arrangement into a money purchase arrangement.

- Transfer of sums into a money purchase arrangement from somewhere other than another pension arrangement of the member.

A transfer of pension rights pursuant to a pension sharing order in connection with divorce proceedings is exempt.

Permitted transfers

11.31   A permitted transfer would take place where some or all of the benefits under a defined benefit or a money purchase arrangement are transferred to a money purchase arrangement. The value of the sums and assets received by the money purchase arrangement must be actuarially equivalent to the rights being transferred.

Partial transfers may be effected without losing enhanced protection. Under the original wording of the *Finance Act 2004* partial transfers would have caused the loss of enhanced protection. The *Finance Act 2007* introduced an amendment to remove the bar on partial transfers. The amendment is deemed to have effect from 6 April 2006.

A transfer from one defined benefit arrangement to another is permitted in certain circumstances. These are where:

- A scheme is winding up and a transfer is made to another defined benefit scheme relating to the same employment.

- A business or undertaking is being transferred from one person to another, it involves the transfer of at least 20 employees and the transferor and transferee are not treated as members of the same group of companies.

Otherwise a transfer to a defined benefit scheme is not a permitted transfer, and enhanced protection would be lost.

Note that upon a transfer from a defined benefit arrangement to a money purchase arrangement, the transfer value must be tested against the appropriate limit (see **11.29**). Although the transfer may be a permitted transfer, if the transfer value exceeds the appropriate limit, it will cause the loss of enhanced protection.

Any transfer of rights which is made to a scheme for an ex-spouse following a pension sharing order is a permitted transfer.

MODIFICATION OF SCHEME RULES

Scheme protection

11.32   Much has been made of the fact that removal of the existing HMRC benefit restrictions on 6 April 2006, especially the *Finance Act 1989* earnings cap, could leave scheme sponsors exposed to a significant increase in liability. Phrases such as '… as will not prejudice the tax approval of the scheme …' are scattered throughout occupational pension scheme rules concerning payment of benefits or certain other duties or discretions conferred on trustees.

Furthermore, scheme rules may even compel trustees to make a payment which would be unauthorised under the new tax regime.

To address these issues, HMRC published the *Pension Schemes (Modification of Rules of Existing Schemes) Regulations 2006 (SI 2006/364)*. They are for the purpose of providing transitional protection for schemes whose documentation has not been amended to comply with the post 6 April 2006 tax rules. The general effect is explained in the following.

Modification provisions

11.33

(a)   If the rules of a scheme would require the trustees to make what would be an unauthorised payment, then the trustees have discretion whether or not to make that payment. If, before A-Day, the consent of the sponsoring employer was required before making the payment in question, that consent is still required. Where such payment is made, that part of it relating to pre-A-Day rights will not be a scheme chargeable payment.

(b)   If any scheme rule limits benefit by reference to the earnings cap (in whatever terms), then that rule should continue to be construed as limiting the benefit post A-Day as if the earnings cap legislation had not been repealed.

(c)   If the rules provide for a certain pension to be paid and mention that a greater payment may be made subject to not prejudicing approval, then post A-Day the trustees can pay up to the HMRC maximum benefit as if pre-A-Day limits were still in place, but they are prohibited from paying a sum greater than the pre-A-Day maximum benefit. If, before A-Day, the consent of the sponsoring employer was required before making the augmentation, then it is still required post A-Day.

(d)   If the rules provide for any payment to be made of such amount as would not prejudice approval, then post A-Day the trustees are prohibited from making a payment which would be greater than HMRC maximum benefits calculated as if pre-A-Day limits were still in place.

(e)   If the rules do not permit the trustees to recover from a member any lifetime allowance charge for which the trustees are liable, then post A-Day the trustees are able to reduce the member's benefits to reflect the amount of tax paid, such reduction to be determined in accordance with 'normal actuarial practice'.

(f)   Transfers may be made only to the extent that the payments would have been authorised by the rules immediately before the coming into force of the Regulations, and subject to not prejudicing the scheme's approval.

These modification provisions may continue in effect until 6 April 2011 or, if earlier, until the trustees specifically disapply any particular modification by making an appropriate amendment to the relevant scheme rule.

In addition to these HMRC regulations, the *Occupational Pension Schemes (Modification of Schemes) Regulations 2006 (SI 2006/759)* give trustees power to make a permanent modification by resolution to give effect to most of the above (if they do not already have the power) and to exempt certain modifications from *s 67, PA 1995* by disapplication.

Examples reproduced from RPSM

11.34   The following examples and text are reproduced from Chapter 3 of the Technical Pages of the HMRC Registered Pension Schemes Manual (RPSM). They have been referred to earlier in this chapter to help illustrate various aspects of the protections available under the new tax regime. The examples appear here in their numerical order. The complete RPSM can be found on the HMRC website at:

www.hmrc.gov.uk/manuals/rpsmmanual/index.htm

RPSM03101040 Crystallised rights: income drawdown

If the individual has 'relevant existing pensions' that are being paid under income drawdown from

●   a retirement benefit scheme or

●   a deferred annuity contract (section 32 policy)

the annual rate at which the pension is payable on 5 April 2006 is to be taken to be the maximum that could be drawn as income from the pension scheme or contract concerned – the actual drawings are not material.

Example 1

An individual is drawing a pension of £5,000 under drawdown, but the maximum annual rate of this pension is £10,000. The value of the crystallised rights in these circumstances is £250,000 (25 × £10,000 = £250,000).

Example 2

Alan had a fund of £1.6 million. He took a lump sum of £400,000 in January 2006. From the remaining fund of £1.2 million he takes a pension of £91,200 a year under income drawdown. This is the maximum pension that could have been taken under income drawdown. (Alan is assumed to be age 60 and gilt yields are assumed to be 4.5% per annum.)

Alan's pension is therefore valued at £2,280,000 (25 × £91,200 = £2,280,000).

There is no requirement to perform a valuation/review as at 5 April 2006 to determine the maximum amount of pension payable. The maximum amount determined by the most recent valuation/review may be used.

The same principle applies in the case of an individual taking income withdrawal from a **personal pension scheme**. The crystallised value will be 25 times the maximum amount that could be taken as income drawdown on 5 April 2006. It is not 25 times the amount of income actually being drawn.

RPSM03101551 Retirement benefits scheme limit: preservation limit for retirement benefits schemes – Practice Notes published 1 October 1974

Following on from RPSM03101531 and RPSM03101550 if 5 April 2006 falls before an individual's normal retirement date in a retirement benefits scheme and the individual has employer sponsored money purchase rights in the scheme, the calculation of MPP should be carried out on the basis that preservation applies to the benefits.

The relevant preservation calculation will be the one published in the IR 12 'Occupational Pension Schemes Practice Notes' at the time the scheme was approved.

The following is a direct copy of the advice published in the version of IR 12 'Occupational Pension Schemes Practice Notes published on 1 October 1974.

It applies to any schemes approved under *s 591 ICTA 1988* (previously *s 20 FA 1970*) before 1 May 1979.

PN 13.4

"A scheme of the type to which Regulation 5 of the Occupational Pension Schemes (Preservation of Benefit) (No2) Regulations 1973 (SI 1973 No 1784) applies (whether or not in existence on 6 April 1974), i.e. a scheme providing benefits based on final remuneration but funded by means of a policy or policies with level annual premiums securing benefits based on current remuneration, may give a member leaving service the amount of deferred pension actually secured by premiums paid up to date of his withdrawal even if this is somewhat in excess of the amount calculated under N/NS × P formula. A money purchase scheme, or a scheme using earmarked policies (see paragraphs 18.10–18.20) must test leaving benefits against the N/NS × P formula unless

the member's earnings while a member of the scheme have not exceeded £5,000 in any year or

at the time of leaving he is less than 45 years of age or

such a restriction would infringe the preservation requirements of the Social Security Act 1973."

When calculating the limit above, final remuneration shall be determined by reference to the maximum amount of earnings allowed under the rules of the scheme for the purposes of calculating the maximum retirement benefits for that individual.

RPSM03101560 Retirement benefits scheme limit: preservation limit for retirement benefits schemes – Practice Notes published 1 May 1979

Following on from RPSM03101531, RPSM03101550 and RPSM03101551 if 5 April 2006 falls before an individual's normal retirement date in a retirement benefit scheme and the individual has employer sponsored money purchase rights in the scheme, the calculation of MPP should be carried out on the basis that preservation applies to the benefits.

The relevant preservation calculation will be the one published in the IR 12 'Occupational Pension Schemes Practice Notes' at the time the scheme was approved. The following is a direct copy of the advice published in the version of IR 12 'Occupational Pension Schemes Practice Notes published on 1 May 1979.

It applies to any schemes approved under *s 591 ICTA 1988* (previously *s 20 FA 1970*) after 30 April 1979 and before 29 November 1991.

PN 13.4

'Because of the preservation requirements of the Social Security Act 1973 it may not be possible for certain schemes to restrict the benefits of an early leaver by reference to the 1/60th of final remuneration or N/NS × P formula, above viz:

(a) schemes giving a benefit of a constant proportion of final or average earnings for each year of service, at an accrual rate greater than 1/60th (Memorandum No 18 paragraphs 111–121)

(b) money purchase schemes and insured level annual pension premium schemes set up before 6 April 1974 (ibid paragraphs 127 and 137)

(c) "proceeds of policy" schemes (Memorandum No 78 paragraphs 251–259)

In such cases, the Inland Revenue limit will bite only if it is desires to give greater benefits that the minimum short service benefit.

Other schemes funded by level annual premium policies and securing benefits not exceeding the maximum approvable fraction of current remuneration may also give an early leaver the amount of deferred pension actually secured by premiums paid up to the date of his withdrawal, even if in excess of the amount calculated under the N/NS × P formula.'

When calculating the limit above, final remuneration shall be determined by reference to the maximum amount of earnings allowed under the rules of the scheme for the purposes of calculating the maximum retirement benefits for that individual.

RPSM03101570 Retirement benefits scheme limit: preservation limit for retirement benefits schemes – Practice Notes effective from 29 November 1991

Following on from RPSM03101540, and RPSM03101550 to RPSM03101560 if 5 April 2006 falls before an individual's normal retirement date in a retirement benefit scheme and the individual has employer sponsored money purchase rights in the scheme, the calculation of MPP should be carried out on the basis that preservation applies to the benefits.

The relevant preservation calculation will be the one published in the IR 12 'Occupational Pensions Schemes Practice Notes' at the time the scheme was approved. The following is a direct copy of the advice published in the version of IR 12 'Occupational Pension Schemes Practice Notes published on 1 September 1991.

It applies to any schemes approved under s 591 ICTA 1988 on or after 29 November 1991.

10.13

'The maximum benefits an approved money purchase scheme may provide at normal retirement date for a member (whether or not entitled to continued rights) who left pensionable service prior to that date, is a deferred pension (including the pension equivalent of any deferred lump sum benefits) of the greater of:

(a) 1/60th of final remuneration for each year of service (up to 40 years) increased in accordance with paragraph 10.12 [PN10.12 – at a fixed rate not exceeding 5% per annum compound, or by a greater percentage but restricted so as not to exceed the increase in the retail prices index during the period of deferment], and

(b) the total benefit the member could have expected to receive at normal retirement date calculated on the same basis as applies for incapacity (see paragraph 6.2) [PN6.2 – the fraction of final remuneration the employee could have received had he or she remained in service until normal retirement date] together with any statutory revaluation increases required by the relevant Social Security legislation.

NB A power of augmentation cannot be used to increase a member's benefit up to this limit: an increase in benefit up to the limits set out in paragraphs 7.4 and 7.36 is, however, permissible.'

The following text was added to the end of paragraph 10.13 on 23 March 2001 (via the revised Practice Notes issued with Update 90).

"Where the member has a pension debit in relation to the scheme and does not fall within the administrative easement described in paragraph 7.7, the maximum benefits calculated in accordance with the requirements of this paragraph must be reduced by the pension debit (see paragraph 16.56)."

When calculating the limit above, final remuneration shall be determined by reference to the maximum amount of earnings allowed under the rules of the scheme for the purposes of calculating the maximum retirement benefits for that individual.

RPSM03102030 Protection from the lifetime allowance charge – taking benefits at different times

Where an individual takes benefits at different times the balance of the personal lifetime allowance will be indexed at the same rate that the standard lifetime allowance has been indexed.

Example

Jacob had £3 million of pension rights protected under primary protection on 5 April 2006, giving an additional lifetime allowance factor of 1.

He took benefits worth £1.8 million in 2011 when the standard lifetime allowance was £1.8 million. At that time, Jacob's primary protection was worth £3.6 million (standard lifetime allowance of £1.8 million plus additional lifetime allowance factor of £1.8 million). So Jacob used up 50% of his personal lifetime allowance.

In 2023 Jacob took the rest of his benefits that were worth £2 million. The standard lifetime allowance (SLA) in 2023 was £2.1 million. Jacob's primary protection was then worth £4.2 million (SLA plus a factor of 1).

Jacob has already used up 50% of his protection so has £2.1 million available. In taking £2 million Jacob has no lifetime allowance charge to pay. This is because the amount taken is within the amount of protection still available to him.

In describing how the individual gets a lifetime allowance that is greater than the standard lifetime allowance, it has been assumed that the individual's rights when valued were within 'HMRC limits'. The valuation section of this guidance at RPSM03101510 explains how only rights valued on 5 April 2006 within 'HMRC limits' can be taken into primary protection.

RPSM03104590 Relevant benefit accrual in defined benefits and cash balance arrangements: example

David is a member of a contracted-out defined benefits arrangement with an accrual rate of one sixtieth for each year of service. On 5 April 2006, David has 30 years' service and his pensionable earnings are £120,000. He takes benefits in April 2011. The arrangement uses the 20:1 valuation factor in s 276 FA 2004.

Step 1

On 5 April 2006, David's rights are valued at £1.2 million (30/60 × £120,000 × 20).

Step 2

Calculate the 'appropriate limit' using the value from Step 1. Two calculations need to be done: the higher of the two is the 'appropriate limit'.

The first calculation is increasing £1.2 million by an indexation figure. The indexation figure is the highest figure obtained from a calculation over the period between 6 April 2006 and the date of the relevant event. The indexation figure is the highest of

- 5% annual compound interest over the period,

- $[RPI(2) - RPI(1)] / RPI(1)$

- where RPI(2) is the **RPI** for the month in which the first relevant event occurs and RPI(1) is the RPI for April 2006; or

- for contracted-out rights, the percentage rate specified in the Registered Pension Schemes (Uprating Percentages for Defined Benefits Arrangements and Enhanced Protection) Regulations 2006 – SI 2006/130.

Assume the highest figure is arrived at by using 5% compound for the five years between April 2006 and April 2011. Indexing £1.2 million in this way gives a figure of £1,531,538.

The second calculation is to use David's pensionable earnings in April 2011 and apply David's accrual rate under the arrangement to this. In this instance, the scheme rules would not apply an early retirement factor to David's pension rights when they come into payment in 2011. David's pensionable earnings are now £160,000. Assume that this pensionable earnings figure does not exceed the limit on post-commencement earnings. David's pre 6 April 2006 rights have a value of £1.6 million (30/60 × £160,000 × 20).

The amount of £1.6 million from the earnings re-calculation is higher than £1,531,400 figure from the indexation calculation. So the appropriate limit is £1.6 million.

Step 3

Compare the value of the benefit crystallisation event in April 2011 with the appropriate limit.

Scenario 1: The benefit crystallisation event in April 2011 is worth £1.75 million. Enhanced protection is lost but there is no lifetime allowance charge because the standard lifetime allowance is £1.8 million.

Scenario 2: The benefit crystallisation event in April 2011 is worth £2 million. Enhanced protection is lost and there is a lifetime allowance charge.

RPSM03104600 Example 1 of benefit increases after 5 April 2006 that are not relevant benefit accruals: low salary increases

The example here and on RPSM03104610 show where relevant benefit accrual as defined in paragraph 13, Schedule 36 FA 2004 has not occurred and consequently the individual has not lost enhanced protection.

Example 1 Accrual after 5 April 2006, but low salary increases

Anthony had 30 years service on 5 April 2006. The scheme's accrual rate was 1/60th for each year of service. His final pensionable salary, as defined on that day in the scheme documentation, was £240,000. He therefore registered £2.4 million (£120,000 × 20) for enhanced protection.

Anthony remained an active member of the pension scheme for another five years until he reached normal retirement age. By this time, his final pensionable salary had grown to £252,000 giving a pension of £147,000 (35/60 × £252,000). The value of the benefit crystallisation event is £2.94 million (£147,000 × 20).

The test for relevant benefit accrual is whether the value of the benefit crystallisation event is greater than the value of the appropriate limit.

The appropriate limit is the greater of

- indexation of £2.4 million (× 5% compound, RPI or the percentage rate specified in The Registered Pension Schemes (Uprating Percentages for Defined Benefits Arrangements and Enhanced Protection) Regulations 2006 – SI 2006/130, and

- a recalculation of the pension accrued at 5 April 2006 reflecting current final pensionable salary and the scheme early retirement factor (where appropriate) for the current age and a valuation factor of 20.

For the purposes of this example it has been assumed that indexation at 5% compound gives a higher figure than the recalculation.

The value of the appropriate limit is £3,063,076 (£2.4 million indexed at 5%) which is more than the value of the benefit crystallisation event (£2.94 million). Therefore relevant benefit accrual has not occurred and enhanced protection is retained.

RPSM03104610 Example 2 of benefit increases after 5 April 2006 that are not relevant benefit accruals: early retirement factor applied

Early reduction factor where the member retires before normal retirement date

Matthew had 30 years' service on 5 April 2006. The scheme's accrual rate was 1/60th for each year of service. His final pensionable salary, as defined on that day in the scheme documentation, was £240,000. He therefore registered for enhanced protection.

He remained an active member of the pension scheme for another five years until age 55. His final salary grew to £300,000. The scheme operated a normal retirement age of 60. If the accrued pension had been taken as a deferred pension at age 60 the scheme would have paid £175,000 per annum (35/60 × £300,000). However Matthew wanted an immediate pension. The scheme applied its own early retirement factor of 4% per annum for each year that benefits were taken before age 60. Matthew was therefore paid a pension of £140,000, which has a capital value of £2.8 million (£140,000 × 20).

The test for relevant benefit accrual as in example 1 in RPSM03104600 meant that a pension of £153,154 per annum (valued at £3,063,076) could have been paid without causing the loss of enhanced protection. Matthew retains enhanced protection.

RPSM03105160 Protection of lump sums with primary protection: taking benefits at more than one time – some lump sum benefits are not tax-free: example of a stand-alone and then a pension commencement lump sum payment

Sally has lump sum rights of £1 million on 5 April 2006 and has primary protection on pension rights of £5 million. She has rights in two arrangements. Her lump sum rights are payable by commuting pension rights.

She takes benefits on 3 April 2011, her 55th birthday, from the smaller of the two arrangements. The standard lifetime allowance in 2010–2011 is £1.8 million. The amounts of her protected pension and lump sum have increased in line with the increase in the standard lifetime allowance to £6 million and £1.2 million (each amount being multiplied by £1.8 million/£1.5 million).

As the smaller arrangement, a money purchase arrangement, is valued at £600,000 she chooses to take all her benefit as a stand-alone lump sum.

Sally takes benefits from her second arrangement in 2017 when the standard lifetime allowance is £2.1 million. The amounts of her protected pension and lump sum have increased in line with the increase in the standard lifetime allowance to £7 million and £1.4 million (each being multiplied by £2.1million/£1.5 million).

Sally has taken benefits previously so the amounts of benefits currently protected must be reduced by the value of the earlier benefits. The value of the earlier benefits must be increased in line with the increase in the standard lifetime allowance from its value when the benefits were taken to its current value. In this example, the standard lifetime allowance has increased from £1.8 million to £2.1 million. The value of the £600,000 stand-alone lump sum taken in 2011 is therefore £700,000 (£600,000 × £2.1/1.8 million).

Sally's available protected pension and lump sum are therefore £6.3 million (£7 million – £700,000) and £700,000 (£1.4 million – £700,000) respectively.

Her second arrangement is a money purchase arrangement worth £8.3 million. She takes a pension commencement lump sum of £700,000 and uses the remainder of her protected pension rights, £5.6 million, to buy a lifetime annuity.

The residue of £2 million in the arrangement (£8.3 million less protected pension rights of £6.3 million) is liable to the lifetime allowance charge. From this residue she takes a lifetime allowance excess lump sum of £900,000 after tax of £1.1 million.

RPSM03105170 Protection of lump sums with primary protection: taking benefits at more than one time – some lump sum benefits are not tax-free: example 1

Jane has primary protection for her pension rights, and her lump sum rights on 5 April 2006 exceeded £375,000. She has already taken some benefits after 5 April 2006 under primary protection.

Her remaining rights are in a money purchase arrangement, which are valued at £1 million. Her available protected pension rights are valued at £600,000, which means her available personal lifetime allowance is £600,000. The amount of protected lump sum is £700,000 – her protected lump sum rights are greater than her available personal lifetime allowance.

Jane takes a pension commencement lump sum of £700,000, using up all of her available lifetime allowance. She takes the balance of the £1 million (£300,000), as a lifetime annuity. £600,000 of her pension commencement lump sum is free of income tax, but £100,000 is liable to the lifetime allowance charge under section 214 Finance Act 2004. So she receives £600,000 tax-free and a further lump sum of £45,000 after tax under the lifetime allowance charge.

Jane cannot take all of her protected lump sum amount tax-free because the maximum amount of pension commencement lump sum exceeds the amount of her available lifetime allowance.

Because Jane took too little lump sum when she took her earlier benefits, the full aggregate lump sum available under protection was not paid entirely free of income tax.

RPSM03105180 Protection of lump sums with primary protection: taking benefits at more than one time, some lump sum benefits are not tax-free: example 2

Dean had registered pension rights of £3 million and lump sum rights of £800,000 by commutation under primary protection on 5 April 2006. £3 million was the equivalent of the **standard lifetime allowance** (£1.5 million) plus an additional factor of 1.

In 2011, Dean took pension rights worth £3 million plus a lump sum of £600,000. In 2011 the standard lifetime allowance was £1.8 million. So Dean's personal lifetime allowance is £3.6 million (this being the standard lifetime allowance of £1.8 million at the time plus a factor of 1) and his maximum protected lump sum is £960,000 (£800,000 × £1.8 million/£1.5 million). Dean has now used up all of his personal lifetime allowance.

In 2013, Dean took further benefits including a lump sum, and paid a lifetime allowance charge on the whole of the benefits that he took.

Although Dean originally had a lump sum right of £800,000, he did not use this up whilst he had some personal lifetime allowance remaining. The result is that any lump sum taken after his personal lifetime allowance has been used up in full is not a pension commencement lump sum. The payment will be a lifetime allowance excess lump sum and so it is subject to the lifetime allowance charge.

RPSM03105210 Protection of lump sum rights with enhanced protection: example 1

Sally has uncrystallised lump sum rights of £400,000 and uncrystallised pension rights of £2 million on 5 April 2006. This gives (VULSR ÷ VUR) of 20%. She takes benefits from three schemes on different dates whilst retaining enhanced protection.

Sally takes benefits from the first scheme, which are worth £1 million, by taking unsecured pension using income withdrawal. She designates assets valued at £800,000 for the payment of her unsecured pension and takes a lump sum benefit of £200,000. This is the maximum permitted by (VULSR ÷ VUR) multiplied by the value of the funds designated for the payment of unsecured pension plus the lump sum – paragraph 29 (2) of Schedule 36 Finance Act 2004. She cannot take the higher amount of 25% under the usual pension commencement lump sum rules. Sally's notification of enhanced protection has changed the maximum amount of lump sum she can be paid when she crystallises benefits.

Sally takes benefits from the second scheme worth £750,000 in the form of a lifetime annuity bought for £600,000 and a lump sum benefit of £150,000. This is the maximum permitted by (VULSR ÷ VUR) multiplied by the value of the annuity purchase price plus the lump sum – paragraph 29 (2) of Schedule 36 Finance Act 2004.

Sally takes benefits from the third scheme (which is a defined benefits arrangement) as a scheme pension of £20,000 plus a lump sum benefit of £100,000. The scheme pension is valued at £400,000 (20 × the annual pension of £20,000). And the lump sum is the maximum permitted by (VULSR ÷ VUR) multiplied by the value of the scheme pension plus the lump sum – paragraph 29 (2) of Schedule 36 Finance Act 2004.

If one of Sally's schemes paid her a lump sum of 15% of the combined value of her lump sum and pension benefits (because scheme rules did not permit a larger lump sum) her other schemes could not pay her a lump sum greater than 20% to make up the 'shortfall'.

Chapter 12

SSASs, SIPPS and IRPS

INTRODUCTION

12.1   The tax rules for schemes which were formerly designated as SSASs and SIPPs under the legislation which applied up to A-Day now fall within the single tax regime and the special category of investment-regulated pension schemes (IRPS).

As stated in **12.6**, the post A-Day investment rules rely to a large extent on the prudent man principle. This has facilitated the removal of the role and status of the pensioneer trustee, which had effectively acted as HMRCs watchdog.

IRPS are described in *Finance Act 2004, Sch 29A,* as amended by *Sch 21, Finance Act 2006*. They can incur prohibitive tax charges if they invest in taxable property. The meaning of taxable property, and the exemptions and exclusions which apply, is given in **12.5** to **12.9**.

There are also some exceptions from taxable property under transitional protection (see **12.10**). The past exemptions for certain small schemes from some of the provisions of the *Pensions Act 1995* are largely retained. Additionally, special provisions apply to schemes with fewer than 100 members under *IORPS Directive* (see **Chapter 5**).

The permitted investments for SSASs and SIPPS pre A-Day are summarised in **Appendix 5**.

REGISTERING FOR ENHANCED PROTECTION

12.2   Members of IRPS with aggregate pension savings in excess of the lifetime allowance at A-Day are likely to have registered for enhanced protection (see **Chapter 11**). In such cases it is important to ensure that no relevant benefit accrual has taken place, or takes place, from A-Day or that protection will be lost. Notice of intention to rely on enhanced protection, including pre-commencement pension credit on divorce, must be given no later than 5 April 2009.

Alternative benefit provision

12.3   An employer may wish to offer different benefits for its employees who have registered for enhanced protection in the future, such as cash, share schemes or unfunded arrangements etc. Further details are given in **Chapter 13**.

Description of an IRPS

12.4   An IRPS is a scheme or arrangement which falls within one of the categories listed below. It is important to ensure that the design and administration of a scheme is given careful consideration if the categories are to be avoided. The main feature of an IRPS is that the member(s) or related person(s) have power to direct or influence investment activity.

The categories are:

- In the case of a scheme other than an occupational scheme, one or more members, or a person related to the member is or was able to (directly or indirectly) direct, influence or advise on investments for the purpose of the scheme under an arrangement for that member.

- In the case of an occupational scheme, a scheme with 50 or fewer members and at least one meets the following condition (an alternative requirement 'or 10% or more of the members of a scheme meet that condition' under *Finance Act 2004, Sch 29A, para 2*, was removed by *Finance Act 2004, Sch 29, para 3*).The condition is that one or more of those members or a person related to one of those members is or was able to (directly or indirectly) direct, influence or advise on investments held by the scheme

- An arrangement, within an occupational scheme which is not an IRPS itself, has one or more members or a person related to one of the members who is or was able to (directly or indirectly) direct, influence or advise on investments which are linked to an arrangement relating to that member. The term 'linked' means the sums or assets are held for the purpose of an arrangement under the scheme relating to that member, but not merely by virtue of apportionment of scheme assets.

The following expressions have the following meanings:

- 'related person': a person is related to a member if the member and the person are connected persons within the meaning of the *Income and Corporation Taxes Act 1988, s 839*, or the person acts on behalf of the member or a person connected to the member, within that meaning;

- 'held for the purposes of an arrangement': sums or assets which are held other than for administration or management of the scheme and would not otherwise be treated as held for the purpose of an arrangement. These sums or assets are to be treated as held for the purpose of an arrangement by reference to the respective rights under the scheme of the member to which the arrangement relates.

A welcome clarification was announced in the pre-Budget Report 2007. With effect from 6 April 2006 the definition of an IRPS now excludes schemes in which the individual members could not realistically be expected to influence scheme decisions to invest in taxable property (*Finance Act 2008, Sch 29*).

TAXABLE PROPERTY

12.5   The legislation states that taxable property is 'residential property' and most 'tangible moveable property'.

Residential property means:

- a building which is used, or can be used, as a dwelling;

- lands and gardens surrounding residential property;

- land under or forming part of the garden or grounds of such a building or used or intended for use in connection with such a building;

- hotels;

- beach huts;

- holiday homes;

- leaseholds over hotel rooms or accommodation;

- converted non-residential property;

- buildings which are not in such current use but which were last used for such a purpose, or which have never been used for such a purpose but are more suitable for such use than for other uses, regardless of their suitability for use as a dwelling.

Defining tangible moveable property unhelpfully relies heavily on what it does not include (see **12.7**). As a guide, tangible moveable property is generally likely to encompass things that you can touch and move. Examples would be:

- works of art;

- antiques;

- jewellery;

- fine wine;

- classic cars;

- yachts;

- stamps;

- autographs;

- gems;

- certain machinery

Residential property – exemptions and exclusions

12.6 The following types of residential property do not fall within the category of taxable property:

- where the property is occupied by an employee who is not a member of the pension scheme which owns the property and who is not connected to a member of the scheme, within the meaning of the *Income and Corporation Taxes Act 1988, s 839;* and

- where the employee is not connected with the employer within the meaning of *s 839;* and

- where the occupying employee is required to do so as a condition of their employment.

The following property is excluded from the category of residential property:

- where it is occupied by someone who is not a member of the pension scheme which owns the property and who is not connected to a member of the scheme within the meaning of *s 839;* and

- where it is used in connection with business premises held as a scheme investment.

Tangible moveable property – exemptions

12.7   The specific exemptions from the meaning under the *Investment-regulated Pension Schemes (Exception of Tangible Moveable Property) Order 2006 (SI 2006/1959)* are:

- gold bullion;

- items with a market value of £6,000 or less which no member of the scheme or connected person has a right to use or occupy, and which the scheme does not hold an interest in directly, and which is held by a 'vehicle' (meaning a person described under the *Finance Act 2004), para 20, Sch 29A* for the purpose of management or administration of that vehicle).

Genuinely diverse commercial vehicles

12.8   The taxable property provisions cover property held directly or indirectly, except through genuinely diverse commercial vehicles. Examples of diverse commercial vehicles are:

- Collective schemes which provide an arm's length vehicle for investment in properties, but normally rent must be paid. The rent is taxable on the investor after costs, repairs and interest offsets. There is no capital gains tax on the first £8,500 of annual profit on each title-holder, and taper relief applies on chargeable disposals. There are different capital gains rules for property which is rented out to holidaymakers and for furnished lettings.

- REITs *(Finance Act 2006, Pt 4 (Real Estate Investment Trusts))*: These offered a means of investment in residential property investment without attracting taxable property charges. However, the government introduced a special restriction with effect from 1 January 2007 on IRPS. The underlying exemption from the charge on indirect holdings unless such investment is made to enable a scheme member or a connected person to occupy or use residential property does not apply to IRPSs if the holding is 10% or more. The test of what is meant by a holding is described in *s 24(5), Finance Act 2004,* and the required statutory power was included in the *Finance Act 2007*

Other diverse property investment vehicles

12.9   Taxable property charges do not apply to diverse property investment vehicles where such property is held by a scheme directly or indirectly in a vehicle, subject to the prescribed limits on maximum holdings described below, in which:

- the total value of assets held directly by the vehicle is at least £1 million, or the vehicle holds at least three assets which are residential property and in either case no one asset comprises more than 40% of the total assets; and

- the vehicle is a UK resident company, or is not UK resident but would not be a classed as a close company if it were UK resident; and

- the vehicle does not have as one of or its main purpose the direct or indirect holding of animals for sporting purposes.

'Maximum holdings' means:

- the scheme must not hold the interest in the vehicle for the purpose of enabling a scheme member or person connected to that member to use or occupy the property of the vehicle; and

- either *Condition B* or *Condition C* is met.

Condition B

The scheme is an occupational scheme and does not alone or together with associated persons (as described below) hold an interest in the vehicle which is:

- 10% or more of the share capital or issued share capital of the vehicle; or

- 10% or more of the voting rights of the vehicle; or

- an entitlement to 10% or more of any distribution of the vehicle; or

- an entitlement to 10% or more of the assets of the vehicle on wind up or otherwise; or

- an interest which gives rise to income or gains from a specific property of the vehicle.

Condition C

The scheme is not an occupational scheme and no arrangement under the scheme either alone or with one or more associated persons holds an interest in the vehicle which is:

- 10% or more of the share capital or issued share capital of the vehicle; or

- 10% or more of the voting rights of the vehicle; or

- an entitlement to 10% or more of any distribution of the vehicle; or

- an entitlement to 10% or more of the assets of the vehicle on wind up or otherwise; or

- an interest which gives rise to income or gains from a specific property of the vehicle.

For the purpose of deciding at arrangement level within a non-occupational pension scheme whether a holding is within the limits at *Condition C* above, only the holding in that arrangement, together with interests held by other associated persons, is counted. There is further provision exempting otherwise taxable property where those assets are held under insurance policies.

TRANSITIONAL PROVISIONS

12.10   There are transitional provisions for property held before A-Day, where:

- the scheme held an interest in a property on A-Day which it had acquired before that date, and which it was not prohibited from holding up to 5 April 2006; or

- before A-Day the property was held by a person other than the scheme and the scheme was not prohibited from holding the interest it held in that person at that time; or

- the scheme or a person in whom the scheme directly or indirectly held an interest entered into a contract to acquire an interest in such property before 5 April 2006 and was not at that time prohibited from acquiring such an interest, but acquires the property on or after that date.

However, exemption is lost on a change in occupation or use, or where there is a change in the scheme's interest in any person who holds a direct interest in the property or in anyone who has entered into a contract to acquire the property if the change would not have met pre-A-Day conditions.

Meaning of directly holding taxable property

12.11   A scheme or person will be deemed to hold taxable property directly if they alone or jointly or in common:

- hold the property or any rights power or interest in or over the property; or

- have a right to use or participate in arrangements relating to the use of the property itself or a description of property to which that property belongs; or

- have the benefit of any obligation restriction or condition affecting the value of any interest in, powers or rights over the property; or

- are entitled to receive payments determined by the value of the property or by the income from the property.

There is an exemption where a scheme or person owns or jointly owns hotel accommodation in its entirety. Hotels, inns etc are regarded as commercial property and are therefore acceptable investments. Also most property underlying certain insurance contracts is deemed not to be directly held taxable property.

Meaning of indirectly holding taxable property

12.12　A scheme or person is deemed to hold taxable property indirectly if it does not hold the property directly, and either alone jointly or in common it:

- holds an interest in a person who holds the interest in the property directly; or
- holds an interest in a person who holds the interest in the property indirectly in accordance with the above condition.

An interest is deemed to exist where a person:

- holds an interest, right or power in or over that person; or
- lends money to that person to fund an acquisition of taxable property.

Similar provisions apply to schemes or persons holding an interest in a company, a collective investment scheme or a trust.

Person in whom interest is held is a company, collective investment scheme or trust

Company

12.13　Where the person in whom a scheme or person is deemed to hold an interest in an indirect holding under the *Finance Act 2004, para 16, Sch 29A,* is a company, the scheme or person holds an interest if:

- it holds or is entitled to or will become entitled to acquire shares or voting rights in the company; or
- it holds or is entitled to or will become entitled to acquire a right to receive or participate in distributions; or
- it is entitled to or will become entitled to secure that current or future income or assets of the company will be applied to its benefit; or
- it controls the company alone or with others within the meaning of the *Income and Corporation Taxes Act 1988, s 416.*

Collective investment scheme

12.14　Where the person in whom a scheme or person is deemed to hold an interest in is a collective investment scheme, the scheme or person holds an interest if hor it is a participant in that collective investment scheme. The *Financial Services and Markets Act 2000, s 236, defines* collective investment schemes and their participants.

Trusts

12.15　Under the *Finance Act 2004, paras 17,18, Sch 29A,* where the person in whom the scheme is deemed to hold an interest is a trust, the scheme holds an interest in that trust if:

- the scheme, has a relevant interest in the trust; and

- the scheme, or a scheme member or person connected to a scheme member, has made a payment to the trust on or after acquisition of the above interest.

A payment which is part of an arm's-length transaction in return for property or a benefit, and which is not paid to enable a scheme member or person connected to a member to occupy or use any property, is disregarded for the above criteria.

Where the person in whom the scheme is deemed to hold an interest is a trust, the scheme also holds an interest in that trust if:.

- a scheme member or person connected to a member holds a relevant interest in the trust; and

- the scheme has made a payment to the trust on or after acquisition of the above interest.

However, a payment which is part of an arm's length transaction in return for property or a benefit, and which is not paid to enable a scheme member or person connected to a member to occupy or use any property, is disregarded for the above criteria.

Where the person whom the scheme is deemed to hold an interest in is a trust, a person other than the pension scheme holds an interest in a trust if:

- the person holds a relevant interest in the trust; and

- the person has made a payment to the trust on or after acquisition of the above interest.

A payment which is part of an arm's length transaction in return for property or a benefit, and which is not paid to enable a scheme member or person connected to a member to occupy or use any property, is disregarded for the above criteria.

The trust rules above are contained in *para 19,* but they do not apply to a unit trust scheme within the *Financial Services and Markets Act 2000, s 237(1).*

What are the taxable property charges?

12.16   The taxable property rules include the following:

- The use of funds to acquire, improve, convert or adapt taxable property is deemed to be an unauthorised member payment by the scheme, so triggering an unauthorised payment charge at 40% on the member, and a 40% scheme sanction charge on the scheme administrator.

- The scheme sanction charge may be reduced to 15% when the member has paid his tax.

- The member may also face a further 15% unauthorised payment surcharge if the taxable property is a wasting asset within the meaning of *TCGA 1992, s 44*, eg a leasehold interest in property for less than 50 years or plant and machinery.

- A combination of the above charges may also trigger de-registration of the scheme by HMRC, resulting in a further charge on the administrator of 40% of the scheme value.

- Income from taxable property will be charged on the scheme administrator. This will be a charge under the scheme sanction charge and will be taxed at a rate of 40%. If the net income from the property is less than 10% of the value of the property then in place of the actual income the scheme administrator will be taxed on a deemed income. The amount of the deemed income will be 10% of the value of the property. If there is no actual income, deemed income is used to determine the tax chargeable.

- Capital gains apply arising on disposal of taxable property will also be taxed on the scheme administrator as a scheme sanction charge and this will be charged at 40%. The gain will be calculated as if it had been made by a UK resident and domiciled person.

- The scheme sanction charge also applies in the circumstance of a member of a registered pension scheme which is established outside the UK, which holds an interest in taxable property outside the UK, in respect of income and gains from that property.

Chapter 13

Tax planning

INTRODUCTION

13.1   This chapter highlights some of the tax planning issues that members of registered pension schemes, advisers and employers may want to consider in the wake of the introduction of the post 6 April 2006 tax regime. It sets out some of the advantages to be had from the new easements and some of the pitfalls that may need to be avoided.

MEMBERSHIP AND CONTRIBUTIONS

Membership

13.2   The new tax regime from 6 April 2006 (A-Day) opened up tax-advantaged schemes to a wide range of individuals and employers. Registered pension schemes may be open (dependent on their own rules) to anyone without restriction, and tax relief is available on a scheme's investments regardless of a member's tax residence.

Individuals can be members of more than one type of registered scheme at the same time, whether or not they are employees of the participating companies. The new tax regime brought in full concurrency.

Some examples of the wide class of permitted members for whom contribution relief is available are:

- a non-working spouse or minor for whom contributions are paid by a third party, eg a working spouse, parent or grandparent;

- a self-employed individual in membership of an occupational scheme of which he is the sponsoring employer in the role of a sole trader or partnership in relation to his self-employed earnings.

UK earnings, upon which tax-relievable contributions can be paid, are widely drawn. They can include patent income, share options treated as employment income, the taxable element of a golden handshake over £30,000, and earnings of directors and members of their families who are employees of private investment or property companies.

The old restrictions which were imposed on centralised schemes for both associated employers and for non-associated employers have been removed, which means that employers may be able to minimise administrative and overhead costs.

There is no longer any prohibition on transferring pensions in payment from one scheme to another. This may have particular application for members in receipt of income withdrawal, who may wish to move their funds from one provider to another.

Contributions

13.3   There are no limits on members' contributions to registered pension schemes. Member contributions are no longer limited to a percentage of remuneration, but the tax relief available on member contributions is instead capped at 100% of earnings or the annual allowance if lower. Nonetheless, this will be an attractive facility for a number of high earners.

Large contributions

13.4   The ability to nominate the end date for pension input periods means that there is scope to make large contributions at the most tax efficient time for the contributor concerned. Ending a pension input period early can allow two payments to be made within one tax year which, in total, exceed the annual allowance. (See **Chapter 10** for input periods and the annual allowance.)

For example, if a member of a money purchase scheme nominated an end date of, say, 28 February 2007 for his first input period, he would be able to make contributions up to a maximum of £440,000 in the 2006/07 tax year, given sufficient taxable earnings. A contribution of £215,000 could be made before 28 February 2007 and an additional contribution of £225,000 could be paid between 1 March and 5 April 2007. If the second input period is ended shortly into the next tax year, say, on 7 April 2007, the third input period would run from 8 April 2007 to 7 April 2008 (ending in the 2008/09 tax year), thereby enabling a contribution of £235,000 to be made as early as 8 April 2007, subject of course to sufficient taxable income being available. A further contribution could not be made until 8 April 2008.

Note that start and end dates in the past may be nominated for a pension input period. Note also that just because large contributions can be made, for example by sacrificing bonuses and manipulating the annual allowance, it does not always mean it is a sound course of action. If an employee contributes too much early on, he may not be able to benefit fully from contributions an employer may make on his behalf later. Careful consideration will be required when dealing with large contributions.

Contributing while overseas

13.5   Individuals who joined a UK scheme and who were resident in the UK at some time in the last five tax years still qualify for tax relief on contributions through the relief at source provisions even though they are no longer UK resident and have no UK chargeable earnings. However, the maximum relievable contribution is limited to £3,600.

This may have an impact on overseas members of personal and stakeholder pension schemes. Before A-Day relievable contributions could be based on UK chargeable earnings immediately before going abroad, and this was available for up to five years. If the gross contribution being made before A-Day was more than £3,600, the position of such members may need to be revisited.

It may still be possible for someone subject to income tax in a foreign country to contribute to a UK registered pension scheme and receive tax relief against his earnings in the foreign country under the provisions of a double taxation agreement. The UK has many double taxation agreements with other countries although not all of them cover tax relief on pension contributions.

Someone who has come to the UK to work may continue to contribute to an overseas scheme of which he was a member before coming to the UK. In such a case, contributions will be relievable against UK tax. See **Chapter 9** for more information on migrant member relief.

In specie contributions

13.6   It is possible to transfer an asset into a registered scheme, if the rules so permit. This will effectively be a gift and so will not enjoy tax relief.

However, a member or employer may agree to pay a monetary contribution to a pension scheme but then transfer an asset in settlement of the debt. The agreement to pay the contribution must be legally enforceable so that the scheme administrator can pursue the member or employer for payment. HMRC requires the value of the asset to match the amount of the debt. If there is a discrepancy, the scheme administrator should either refund the excess or require a further payment. If the scheme administrator does not pursue a shortfall, it may be treated as an unauthorised payment.

Making *in specie* contributions was a popular method of transferring assets into a Self-Invested Personal Pension (SIPP), but many SIPP providers no longer accept them due to the complications mentioned above and increased HMRC scrutiny. Some SIPP providers will offer a 'Bed-and-SIPP' facility. A SIPP provider with stockbroker services may sell the shares a member has outside his SIPP and repurchase them immediately on behalf of the SIPP. This avoids the disadvantages of making an in specie contribution and, if done quickly, may minimise out of market risk.

The new tax regime does explicitly allow one form of in specie contribution. Shares granted in an employer's share incentive plan or under an SAYE share option scheme may be transferred to a registered pension scheme within 90 days of entitlement and will be treated for tax relief as if they were a contribution made by the member. Tax relief is available on the market value of the shares. There is therefore some scope to use a share incentive plan or SAYE scheme in conjunction with a company's pension scheme or a SIPP.

Recycling tax-free lump sums

13.7   The new tax regime restricts the recycling of tax-free lump sums taken upon retirement. HMRC was concerned that members above normal minimum pension age could vest benefits, draw a tax-free lump sum and immediately re-invest it in a registered scheme. The lump sum contributions would obtain tax relief, and the member could then take another tax-free lump sum to enable the cycle to be repeated. Such arrangements are blocked by the legislation, which removed the tax advantages relating to any lump sums artificially recycled.

HMRC states that it is not intended to affect cases where an individual takes a tax-free lump sum as part of the normal course of taking pension benefits. The legislation only applies to contributions which are greater than 30% of the lump sum. In such circumstances the whole of the lump sum would be treated as an unauthorised payment and subject to the unauthorised payments tax charge. However, if it is less than 1% of the lifetime allowance, it is exempt.

Removal of funding rules

13.8   There are no longer any statutory HMRC funding rules. Accordingly, the need to obtain actuarial advice arises mainly for the purpose of compliance with DWP legislation.

Salary sacrifice

13.9   Salary sacrifices were popular before A-Day primarily for those employees who wished to avoid the restriction that limited contributions to a percentage of remuneration. The introduction of relief of up to 100% of remuneration alleviates this, but there is still good reason in paying contributions by salary sacrifice due to the National Insurance savings that can be made.

Pension contributions that an employer makes are not subject to employee or employer National Insurance. By making his contribution through the salary sacrifice route, an employee therefore saves 11% National Insurance on the amount of his contribution if he is not contracted-out and earns under the upper earnings limit. The saving is only 1% if he earns above the upper earnings limit. An employer saves 12.8% National Insurance on the contribution whether or not the member earns above the upper earnings limit, assuming not contracted-out employment. Some or all of the employee and employer National Insurance saving can be directed into the pension scheme. This therefore makes salary sacrifice an attractive proposition.

If a salary sacrifice is to be effective, an employee's contractual right to cash pay must be reduced. This means:

- The employee must give up his potential future remuneration before it is treated as received for tax and National Insurance purposes, and

- The true construction of the revised contractual arrangement between employer and employee is that the employee is entitled to lower cash remuneration and a benefit.

Any right an employee retains to be able to claim his original level of cash pay will normally invalidate the salary sacrifice. However, HMRC will allow employees to revert to their original level of cash pay once a year without invalidating the effectiveness of the arrangement.

Although the National Insurance savings may seem good financial sense, employers thinking of implementing a salary sacrifice scheme need to remember that a reduction in employees' earnings could have adverse consequences for their state benefits, such as the additional state pension. Employers therefore need to be aware of the risks involved.

Before A-Day, salary sacrifices of £5,000 or more to an occupational pension scheme had to be reported to HMRC. This requirement fell away with the introduction of the new tax rules on 6 April 2006.

AVOIDING A LIFETIME ALLOWANCE CHARGE

13.10 The most obvious method of reducing exposure to a lifetime allowance charge is to make use of the transitional protection that exists for those with large pension rights at A-Day – primary and enhanced protection. However, that will not be of benefit to those who will accrue large rights in the future. Given the overarching nature of the lifetime allowance, it is probably not possible to avoid it completely, but there are some ways in which exposure to a lifetime allowance charge can be reduced in cases which are marginal.

Scheme pension

13.11 This may be of use where a lifetime annuity is purchased under a money purchase arrangement. Normally the amount crystallised by a lifetime annuity is the purchase price of the annuity. However, in order to ensure a level playing field with defined benefit arrangements, the new tax rules allow an annuity to be valued in the same way as a defined benefit pension as long as the annuity meets the same conditions that apply to a 'scheme pension' payable under a defined benefit arrangement (see **4.3**). This allows a lifetime annuity to be valued at 20:1 instead of at the purchase price. If it costs more than £20 to buy £1 per annum of annuity, valuing it at 20:1 crystallises a lower amount. This is demonstrated in the following example.

The lifetime allowance is £1,800,000. The fund value of a member of a money purchase arrangement is £2,250,000. The member is buying an annuity at a cost of £25 per £1 per annum. In the normal course of events the lifetime allowance would be exceeded by £450,000 (£2,250,000 – £1,800,000). However, the annuity that is purchased amounts to £90,000 per annum (£2,250,000 / 25). Valuing the £90,000 annuity as a scheme pension, at 20:1, results in a benefit crystallisation amount of only £1,800,000.

Dependant's pension

13.12 Most defined benefit pension schemes allow members to surrender part of their own pension at retirement in exchange for a higher dependant's pension payable on their death after retirement. Reducing member pension in this way also reduces the amount of benefit crystallised.

If this is being considered, it should be remembered that a dependant's pension upon death after age 75 should not exceed 100% of the member's pension plus 5% of the retirement lump sum (see **4.33**).

Pension increases

13.13   The HMRC valuation factor of 20 for a scheme pension allows for pension increases of the higher of 5% per annum and the rise in the Retail Prices Index. Few defined benefit schemes have increases as high as this. Exchanging a pension with low pension increases for a lower pension with higher increases will reduce the amount of benefit crystallised for lifetime allowance purposes. The consent of the scheme's trustees and/or sponsoring employer may be required, but at least one large occupational scheme in the UK has already amended its rules to give members the choice for the purpose of reducing exposure to a lifetime allowance charge.

Tax-free lump sum

13.14   If a defined benefit scheme provides a retirement lump sum by commutation of member pension, drawing a lump sum and reduced pension may reduce exposure to a lifetime allowance charge by reducing the value of benefits crystallised. This will be possible where the scheme commutes pension for lump sum at a rate less than £20 for each £1 of pension given up.

For example, if the lifetime allowance is £1,800,000 and a member of a defined benefit scheme is entitled to a pension of £95,000 per annum, this would normally incur a lifetime allowance charge on £100,000 (£95,000 × 20 = £1,900,000 – £1,800,000 = £100,000). However, if the scheme commutes pension for cash at the rate of £15 for each £1 per annum given up, the amount crystallised by drawing the maximum lump sum of £438,461 and a reduced pension of £65,769 per annum is only £1,753,841 (20 × £65,769 + £438,461 = £1,753,841).

Overseas transfer

13.15   Even though no more contributions might be paid into a money purchase pension scheme by or on behalf of a member, the fund may still grow beyond the lifetime allowance. If the fund is transferred to a qualifying recognised overseas pension scheme (QROPS) (see **Chapter 9**), it is tested against the lifetime allowance only once, at the point of transfer. Early transfer to a QROPS, when the fund is just below the lifetime allowance, would permit investment growth in the QROPS vehicle unrestricted by the UK lifetime allowance.

Loss of enhanced protection

13.16   If loss of enhanced protection cannot be avoided, it may make sense to crystallise benefits under other arrangements, so that they benefit from enhanced protection, before crystallising benefits from the arrangement that loses all enhanced protection.

Second lifetime allowance test

13.17   Someone taking income withdrawals will have had his crystallised benefits tested against the lifetime allowance whenever he first started income withdrawal. Unfortunately, this is not the end of the matter as far as the lifetime allowance is concerned as the new tax rules are designed to ensure that members draw income from their tax-advantaged pension savings.

An income withdrawal fund will be tested again against the lifetime allowance when the member reaches the age of 75 or upon purchase of an annuity if earlier.

Upon a member reaching age 75 while still in receipt of income withdrawal, the amount tested against the lifetime allowance is the remaining fund less the original amount crystallised by going into income withdrawal. If the member has not drawn enough income in the meantime, this could result in some funds being exposed to a lifetime allowance charge. It may therefore be advisable to draw income rather than face additional tax.

An alternative may be to transfer the income withdrawal fund to a drawdown arrangement under a qualifying recognised overseas pension scheme. There will be a lifetime allowance test on the funds at the point of transfer but no other lifetime allowance test will be applied in the receiving overseas scheme.

INHERITANCE TAX

13.18   It is prudent to avoid the prospect of a charge to inheritance tax (IHT) on lump sum death-in-service benefits. For certainty, the benefit must be dispensed through a discretionary trust, meaning that the trustees have discretion to decide to whom the benefit is paid. Members should be asked to complete an expression of wishes form, indicating the person/s or body/ies that they would like to benefit. The trustees are not to be bound by this statement, but they will usually be guided by it.

13.19   The following special rules apply to IHT:

- *FA 2006* states that monies held in an alternatively secured pension (ASP) by an investor aged 75 or over will be subject to inheritance tax at 40% when the investor dies, deducted directly from the fund by the administrator. The charge is based on the value of the taxable property at the time the charge arises, calculated by reference to the assets over the nil-rate band and the rate of tax at the time. Funds passed to charities escape the tax, and funds paid to provide pension benefits for a spouse, civil partner or financial dependant will not be chargeable until the entitlement to the benefit ceases.

- *FA 2006* also states that ASP funds which are passed on at death (eg to other family members) have been prohibited. The minimum ASP withdrawal level was increased from nil to 55% of the notional annuity, and the maximum level was increased from 70% to 90%.

- In mitigation of the above, there may be merit, where another family member is earning, in a member drawing maximum income and paying it directly into an arrangement for that person. The family member will obtain tax relief on the contribution, and payments out of income, including income from ASP, are free from inheritance tax.

- *FA 2008* states that tax relieved pension savings diverted into inheritance using scheme pensions and lifetime annuities in other circumstances than ASP will be subject to unauthorised payment charges and inheritance tax where appropriate. This applies to transfers and assignments after 10 October 2007 or increases in pension rights attributable to the death of a member when the member dies on or after 6 April 2008. The charges will not apply where the pension scheme has at least 20 members whose rights are increased at the same rate because another member has died.

- *FA 2006* legislated an existing 1992 concessionary practice in relation to an IHT charge which can arise when a person aged under 75 exercises a choice which reduces his chargeable estate and increases that of another (unless on an arm's length basis, and so excepted as a transfer of value). The exemption can apply in a pension scheme where the member exercised his right not to take pension. For example, where the member was in good health when the decision was made, but subsequently his life expectancy was seriously impaired and an enhanced death benefit is paid. The Act also extends the concession to dispositions to charities.

- *FA 2008* provides for inheritance tax relief from 6 April 2006 on savings in certain overseas pension schemes. Effectively this will protect monies in qualifying recognised overseas pension schemes, *s 615(3)* schemes and schemes which provide a pension for life.

REVIEW EXISTING SCHEMES

13.20   From A-Day all approved schemes were re-designated as registered schemes, unless they opted out of the new regime. These schemes are subject to the overriding modification regulations until 6 April 2011 (see **11.32**). The *Registered Pension Schemes (Modification of Rules of Existing Schemes) Regulations 2006, SI 2006/364* provide a rule of construction and give the trustees discretion over whether or not to make a payment which would fall to be treated as an unauthorised payment under the new regime. However, from a tax-planning perspective it is advisable to review existing documentation and make any desirable revisions, after seeking appropriate legal advice, at an early date. For example:

- any changes in the level of pensionable pay and the method of calculation;

- whether or not to put in place the scheme's own earnings cap as a means of controlling maximum benefit accrual;

- how the removal of HMRC limits is to impact on intended member benefits;

- whether to extend the scheme to overseas employers and employees;

- whether to widen the transfer powers and income withdrawal facilities to take advantage of the new freedoms;

- how the new tax rules affect benefit payments, eg transfers and income withdrawal;

ALTERNATIVE BENEFITS

13.21   In view of the potential impact of the lifetime allowance charge on senior employees who have accrued or will accrue significant pension entitlements, employers may wish to consider providing alternative means of reward or benefit for such persons in the future.

Cash payments

13.22   A company may consider making a direct cash payment to employees who no longer benefit tax efficiently from a registered pension scheme. This may be attractive as it provides ready access to monies and freedom of choice on expenditure. However, paying cash is more expensive than a pension contribution. Employers must pay 12.8% National Insurance on the cash payment, and employees suffer income tax and 1% National Insurance. The employee's cash payment might also be reduced by the employer to reflect the increased National Insurance paid the employer.

Benefits-in-kind, share schemes etc

13.23   Many companies have found that the provision of benefits to employees, such as cars, accommodation, membership fees and school fees attracts new personnel. There will be tax charges on the recipients of such benefits, but these are mitigated by certain allowances and exemptions. In addition, any such expenditure which is deemed to be for the furtherance of the company's trade or undertaking will secure tax reliefs for the company. Other popular means of providing incentives to employees, and increased performance, include bonuses; share incentive schemes and share options.

Excepted group life policies

13.24   Excepted group life policies (EGLPs) can be an attractive alternative to providing death-in-service benefits through a registered scheme. They share the same tax advantages of a registered scheme but are not subject to the lifetime allowance. There is no BIK income tax charge on the premiums paid, they can provide tax-free lump sum death benefits and they can be efficient on IHT where a discretionary trust is in place. Employer contributions should be tax-relievable under the 'wholly and exclusively' test.

13.25   EGLPs are not subject to the punitive taxation that applies to employer-financed retirement benefit schemes. There is no need to register an EGLP with HMRC and no need to comply with the new regime's reporting requirements. Since EGLPs sit outside the registered pension scheme tax regime, they could therefore be used to provide lump sum life cover for:

- Employees whose group life cover already exceeds their lifetime allowance.

- Employees whose group life cover, together with lump sum death benefits from other registered pension schemes, exceeds their lifetime allowance.

- Employees with enhanced protection where payment of the lump sum insured would jeopardise enhanced protection.

- Employees with enhanced protection where payment of life assurance premiums would jeopardise enhanced protection.

- Employees with primary protection where primary protection may not fully protect against a lifetime allowance charge.

- New employees who have enhanced protection and would lose it if they became members of a registered pension scheme for life assurance benefits.

A similar policy may be put in place where it covers only one employee, known as a 'relevant life policy'.

Inducement offers

13.26   Inducement payments are payments by employers or registered schemes to incentivise scheme members into giving up certain rights in place of alternative provision or benefit enhancement. In the past some arrangements had been accepted by HMRC as not attracting tax or National Insurance charges. The arrangements had demonstrated that the offer had been fairly communicated to the members, and that the relevant advisers had agreed that the payments were fair deals for all parties.

HMRC issued an announcement in January 2007 entitled 'The tax and National Insurance treatment of employer cash inducement payments to pension scheme members'. The announcement stated that the payment of cash sums 'in connection with the surrender or exchange of rights' is employment income and chargeable to income tax, regardless of the age of the recipient or whether or not the recipient is retired, as they are deemed to fall within the meaning of relevant benefits payable from an employer-financed retirement benefit scheme. Existing arrangements, already agreed with HMRC, are not disturbed. HMRC considers that the payment of a cash sum attracts National Insurance if it is deemed to be 'earnings'. Earnings 'paid to or for the benefit of the individual' (payments made direct from employer to individual) attract Class 1 National Insurance. Where payment is made by the employer into the registered scheme it attracts neither Class 1 nor Class 1A National Insurance.

By way of exception, HMRC stated that the above does not apply to payments that 'enhance the transfer value of the pension fund and which are included in the funds transferred between schemes'.

Qualifying recognised overseas pension schemes

13.27   There is no doubt that there are considerable funds which are tied up in UK pension schemes for internationally mobile employees, expatriates and employees of overseas companies. Before A-Day there was little that could be done to move these monies to an overseas scheme. *FA 2004* introduced sweeping changes, and these have yet to be fully explored by many.

A key opportunity for members lies in joining a qualifying recognised overseas pension scheme (QROPS). The advantages are that pension monies may be transferred to and from UK registered schemes without tax charge, and tax reliefs are available on contributions to such schemes. Future accrual of benefits from monies which have received no UK tax reliefs will not attract the lifetime allowance charge.

The transfer rules are far more flexible than before A-Day, and are attracting increasing interest. A transfer to a QROPS is a 'recognised transfer' under *FA 2004, s 169* which includes alternatively secured pensions and other pensions in drawdown. Additionally, there are wide potential tax savings for individual members on their benefits, dependent on their residence and/or domicility status.

There are no specific UK restrictions on borrowing by QROPS. However, if a member borrows money back from funds he has transferred, it will trigger an unauthorised payment charge.

Chapter 9 contains further information about QROPS.

Hancock annuities and EFPOS

13.28 A Hancock annuity is an immediate annuity for a retiring employee. This is still available post A-Day as a registered scheme and would be subject to the lifetime allowance. Alternatively, a Hancock may be paid as an employer-financed pension only scheme (EFPOS), which sits outside the registered pension scheme regime.

An EFPOS is not an employer-financed retirement benefit scheme as it provides only a pension. An EFPOS enjoys exemptions from National Insurance charges both on the employer contribution/premium and the benefit paid from the scheme. It is therefore a method employers could consider for providing senior employees with an unfunded pension.

Chapter 14

Unauthorised payment tax charge

INTRODUCTION

14.1   Although the post A-Day legislation refers to 'authorised' and 'non-authorised' payments, such terms are, in strictness, misnomers. The removal of HMRCs discretionary powers means that it is for registered schemes to make such payments as they deem appropriate. Tax charges and penalties are incurred on any payments which are, or are deemed to be, so chargeable under the governing legislation and codes of practice.

Details of tax-relievable benefits are given in **Chapter 4**. Authorised member payments are described in **14.2** and authorised employer payments are described in **14.3**.

The general rules which apply to unauthorised payments are described in **14.4**, the meaning of 'payments' is given in **14.5**. Actual and 'deemed' unauthorised member payments are described in **14.6** to **14.14** and the tax charges on unauthorised payments are described in **14.15** to **14.27**.

AUTHORISED MEMBER PAYMENTS

14.2   The *Finance Act 2004* describes seven types of payment, under the sections referred to below, which may be made to registered pension scheme members, or former members, which are classified as authorised member payments. Any other type of member payments will attract unauthorised payment charges. The authorised member payments are:

- lifetime pensions and pensions on death which fall under the *Finance Act 2004, ss 165* and *167* respectively;

- lump sums and lump sum death benefits which fall under the *Finance Act 2004, ss 166* and *168* respectively;

- recognised transfers which fall under the Finance Act 2004, s 169;

- scheme administration member payments which fall under the *Finance Act 2004, s 171*;

- payments which fall under various regulations and statutes, including:.

    - the *Registered Pension Schemes (Authorised Member Payments) Regulations 2006 (SI 2006/137)*;

    - the *Registered Pension Schemes (Authorised Member Payments) Regulations 2006 (SI 2006/137)*;

– the *Registered Pension Schemes (Authorised Member Payments) (No 2) Regulations 2006 (SI 2006/571)*;

– the *Registered Pension Schemes (Authorised Member Payments) Regulations 2007 (SI 2007/3532)*;

– the *Registered Pension Schemes (Authorised Payments) Regulations 2006 (SI 2006/209)*;

– the *Registered Pension Schemes (Authorised Payments – Arrears of Pension) Regulations 2006 (SI 2006/614)*;

– the *Registered Pension Schemes (Authorised Payments) (Transfers to the Pension Protection Fund) Regulations 2006 (SI 2006/134)*;

– the *Registered Pension Schemes (Meaning of Pension Commencement Lump) Regulations 2006 (SI 2006/135)*.

Additionally, the Finance Act 2008, para 1, Sch 29, inserted s 164 (2) in the Finance Act 2004 in respect of authorised member payments, as follows

'(2) Regulations under subsection (1) (f) may –

(a) provide that for the purposes of Part 9 of ITEPA 2003 all or part of a prescribed payment is to be treated as pension under a registered pension scheme, or as a lump sum of a prescribed description,

(b) provide that all or part of a prescribed payment is subject to the short service refund lump sum charge or the special lump sum death benefits charge,

(c) provide that a prescribed event in relation to a prescribed payment is to be treated for the purposes of the lifetime allowance charge as a benefit crystallisation event, and make provision as to the amount crystallised by that event,

(d) include provision having effect in relation to times before the regulations are made if that provision does not increase any person's liability to tax,

and "prescribed" means prescribed in regulations under subsection (1) (f).'

AUTHORISED EMPLOYER PAYMENTS

14.3   The *Finance Act 2004, s 175*, describes six types of payments which may be made to a current or former employer of a registered pension scheme under the sections referred to below. The authorised employer payments are:

● public service scheme payments which fall under the *Finance Act 2004, s 176*;

● authorised surplus payments which fall under the *Finance Act 2004, s 177* (see 14.28);

● compensation payments which fall under the *Finance Act 2004, s 178*;

- authorised employer loans which fall under the *Finance Act 2004, s 179*;

- scheme administrator employment payments which fall under the *Finance Act 2004, s 180*;

- payments prescribed by legislation.

Unauthorised payments – general

14.4   The *Finance Act 2004, s 160*, describes four types of unauthorised payments. The unauthorised payments are:

- a payment to a current or former member which is not an authorised payment;

- a deemed payment to or in respect of a current or former member which is specified as an unauthorised payment;

- a payment by an occupational pension scheme to a current or former sponsoring employer which is not an authorised payment;

- a deemed payment by an occupational pension scheme to a current or former sponsoring employer in respect of value-shifting (see in **14.14**).

The categories can be further broken down to include the following:

- benefits taken before age 50 from A-Day and age 55 from 2010;

- cash lump sum benefits in excess of the permitted maximum;

- assignments or surrenders of pension;

- recycled cash lump sums;

- reductions or stopping of a pension, other than in certain circumstances;

- lump sum death benefits paid to a person not in existence at the death of a member;

- deceased member's rights used to increase the rights of a connected person;

- dependant's pension in excess of the member pension limit;

- transfers to non-registered pension schemes, other than in certain circumstances;

- unauthorised loans;

- winding-up lump sum death benefits paid to non-dependants;

- trivial commutation in excess of the permitted limit;

- payments to migrant members who have benefited from UK tax relief, other than in certain circumstances;

- debts payable by members to a scheme which are not on arm's-length terms (including debts payable by a person connected with the member);

- payments to a sponsoring employer out of a surplus which arises where a member surrenders his pension benefits (such a device can attract an income tax charge of up to 70%);

HMRC's Pensions Tax Simplification Newsletter No 29, dated 31 August 2007, stated that the amount of the unauthorised payments charge from 2007/08 will be the actual payment increased by any amount withheld to cover the scheme administrator's liability to pay the scheme sanction charge. However, any additional payment to the member representing all or part of the amount withheld is not an unauthorised payment if paid within a specified time.

Meaning of 'payments'

14.5   The *Finance Act 2004, s 161(2)*, describes payments as including transfers of assets or other money's worth. *Sub-sections 161(3)* and *(4)* include:

- a payment or benefit in respect of scheme assets;

- payments made to persons connected with the member or the sponsoring employer;

- payments made to persons who are not members or a sponsoring employer;

- certain assets, increases in value or reductions in liability of a member or sponsoring employer or connected person

even where the scheme or arrangement has wound up.

A 'connected person' has the meaning within the *Income and Corporation Taxes Act 1988, s 839.*

Unauthorised member payments

Actual and 'deemed' unauthorised member payments

14.6   Under the *Finance Act 2004*, an unauthorised member payment may be deemed to have been made whether or not money has been paid out. The main circumstances are as listed below, and are described in **14.8** to **14.14**:

- an assignment of benefits or rights;

- a surrender of benefits or rights;

- an increase in rights of a connected person on death;

- an allocation of an unallocated employer's contribution;

- an increase in a member's benefits beyond the statutory limit;

- a member's use of assets;

- value-shifting;

- taxable property held by an IRPS (see **Chapter 12**).

Assignment of benefits or rights

14.7 Under the *Finance Act 2004, s 172*, an unauthorised payments charge based on the market value of the assigned benefits or rights of a member or dependant of that member, or any sums or assets assigned by such person under the scheme or arrangement, will fall on the member or, where deceased, the personal representative. It does not extend to assignments by spouses and civil partners. (However, see **14.11** concerning increase in rights on death arising from an ASP fund etc.)

Exclusions include assignments under pension-sharing orders and pensions payable under a death guarantee payment.

Surrender of benefits or rights

14.8 Under the *Finance Act 2004, s 172A*, an unauthorised payments charge based on the market value of the surrendered benefits or rights of a member or dependant of that member, or any sums or assets assigned by such person under the scheme or arrangement, will fall on the member or, where deceased, the personal representative. It does not extend to assignments by spouses and civil partners. (However, see **14.11** concerning increase in rights on death arising from an ASP fund etc.)

Other exclusions include:

- surrenders under pension-sharing orders;

- a surrender to provide for a dependant after death;

- a transfer to another arrangement under the scheme relating to the member or a dependant of the member (but see **Chapter 13** concerning tax planning and inheritance tax);

- a surrender to pay an authorised surplus payment;

- a surrender made as part of a retirement benefit activities compliance exercise;

- a surrender permitted by regulations.

Increase in rights of a connected person on death

14.9 Under the *Finance Act 2004, s 172B*, if a member's benefits are increased as a result of another member's death, an unauthorised payments charge based on the value of the increase will fall on that member if he is a connected person within the meaning of the *Income and Corporation Taxes Act 1988, s 839*. This applies where the deceased member's rights were uncrystallised, or unsecured or a dependant's unsecured pension.

Exclusions include:

- where, at the member's death there were at least 20 scheme members and each had their benefit entitlements increased at the same rate;

215

- any transfer lump sum death benefit received from the deceased member;

- any pension or lump sum death benefit received from the deceased member;

- any other sums specified in regulations.

Under the *Finance Act 2004, s 172BA*, which was inserted by the *Finance Act 2007, Sch 19, para 13*, if after the death of a member or dependant (and after 6 April 2007) another member becomes entitled to an ASP in relation to an entitlement of that member or dependant an unauthorised payments charge based on the consideration that might be expected to be received for that benefit value of the increase will fall on the other member or personal representative. The amount may be reduced by so much excess as arises from the other member becoming entitled to any pension or lump sum death benefit received from the deceased member. Before 6 April 2007, ASP was included in the exceptions in **14.9**.

Additionally, *Finance Act 2008, s 901, Sch 28*, introduced an additional restriction. It stipulates that tax-relieved pension savings which are diverted into inheritance tax using scheme pensions and lifetime annuities in other circumstances than ASP (see 46.27) will be subject to unauthorised payment charges and inheritance tax where appropriate. The charge applies to transfers and assignments after 10 October 2007 or increases in pension rights attributable to the death of a member when the member dies on or after 6 April 2008. The charges will not apply where the pension scheme has at least 20 members whose rights are increased at the same rate because another member has died.

Allocation of an unallocated employer's contribution

14.10 The charge falls under the *Finance Act 2004, s 172C*. It applies where:

- the scheme is an occupational pension scheme and the member and employer are connected or the member and a person connected to the employer are connected (as described in the *Income and Corporation Taxes Act 1988, s 839*; and

- the pension arrangement is money purchase and not cash balance, or if it is a hybrid arrangement providing both money purchase and cash balance benefits.

Where the amount of any previously unallocated employer payments which are allocated to a member or members exceed the following permitted maximum, the excess of the allocated contributions is taxed on the member as an unauthorised payment.

The permitted maximum is the amount of tax relief which would have been available to the member in the relevant tax year, disregarding any member contributions paid but including any employer contributions paid in that period. Where the member belongs to more than one scheme, the permitted maximum must be divided by the number of schemes.

Increase in a member's benefits beyond the statutory limit

14.11   The charge falls under the *Finance Act 2004, s 172D*. It applies where:

- the scheme is an occupational pension scheme and the member and employer are connected or the member and a person connected to the employer are connected (as described in the *Income and Corporation Taxes Act 1988, s 839*; and

- the pension arrangement is defined benefit, or if it is a hybrid arrangement providing both defined benefit and cash balance benefits.

Where the pension input amount for the input period (see **Chapter 10**) exceeds the following notional unconnected person input amount, the excess is taxed on the member as an unauthorised payment.

The notional unconnected person input amount the notional pension input amount which would have applied if the member and employer had not been connected or the member and a person connected to the employer had not been connected as described in *s 839*.

Member use of assets

14.12   The charge falls under the *Finance Act 2004, s 173*. It applies where a scheme's assets are used to provide a benefit (other than a payment) to a person who is or has been a member of a pension scheme to:

- that person; or

- a member of the person's family or household, as defined in the *Income Tax (Earnings and Pensions) Act 2003, s 721*.

The cash equivalent of the benefit-in-kind is taxed on the member as an unauthorised payment.

If the benefit is provided by reason of an employment which is not an excluded employment, as defined in the *Income Tax (Earnings and Pensions) Act 2003, s 63(4)*, the charge does not arise.

If the benefit is provided by reason of an employment which is an excluded employment, as defined in *s 63(4)*, the charge only arises if:

- it would have been chargeable under the *Income Tax (Earnings and Pensions) Act 2003* if the employment was not an excluded employment; and

- the scheme that holds the asset or benefit is an occupational pension scheme; and

- the person, or a member of the person's family or household, is a director of and holds a material interest (as described below) in a sponsoring employer.

A material interest is described in the *Income Tax (Earnings and Pensions) Act 2003, s 68,* meaning generally owning 5% of the share capital or having an entitlement to 5% of the assets.

The charge does not apply to taxable property held by an IRPS (see **Chapter 12**).

Similar provisions apply to payments to a person's family or household following that person's death.

Value-shifting

14.13   The charge falls under the *Finance Act 2004, s 174.* It applies to:

• the creation, alteration, release or extinction of rights or powers relating to pension scheme assets or liabilities;

• the exercise, or failure to exercise, any powers, options or rights relating to such assets or liabilities;

• the exercise, or failure to exercise, any power, option or right which is itself a scheme asset 'in a way which differs from that which might be expected if the parties to the transaction were at arm's length' for the benefit of a person who is or has been a member of a pension scheme.

Shifting value from the scheme to a member, or a person connected with the member, will result the excess over 'that which might be expected if the parties to the transaction were at arm's length' being taxed on the member as an unauthorised payment.

Similar provisions apply to unauthorised employer payments under value-shifting by virtue of the *Finance Act 2004, s 181.*

Tax charges on unauthorised payments

14.14   The main impact of the post A-Day regime is that charges to tax, surcharges, penalties etc have become codified. These charges are incurred when an action has taken place which is in breach of the legislation. The charges are summarised under appropriate headings below. Wasting assets will also be regarded as an unauthorised payment.

Payments by registered pension schemes which are not authorised by their rules or legislation (see **14.2** and **14.3** for descriptions of authorised payments) may incur an unauthorised payments charge on the amount paid out or the value of the excess payment or benefit. The tax is chargeable on the member, the recipient or the sponsoring employer, as appropriate.

An unauthorised payments charge arises where a payment (or a deemed payment) is made to or in respect of a current or former member, or a current or former sponsoring employer where the scheme an occupational pension scheme, or to a connected party of either. Additionally:

• an unauthorised payment surcharge may become payable if the unauthorised payment exceeds certain limits;

- a scheme sanction charge is likely to arise on the scheme administrator where an unauthorised payment surcharge has become payable;

- in some situations, a scheme sanction charge can arise on the scheme administrator even if no unauthorised payment surcharge has become payable.

There are some legislative reliefs under legislation, which are described below.

Unauthorised payments charge

14.15   The charge is ring-fenced from other tax offsets, and is 40% on the amount which is paid out (*Finance Act 2004, s 208*). The tax is chargeable on the member, the recipient if the member has died or the recipient if it applies to an unauthorised employer payment. It applies whether or not the member, recipient or scheme administrator is UK resident.

Unauthorised payments surcharge

14.16   An unauthorised payment surcharge (*Finance Act 2004, s 209*) may arise in addition to the unauthorised payment charge described in **14.16**. This charge will be triggered if the unauthorised payment which is made to the member is 25% or more of the value of the member's uncrystallised and crystallised rights under the arrangements within the scheme. The value is described in *ss 211* and *212*. It applies whether or not the member, recipient or scheme administrator is UK resident.

The rate of the surcharge is 15% of the surchargeable unauthorised payment (*s 210*).

Similar provisions apply under *s 213* in respect of surchargeable unauthorised employer payments, based on the amount of the payment divided by the value of the total rights under the occupational scheme.

Period for measuring the charge threshold

14.17   The period over which the charge threshold is measured is described in *ss 210(3)* and *213(3),* and it can straddle more than one tax return year.

Discharge from the unauthorised payments surcharge

14.18   The *Finance Act 2004, s 268,* provides for individual persons and companies who are subject to the unauthorised payments surcharge to seek a discharge if 'in all the circumstances of the case, it would not be just and reasonable for the person to be liable'.

The time limit for applications, under the *Registered Pension Schemes (Discharge of Liabilities under Sections 267 and 268 of the Finance Act 2004) Regulations 2005 (SI 2005/3452)* is:

- 5 years from 31 January following the end of the relevant tax year; or

- where HMRC has raised an assessment, within two years from its date of issue.

The HMRCs decision can be appealed (see **8.15**).

Declaration of liability for the unauthorised payments charge and the unauthorised payments surcharge

14.19   Individual persons and companies must declare any liability for the unauthorised payments charge and the unauthorised payments surcharge on their self-assessment returns, or by separate notification if no return has been received.

The *Registered Pension Schemes (Provision of Information) Regulations 2006 (SI 2006/567)* require companies in receipt of unauthorised employer payments to send the details to their company tax office, not HMRC SPSS.

Scheme sanction charge

14.20   A scheme sanction charge will fall on the administrator of any registered scheme which makes one or more scheme chargeable payments in the year. Under the *Finance Act 2004, s 239,* the rate of tax payable is 40% of the scheme chargeable payment. HMRC will issue a notice of assessment – the charge is not included in the quarterly accounting for tax return. It applies whether or not the liable person is UK resident.

The scheme administrator must pay the charge, although there may be some mitigation where other charges have already been incurred. The provisions which exempt members from charges where they have been duped into making or receiving a chargeable payment, are followed through in the legislation for scheme administrators.

It is a requirement of the *Finance Act 2004* that, in many circumstances, the administrator must be provided with information from the member (for example, the amount of the lifetime allowance which is available). If the administrator has been given false information, he may seek a discharge (see **8.16**). Such application must be made to HMRC.

Payments which attract the scheme sanction charge

14.21   The *Finance Act 2004, s 241*, defines scheme chargeable payments which attract the scheme sanction charge as either:

- an incurred charge in respect of minimum unauthorised borrowing under *s 181A*; or

- unauthorised payments other than payments exempted under *s 241(2)*; or

- unauthorised borrowings under *ss 183* or *185*; or

- income or gains from taxable property under *ss 183A* or *185F* (see **Chapter 12**).

Payments which are excluded from the scheme sanction charge

14.22   The *Finance Act 2004, s 241*, excludes the following unauthorised payments from the scheme sanction charge:

- payments treated as made under *s 173* (see **14.13**) where the asset is not a wasting asset;

- compensation payments under *s 178* (a member's liability to a sponsoring employer in respect of a criminal, fraudulent or negligent act or omission by the member);

- payments made to comply with a court order or an order by a person or body with the power to order the making of that payment;

- payments made on the grounds that a court or any such person or body is likely to order (or would be, if it were asked to do so) the making of the payment;

- payments prescribed by the transitional provisions of the *Registered Pension Schemes (Unauthorised Payments by Existing Schemes) Regulations 2006 (SI 2006/365);*

and lump sums under *para 1(2), Sch 29*, which are not pension commencement lump sums (because they exceeded the permitted maximum) if the payment would not have been unauthorised if:

- for enhanced protection members, *paras 27* and *29, Sch 36* had not applied; or

- for non-enhanced protection members, *para 28, Sch 36* had not applied.

Relief from the scheme sanction charge

14.23   The *Finance Act 2004, s 266B*, permits the scheme administrator to apply for relief from the scheme sanction charge in proportion to the amount of any unauthorised payment subsequently made good under a DWP restitution order (see **14.25**).

Additionally, the Act provides for a discharge from liability if 'in all the circumstances of the case, it would not be just and reasonable for the scheme administrator to be liable'. In all other cases, the criterion is that 'the scheme administrator reasonably believed that the unauthorised payment was not an unauthorised payment'.

The time limit for applications, under the *Registered Pension Schemes (Discharge of Liabilities under Sections 267 and 268 of the Finance Act 2004) Regulations 2005 (SI 2005/3452)* is:

- 5 years from 31 January following the end of the relevant tax year; or

- where HMRC has raised an assessment, within two years from its date of issue.

The HMRCs decision can be appealed (see **8.15**).

Reducing the scheme sanction charge

14.24   The scheme sanction charge is reduced from 40% in cases where the unauthorised payments charge has already been paid. The reduction is the lower of:

- 25% of the scheme chargeable payments on which the tax was paid, and

- the actual amount of tax paid on the unauthorised payment.

A concession is available where the scheme sanction charge is incurred on funds which have been liberated in the member's pension savings through no fault of the member. Where the funds are repatriated, the *Finance Act 2004, s 266* relieves the scheme sanction charge. However, the scheme administrator must claim the relief within one year of the repatriation taking place.

The *Finance Act 2007, para 5, Sch 20*, inserted *ss 160(4A) and (4B)* in the *Finance Act 2004* in respect of unauthorised payments which are reduced by the amount of the scheme sanction charge, as follows:

'(4A) If an unauthorised member payment or unauthorised employer payment made to or in respect of a person would have been greater but for a reduction made in respect of the whole, or any proportion, of the amount which the scheme administrator considers may be the amount of the liability to the scheme sanction charge in respect of it, it is to be regarded for the purposes of this Part as increased by the amount of the reduction.

(4B) But if the amount, or that proportion of the amount, of that liability is in fact less than the amount of the reduction, a subsequent payment of an amount not exceeding the difference between that amount and the amount of the reduction made—

(a) to or in respect of the same person, and

(b) before the end of the period of two years beginning with the date on which the unauthorised member payment or unauthorised employer payment was made,

is not to be regarded for the purposes of this Part as an unauthorised member payment or unauthorised employer payment.

Release of scheme administrator from liability

14.25   The scheme administrator's tax liabilities are passed on at succession (*Finance Act 2004, s 271*). However, if there is no successor, he retains that liability – but may apply to HMRC for a release from liability.

The HMRCs decision can be appealed (see **8.15**).

Surplus repayments

14.26   The *Finance Act 2004, ss 177* and *207* provide that surplus monies may be paid to employers under governing scheme rules. There must be compliance with DWP rules and legislation.

Although not in strictness a penalty, an authorised surplus payment charge must be paid by a registered scheme which makes such a payment to a sponsoring employer. The tax chargeable is 35% of the amount of the surplus.

Chapter 15

Employer-financed retirement benefits schemes

PRE-A-DAY FURBS AND UURBS

Introduction

15.1　Funded unapproved retirement benefit schemes (FURBS) became increasingly popular after the enactment of the *Finance Act 1989*. That Act permitted, for the first time, concurrent membership of approved and non-approved retirement benefit schemes. The reason for this concession was the imposition, also for the first time, of a limit on permitted pensionable earnings under an approved scheme. This major restriction was brought in with seemingly little opposition.

Not only did high earners find themselves faced with a pensionable earnings cap with a 1989 value of £60,000 (the 'earnings cap'), employers in search of senior executives often had to find means of rewarding such key personnel with parallel benefits to those which were already in place for their key men. FURBS were the answer for many, although they were less tax efficient than approved schemes.

Tax advantages of FURBS were steadily eroded over the following years. From A-Day the changes introduced by the new tax regime included the lifetime allowance (see **Chapter 10**) for lifetime-tax relievable funds. The value of the allowance drew heavily on the level of the earnings cap as at A-Day. In effect, the changes also withdrew the advantages of protection for pre *Finance Act 1989* members of approved schemes. Again, rather surprisingly, there was little opposition to this fundamental restriction.

Existing FURBS (and, for a period, consolidated rolled-over UURBS), were able to register from A-Day, bringing them under the tax regime for registered schemes from the date of registration. However, FURBS which did not opt for the new regime are allowed a large degree of protection of their existing pre A-Day rights under transitional arrangements (see **Chapter 11** and **15.3**). The new regime is available to everyone who elects to join it, but note the new lifetime allowance embraces the build up of the post A-Day tax-free fund.

Legislation and guidance

15.2　The main regulations which concern EFRBS are:

- The *Employer-Financed Retirement Benefits (Excluded Benefits for Tax Purposes) Regulations 2006 (SI 2006/210);*

- the *Employer-Financed Retirement Benefits Schemes (Provision of Information) Regulations 2005 (SI 2005/3453)*;

- the *Employer-Financed Retirement Benefits (Excluded Benefits for Tax Purposes) Regulations 2007 (SI 2007/3537)*.

HMRC guidance is difficult to find. The problem is that HMRC SPSS is not empowered to advise on EFRBS (any more than it dealt with FURBS and UURBS in the past). The tax position for such schemes therefore has to be gleaned from various sources and manuals relating primarily to:

- trusts and settlements;

- employment income;

- company and employee tax offices;

- national insurance;

- policy-holders taxation;

- the tax residence of trustees;

- foreign pensions;

- RPSM; and

- an extra-statutory concession.

This Chapter endeavours to summarise the position for FURBS; UURBS and EFRBS based on searches into the above sources.

Transitional protection for FURBS

15.3   Transitional arrangements apply to certain elements of FURBS in respect of unfunded promises made before A-Day. The position is described below:

- if a FURBS ceased to be funded before A-Day, it will not incur any additional charges to tax on the lump sum ultimately payable out of the fund;

- if a FURBS ceased to be funded before A-Day, the entire fund may remain invested, continue to grow and eventually be taken as a tax-free lump sum. Any particular scheme rule that imposes a minimum benefit age or does not permit the partial drawing of benefits may need to be reconsidered if such flexibility is needed;

- the protection of the value of the tax-free lump sum as at A-Day will be index-linked, if the pre A-Day employer contributions were taxed on the member or if all income and gains under the fund have been taxed;

- fund values at A-Day must be based on an 'appropriate fraction', determined from the market value of the assets, on the notional assumption that the scheme had been wound up on that day;

- only those assets which had accumulated in a FURBS under a discretionary trust before A-Day shall benefit from an exemption under inheritance tax rules;

- if further contributions are made post A-Day the exemption relief on benefits will be restricted to the A-Day value of benefits increased by the RPI in the meantime;

- for FURBS which registered on A-Day, the lump sum limit of 25% of the lifetime allowance applies;

- under *SI 2006/210* (see **15.1**) a lump sum benefit is an excluded benefit if it is in respect of the non-accidental death of an employee during service, and already provided for under the rules of a scheme on A-Day;

- *SI 2007/3537*, (see **15.1**) exempts specified non-cash benefits provided to former and current employees under an EFRBS from the charge to tax on employer-financed benefits under the *Income Tax (Earnings and Pensions) Act 2003, s 394.*

The exemptions mainly include:

- living accommodation that had been provided by a local authority employer;

- accommodation that had been provided for the proper performance of the employee's duties

which extend to family members staying on in the accommodation after the employee's death;

- accommodation for ministers of religion;

- accommodation provided because the employee's security was at risk;

- removal expenses, repairs and alterations and council tax;

- replacement accommodation.

The taxation implications for UURBS

15.4   The taxation implications for UURBS were unchanged from A-Day. It is still possible to insure UURBS promises against employer default, and the premium cost will taxed on the member as a benefit-in-kind. UURBS promises need not be tested against the annual allowance or the lifetime allowance.

The main tax details are:

- security and underwriting costs of setting aside assets or securities for UURBS are taxed on the member as a benefit-in-kind;

- payments or benefits-in-kind provided by the scheme are taxable on the employee;

- pension are taxable as earnings, or under *Schedule D, Case V* for certain overseas individuals;

- lump sums are taxable either under the general earnings charging section, the charge for termination payments or under the specific charge for benefits from unapproved schemes:

- if the benefit is received by an individual he is charged to tax;

- if the benefit is received by a person other than an individual, the scheme administrator is charged to tax under *Schedule D, Case VI* at 40% (or such other rate as the Treasury may specify);

- for a cash payment, the amount received is taxed, for a benefit-in-kind the cash equivalent is taxed;

- if notional employer contributions were assessed on an employee in the past, that individual is not taxable under general earnings or under the charge on termination payments on any lump sum benefit paid. However, the payment is not excluded from the specific tax charge on benefits from unapproved schemes (*Income Tax (Earnings and Pensions) Act 2003, ss 393–400);*

- the employer can only obtain tax relief either as a deduction from trading profits or as a management expense if the employee has been charged to income tax on receipt of the benefit.

Transfers to a registered pension scheme

15.5   There is no restriction on a transfer from a pre A-Day FURBS, or an EFRBS, to a registered pension scheme, if the receiving scheme rules allow for it to be done. The payment should not generally be affected by the annual allowance, but it will not attract tax relief. A more tax-efficient method of paying into a registered pension scheme would be, where possible, to draw funds as a tax-free lump sum and pay an equivalent amount to the registered scheme. Tax relief on contributions will only be available up to 100% of earnings or the annual allowance if lower. Therefore, it may be beneficial to draw lump sum benefits in stages where the scheme permits. However, the funds will come within the scope of the lifetime allowance.

The *Finance Act 2004, s 196A* (as inserted by *Finance Act 2005, Sch 10, para 39),* and the *Registered Pension Schemes (Restriction of Employer's Relief) Regulations, SI 2005/3458),* include restrictions to be applied if the transfer value of rights under a registered pension scheme is reduced because of the payment of relevant benefits under an EFRBS.

Tax treatment of EFRBS

15.6   The tax treatment of a contribution to an EFRBS is generally very unfavourable. Although an employee would no longer be taxed on an employer contribution as a benefit-in-kind (as had applied to FURBS), the benefit paid will be subject to income tax, and the employer will not receive tax relief until a taxable benefit is paid. Regulations counter the routing of contributions, through a registered pension scheme, that are intended to fund an EFRBS (*Finance Act 2004, s 196A* as inserted by *Finance Act 2005, Sch 10, para 39,* and the *Registered Pension Schemes (Restriction of Employer's Relief) Regulations, SI 2005/3458*).

In addition, if more than 25% of the benefit is paid as a lump sum, the payment will be subject to National Insurance contributions. For these reasons very few FURBS have stayed open post-A-Day.

Investments will be subject to taxation at the same rates applicable to other trusts, although some advantage may still be gained from separate allowances.

The details are:

- Employers will not receive relief on contributions and administration expenses until benefits come into payment (*Finance Act 2004, ss 245 and* 246, respectively).

- Tax relief on employer's expenses will not be allowed where the provision of the relevant benefits under an EFRBS results in a reduction in the benefits payable to an employee under a registered pension scheme or where a reduction in the benefits payable to an employee under a registered pension scheme results in the provision of the relevant benefits under an EFRBS.

- An employer's cost of insuring benefits against employer insolvency is chargeable to the member as a benefit-in-kind. The employer can claim the cost as an expense against profits at the time it is paid.

- For investment gains, capital gains tax will be taxable at the rate applicable to trusts (RAT), which had already increased for FURBS from 34% to 40% on 6 April 2004, and amounts held in the fund will not be included in the lifetime allowance.

- The basic rate of tax applies on the first £500 of gains from 6 April 2005, which removes one-third of trusts from the RAT (tax returns are only likely to be issued every five years in such cases, although taxable income should be declared if it arises). From A-Day, the first £1,000 of gross income is taxed at the old preferential rates.

- Income tax on funds also applies at the 40% rate (previously 22%) from 6 April 2004.

- Lump sum death benefits will be charged to inheritance tax.

It is understood that there will be no NIC charge on any benefits paid out of non-registered schemes provided they are within the limits of benefits that could be paid out of a registered scheme and all employer and connected employer relationships have ceased.

Provision of information (EFRBS)

15.7 *Statutory Instrument 2005/3453* (see **15.1**) states that HMRC must be notified of the coming into operation of an EFRBS on or before 31 January following the tax year in which it was set up. HMRC must also be informed of benefits provided from an EFRBS by 7 July following the tax year in which the benefits are paid. The report may be done online.

Lists of the benefits should be sent to the HMRC office which deals with any PAYE scheme operated by the EFRBS. They will be treated as employment income in the hands of the employee or former employee unless their overall value is no more than £100.

The relevant reporting individual is extended beyond the scheme administrator to 'responsible persons' under the *Taxes Management Act 1970* where assessments are due on certain payments or actions.

The prescribed information is:

(a)   the name, address and national Insurance Number of the recipient of the relevant benefit;

(b)   the nature of the relevant benefit provided; and

(c)   the amount of the relevant benefit calculated in accordance with *s 398(2)* of *ITEPA 2003*.

Non-reportable benefits

15.8   The following non-cash benefits are not reportable as they do not constitute an EFRBS:

●   continued provision by former employers of accommodation and certain related payments;

●   welfare counselling;

●   recreational benefit;

●   annual parties and similar functions costing up to £150;

●   equipment for former disabled employees;

●   writing of wills costing up to £150;

and benefits, where the right to the continuing benefit arose on retirement before 6 April 1998.

Benefits which are not deemed to be relevant benefits for EFRBS are charged under the *Income Tax (Earnings and Pensions) Act 2003, Pt 9*. Benefits in respect of non-UK schemes are charged under the *Finance Act 2004, Sch 34*.

Excluded benefits are benefits in respect of ill-health, disablement or death by accident during service, benefits under a relevant life policy and benefits excluded by regulation.

Sources of information

Employment Income Manual (EIM)

15.9   The main link source in the manual is EIM15000 – 'Non-approved and "employer-financed" retirement benefits schemes: table of contents'.

EIM15040 states that an *employer's contribution* to a non-approved retirement benefits scheme or EFRBS counts as employment income of an employee to the extent that the contribution is made with a view to the provision of relevant benefits for that employee or others. 'Others' includes:

- the employee's spouse or widow/widower and (from 5 December 2005) civil partner/surviving civil partner;

- the employee's children;

- dependants of the employee;

- the personal representatives of the employee.

Separately identifiable costs incurred by an employer in setting up or administering a scheme are not chargeable on employees as such costs cannot fund the provision of benefits.

If the employer's contribution covers benefits for more than one employee it is apportioned among the employees in accordance with the separate benefits to be provided for each of them.

In more detail, the manual states that:

- relevant benefits are employment income under the *Income Tax (Earnings and Pensions) Act 2003, s 394*;

- the charge on lump sums paid out may be reduced where prior employer contributions have been taxed and where the employee has made contributions;

- a pension is charged separately as pension income under the *ITEPA 2003, Pt 9*, which charges pension income to tax.

In the above, 'relevant benefits' means any lump sum, gratuity or other benefit provided:

- on retirement or on death; or

- in anticipation of retirement; or

- after retirement or death in connection with past service; or

- on or in anticipation of or in connection with any change in the nature of the employee's service; or

- by virtue of a pension-sharing order or provision.

This includes a non-cash benefit, but not:

- pension income within the *Income Tax (Earnings and Pensions) Act 2003, Pt 9*;

- benefits chargeable under the *Finance Act 2004, Sch 34*.

Excluded benefits are benefits:

- in respect of ill-health or disablement of an employee during service;

- in respect of death by accident of an employee during service;

- under a 'relevant life policy' (see in the Policyholder Taxation Manual).

EIM15022 addresses the issue of '*retirement*', and states:

'Deciding whether a payment is given on retirement can be difficult because there is no full statutory definition of the word. Section 612(1) ICTA 1988 states that retirement is to be interpreted according to the way service is defined, but that only means that there cannot be a retirement unless the employment has ended. Consequently, its natural meaning applies.

Payments made in respect of age-related retirement should not cause problems, for example where the typical age of natural retirement in a job is at a fixed age.

But the situation can be less clear where the termination is described as "early retirement" since this is often in fact a dismissal (for example, due to redundancy or inefficiency). A payment in such a case can represent compensation for loss of the employment rather than a payment on retirement and so may be chargeable only under Section 401 ITEPA 2003 (provided that no contractual entitlement exists, see EIM12850). That is so even if the employee also becomes entitled, at the time of termination, to immediate pension benefits from the employer's approved or registered pension scheme (see EIM15030). This could occur, for example, where an approved scheme allows a pension to be paid to persons made redundant at age 50 or over.

If the circumstances of the termination do not suggest that there is a dismissal (including a redundancy), severance, resignation or death, then it is likely that it is a retirement (but see EIM15024 if ill health causes the termination and the scheme is non-approved). There are some further guidelines at example EIM15400.'

Guidance on how annuities, annual payments and non-cash receipts are dealt with is given in EIM15100.

For *overseas schemes*, EIM15060 states:

'Section 397 ITEPA 2003

For this purpose, an overseas scheme is one where **any** of the income and gains of the scheme's investments are or have been outside the charge to UK tax (see Note 1 below).

The treatment of a lump sum from such a scheme depends on whether the scheme was entered into or varied (see below) on or after 1 December 1993.

Treat a scheme as varied if any of its terms change. For example, if a scheme rule that provides for annual contributions of £1,000 to be made is changed to increase the annual contributions to £2,000, that is a variation. By contrast, if contributions are increased automatically by reference to a formula in the scheme that is related to a variable such as earnings, profits or turnover then that is not a variation: the same rule is being applied.

If the scheme was entered into **before** 1 December 1993, follow item 3 of EIM15100.

Otherwise, the charge under Section 394 ITEPA 2003 is calculated by deducting **only the following** from the lump sum:

any sum contributed by the employer on which the employee was chargeable and has been taxed under Section 595(1) ICTA 1988 (see SE15040) or Section 386 ITEPA 2003 (see EIM151040) and

any sum paid by the employee.

There are further rules where the lump sum comes from either the disposal of a part of an asset or the surrender of any part of or share in any rights in any asset and further lump sums may arise from further such disposals or surrenders, see EIM15061.

Note 1: this provision is an anti-avoidance measure. The calculation applies if **any** of the scheme's income or gains are not brought into charge to UK tax. So it applies even if **some** of its income or gains is charged to UK tax.

Note 2: in all the above cases, the charge may be eliminated by Extra-Statutory Concession A10 (see EIM15062).

Note 3: Section 397 has no application for receipts after 5 April 2006. After that date, receipts from employer-financed retirement benefits schemes are charged in full (see EIM15010) subject to transitional provisions (see EIM15125 and subsequent guidance.'

Trusts, Settlements and Estates Manual (TSEM)

15.10 Until A-Day, new FURBS and UURBS were submitted for consideration to HMRC Trusts, Bootle. If a previously approved scheme lost approval because resident trustees had been replaced by non-resident trustees, the case would be referred to CNR (Non-Resident Trusts). Currently, HMRC Trusts are based in Bootle, Edinburgh and London. As technical specialists they form part of HMRC Trusts Head Office. The EFRBS reporting requirements are described in **15.7**.

15.11 The Settlements Legislation in the *Income and Corporation Taxes Act 1988, Pt XV*, was rewritten as part of the Tax Law Rewrite programme. The legislation is now in the *Income Tax (Trading and Other Income) Act 2005, Ch 5, Pt 5*. It will not apply if the scheme is operating on normal commercial lines as part of an employment package. But in certain circumstances HMRC may consider whether the Settlements legislation applies to charge the income and gains of a FURBS or EFRBS on a director. This action will be triggered if the trust is apparently not genuinely to provide retirement benefits. Capital gains tax can be incurred in addition to the settlements charge. The Inspector will submit any matters of doubt to HMRC Trusts, Bootle.

The Settlements legislation may also apply if the relief provided by the *Income and Corporation Taxes Act 1988, s 686(2)(c)*, (now the exemption from taxation on trusts for registered schemes under the *Finance Act 2004)* has been disallowed.

The tax office for the company

Contributions

Information Guidance on whether the contributions into the scheme are allowable is at IM8410 onwards. S76 FA 1989 deals with the timing of any deductions due (see IM8412).

The employer's contributions are allowable only if they are chargeable as employment or pension income on a member or another person. Where due, a deduction is given for the period in which the employer makes the contribution (S76 (4)). This ensures the payer's relief matches the employee's charge as to both time and amount.

Advice If you cannot resolve a problem about this, refer the case to CT and VAT (Trading and Property Income Team).

Action There may be tax avoidance opportunities if a company is 'close' and a member is a participator with a significant interest in the company. You may want to consider whether amounts put into the scheme by the employer are commensurate with a normal commercial provision for the employee concerned.

Action If a trading deduction has been successfully denied because the contribution has not been wholly and exclusively expended for the purposes of the employer's trade, submit the file for the employer to HMRC Trusts Head Office Bootle so that they can consider whether the Settlements legislation applies.

Pensions

Information Pensions that the trustees pay are chargeable as pension income by virtue of s 569 ITEPA 2003 (because of s 393(2) ITEPA 2003).

Advice Refer any problem to PAYE, SA and NICs Group, Employment Income (Technical) Solihull.

Lump sum gratuity or other benefit

Information s394 ITEPA 2003 deals with lump sums gratuities or other benefits that trustees pay. A benefit will be chargeable if it is a relevant benefit within the definition at S393B ITEPA 2003. Where the employee has contributed to the provision of the lump sum the charge may be reduced as set out in S395 ITEPA 2003. It should be noted that up until 5 April 2006 the view taken by HMRC was that non-cash benefits were not within the definition of relevant benefits. From 6 April 2006 the definition of a relevant benefit is within S393B ITEPA 2003 and specifically includes non-cash benefits.

Before 6 April 2006 there was a charge on contributions to a non-approved retirement benefit scheme under S386 ITEPA 2003. Any schemes that continue after 6 April 2006 will now be employer-financed retirement benefit schemes and there is no longer a charge arising on the individual in respect of contributions made after 6 April 2006. There are transitional provisions (paragraphs 53 to 55 Schedule 36 Finance Act 2004) to protect relief for tax paid under S386 ITEPA before 6 April 2006 where the lump sum is paid after 6 April 2006.

Advice Refer any problem to Pension Scheme Services, Yorke House, Castle Meadow Road, Nottingham NG2 1BG

Action Inform HMRC Capital Taxes, Technical Group, Meldrum House, Drumsheugh Gardens, Edinburgh where a member of a FURBS/EFRBS has died, giving full name and date of death.

National Insurance contributions (NICs) position up to and including 5 April 2006

For information about the NICs position on:

an employer's payment into a FURBS; see NIM02157 – NIM02160 SCS106/04 and Newsboard Message 740/05 (which is available via the 'Information Store' on the PAYE, SA and NICs Intranet site); and

payments out of a FURBS, see NIM02161

For advice, contact your PAYE, SA and NICs Technical Newcastle

National Insurance contributions (NICs) position from 6 April 2006

For information about the NICs position on:

an employer's payment into an EFRBS on or after 6 April 2006 see NIM02757; and

a payment out of a EFRBS see NIM02760 (contents)

For advice, contact PAYE, SA and NICs Technical, Newcastle

Disclosure of Tax Avoidance Schemes and AAG Intranet

Employee benefit trusts are often used to facilitate avoidance of PAYE/NI and CT liabilities. The disclosure of tax avoidance schemes introduced on 18 April 2004 requires promoters of schemes subject to the regulations to disclose them to AAG (Disclosure and Risk) within 5 days of their being made available to prospective user. Users of disclosed schemes are identified through notification of an 8 digit Schemes Reference Number (SRN) issued by the AAG. In most instances this is reported direct to the AAG who inform the Lead Office responsible for co-ordinating enquiries. However some employers report the SRN on their CTSA Return or within computations. If you identify an SRN please refer to the Disclosed Scheme pages of the AAG Intranet site, click on the SRN, and follow the advice given. The Current Schemes page also contains details of known employee benefit trust schemes and advice on action to be taken.'

Additionally, the HMRC website contains the following table:

Circumstances	Payments made by an employer to an employer-financed retirement benefits scheme
Class 1 NICs	No
PAYE	No
Enter on P11D	No
Class 1A NICs	No
Enter on P9D	No
Further information	NIM02757 and EIM15040

Form NRT40

15.13 TSEM5355 [Trusts for particular purposes: employment – related trusts – summary for FURBS/EFRBS – non-resident trustees (NRT40)] contains the following extract:

'Contributions

Guidance on whether the contributions into the scheme are allowable is at IM8410 onwards.

S76 FA 1989 deals with the timing of any deductions due (see IM8412).

The employer's contributions are allowable only if they are chargeable as employment or pension income on the member or another person. Where due, a deduction is given for the period in which the employer makes the contribution (S76 (4)). This ensures the payer's relief matches the employee's charge as to both time and amount.

If you cannot resolve a problem about this, refer the case to CT and VAT (Trading and Property Income Team).

However, please note that as non-resident trustees act, there may be tax avoidance opportunities if a company is 'close' and a participator with a significant interest in the company is the member. You may want to consider whether amounts put into the scheme by the employer are commensurate with a normal commercial provision for the employee concerned. Submit the file for the employer to CAR Residency if a trading deduction has been successfully denied because the contribution has not been wholly and exclusively expended for the purposes of the employer's trade.'

TSEM5355 contains the following extract:

'Pensions

Treat pensions that the trustees pay as chargeable as pension income by virtue of s 569 ITEPA 2003 (because of s 393(2) ITEPA 2003).

Refer any problem to PAYE, SA and NICs Group, Employment Income (Technical), Solihull.

Lump sum, gratuity or other benefit

S394 ITEPA 2003 deals with lump sum gratuities and other benefits that trustees pay. A benefit will be chargeable if it is a relevant benefit within the definition at S393B ITEPA 2003. Where the employee has contributed to the provision of the lump sum the charge may be reduced as set out in S395 ITEPA 2003. It should be noted that up until 5 April 2006 the view taken by HMRC was that non-cash benefits were not within the definition of relevant benefits. From 6 April 2006 the definition of a relevant benefit is within S393B ITEPA 2003 and specifically includes non-cash benefits.

Before 6 April 2006 there was a charge on contributions to a non-approved retirement benefit scheme under S386 ITEPA 2003. Any schemes that continue after 6 April 2006 will now be employer-financed retirement benefit schemes and there is no longer a charge arising on the individual in respect of contributions made after 6 April 2006. There are transitional provisions (paragraphs 53 to 55, Schedule 36 Finance Act 2004) to protect relief for tax paid under S386 ITEPA before 6 April 2006 and where the lump sum is paid after 6 April 2006.'

For information about the NICs position on:

– an employer's payment into a FURBS, see NIM02157 – NIM02160, SCS106/04 and Newsboard Message 740/05 (which is available via the 'Information Store' on the PAYE, SA and NICs Intranet site); and

– payments out of a FURBS, see NIM02161

For advice, contact PAYE, SA and NICs Technical, Newcastle

For information about the NICs position on:

– an employer's payment into an EFRBS on or after 6 April 2006, see NIM02757 and

– a payment out of a EFRBS see NIM02760 (contents)

– For advice, contact PAYE, SA and NICs Technical, Newcastle.'

Foreign pensions

15.14   The *Income Tax (Earnings and Pensions) Act 2, s 573*, applies to any pension paid by or on behalf of a person who is outside the UK to a person who is resident in the UK (**EIM74001**).

Section 574 extends the charge under *s 573* to a pension that is paid voluntarily or is capable of being discontinued if the following conditions are met:.

● the pension is paid to a former employee or office holder or to their widow, widower, child, relative or dependant;

● the payment is paid by or on behalf of the person who employed the former employee (or the person under whom the office was held) or by the successors of that person.

Section 575, ITEPA 2003 provides that the taxable amount of a foreign pension is 90% of the actual amount arising in the tax year unless the income is charged on the remittance basis. As foreign pensions are treated as 'relevant foreign income, there is provision for claims to remittance basis, deductions and reliefs and unremittable income.

HMRCs tax guide IR20 is currently being revised.

Extra-statutory concession A10

15.15   This concession is designed to allow exemption on lump sum relevant benefits in like manner to that of exemption or relief for foreign service, under the *Income Tax (Earnings and Pensions) Act 2, s 401*, covering lump sums and commutation options received under the rules of such schemes.

If the employee has served abroad in the relevant employment, charges, if any, under *s 394*, are reduced or eliminated under this concession.

The wording of the concession is as follows:

'Income tax is not charged on lump sum relevant benefits receivable by an employee (or by his personal representatives or any dependant of his) from an Overseas Retirement Benefits Scheme or an Overseas Provident Fund where the employee's overseas service comprises:

(*a*)   not less than 75 % of his total service in that employment; or

(*b*)   the whole of the last 10 years of his service in that employment, where total service exceeds 10 years; or

(*c*)   not less than 50 % of his total service in that employment, including any 10 of the last 20 years, where total service exceeds 20 years.

If the employee's overseas service is less than described above, relief from income tax will be given by reducing the amount of the lump sum which would otherwise be chargeable by the same proportion as the overseas service bears to the employee's total service in that employment.

In addition, income tax is not charged on lump sum relevant benefits receivable by an employee (or by his personal representatives or any dependant of his) from any superannuation fund accepted as being within *s 615, ICTA 1988*.

For the purposes of this concession, the term 'relevant benefits' has the meaning given in *s 612(1), ICTA 1988* and the term 'overseas service' shall be construed in accordance with the definition of 'foreign service' found at *para 10, Sch 11, ICTA 1988*.'

A period of service falling after 5 April 2003 is foreign service if either the earnings from the employment are **not** general earnings to which *s 15* or *s 21, ITEPA 2003*, apply. This will be the case where:

– the employee is **not** resident and ordinarily resident in the UK. So for example if the employee is not resident, neither *s 15* nor *s 21* apply so during that period the employee's service is foreign service; or

– the employee is resident and ordinarily resident in the UK but is not domiciled in the UK, is working for a foreign employer and is carrying out all the duties of the employment outside the UK; **or**

– the employee is a seafarer eligible for 100% deduction from earnings under *Pt 5, Ch 6, ITEPA 2003*.

If there is a period of service when there are no earnings from the employment, it is possible to apply the above rules in the same way as if there were.'

The concession is to be interpreted in the following ways for the post A-Day tax legislation:

●   'overseas retirement benefits scheme' and 'overseas provident fund' are interpreted as overseas employer-financed retirement benefits schemes, as defined in the *Income Tax (Earnings and Pensions) Act 2003, s 393A*;

- The concession continues to apply to lump sums received from schemes within the *Income and Corporation Taxes Act, s 615(6)*;

- 'relevant benefits' are as defined in accordance with the *Income Tax (Earnings and Pensions) Act 2003, s 393B*;

- the concession does not apply to any benefits chargeable under *Finance Act 2004, Sch 34*.

The *Finance Act 2004, s 249* and *Sch 35*, contains various legislative amendments relating to the taxation of non-pension benefits from funded unapproved schemes.

Old Code Schemes

15.16 Any remaining *Income and Corporation Taxes Act, s 608*, schemes fell under the new tax regime at A-Day unless they chose to opt out. As such the annual allowance and the lifetime allowance will have applied from A-Day. If such schemes chose to opt out they will be treated in the same way as non-registered schemes. By way of an alternative, *s 608* schemes (as revised by the *Income Tax (Earnings and Pensions) Act 2003, s 394*) could have chosen to wind up if their rules so permitted, commuting all benefits to a lump sum with a 25% tax free element. However, this option was only available for the first year following A-Day.

The main features of the pre A-Day tax regime

CONTINUED RIGHTS

A large number of differing tax regimes were in place before A-Day. The most significant changes, and complications, were introduced in 1987 and 1989, under the *Finance (No 2) Act 1987* as regards (principally) pension and lump sum accrual, and the *Finance Act 1989 (FA 1989)* as regards (principally) the application of the earnings cap for pension purposes.

In order to protect the interests of existing member entitlements at the dates of change, transitional protection was given in the form of protected rights. The different member classifications which existed were generally referred to as follows:

(a) 'Pre 1987 continued rights members';

(b) '1987 continued rights members'; and

(c) '1989 members';

Controlling directors

Special restrictions were placed on the calculation and payment of pension benefits for controlling directors, who were more closely regulated than those of other members. A controlling director was, broadly, a director who alone or with a number of associates (eg close family members or family trusts) owns or controls 20% or more of the ordinary share capital of the employer company.

Final remuneration

The definition of final remuneration was a key feature of the pre A-Day means of testing benefits against HMRC limits. The main meaning is summarised below:

Final remuneration could be no greater than either:

(a) the highest remuneration for any one of the five years prior to cessation of pensionable service, comprising basic pay for that year plus a three or more year average of fluctuating emoluments (unless received for a shorter period for averaging purposes) expiring at the end of that year. Such fluctuating earnings could include profit-related pay (whether or not relieved from tax), benefits in kind, overtime, bonuses and commissions etc. which were assessable to income tax under Sch E. They could be increased by the rise in RPI to the end of the basic pay year;

(b)   the yearly average of total emoluments for any three or more consecutive years ending not more than ten years before cessation of pensionable service;

Provided that:

- 'golden handshakes' and income from share options/gains etc. (except where the shares or rights were obtained before 17 March 1987) were excluded;

- method (b) had to apply to controlling directors, not method (a);

- method (b) would apply to employees whose income exceeded £100,000 in any year subsequent to 5 April 1987, unless the employee chose a figure of £100,000 to apply;

- final remuneration or other remuneration which related to a year other than the last year in pensionable service could be increased by the rise in RPI to the date of cessation of service, except that any increase given on benefits for pre-1987 continued rights members had always to be applied to the aggregate total benefits;

- final remuneration should not exceed the earnings cap other than for pre-1987 continued rights members or 1987 continued rights members;

- the final remuneration to be used for the purpose of calculating the maximum lump sum for a 1987 continued rights member should not exceed £100,000;

- a member in receipt of much reduced income due to incapacity lasting more than ten years prior to his cessation of pensionable service could have final remuneration calculated under (a) or (b) above as at the cessation of normal pay and increased in line with RPI to the date of cessation of pensionable service;

- an early retirement pension payable by the employer was excluded from final remuneration;

- there was a concession in the method of calculation of remuneration for the 4 × lump sum death benefit described above. Any one of the following methods could be used:

  - the annual basic rate of pay at date of death;

  - method (a) above, plus a three year average of fluctuating emoluments to date of death;

  - the total emoluments, including fluctuating emoluments, paid in any twelve months in the three years prior to date of death.

Full commutation

Full commutation of pension was permitted where the aggregate value of pension benefits was 'trivial' (ie did not exceed £260 pa) and accorded with both the preservation requirements and the contracting-out requirements. Protected rights could not be commuted into lump sum form.

Full commutation of pension was also permitted in exceptional circumstances of serious ill-health, where the member's expectation of life was 'unquestionably very short'. A tax charge arose on excess monies over basic limits.

Retained benefits

Schemes which provided benefits in excess of 1/60ths × final pensionable salary × years of service, had to take retained benefits from other approved schemes into account in testing against the permitted maximum benefits.

Small self-administered schemes and self-invested personal pension schemes (SSASs and SIPPS)

Special restrictions were placed on the permitted investment rules as applied to SSASs and SIPPS. HMRC also required a pensioneer trustee to be in place at all times in order to ensure compliance with the governing rules.

Pre 1987 continued rights members

Maximum pension

The maximum rate of pension build-up was in accordance with the table set out below:

Years of service completed before normal retirement date	Maximum pension fraction of final remuneration
1–5	1/60th for each year
6	8/60ths
7	16/60ths
8	24/60ths
9	32/60ths
10 or more	40/60ths

For such members, immediate pension benefits could be taken on or after normal retirement date (NRD) even where the member remained in service, but, generally, scheme rules would require pensions to be taken not later than age 75. A retirement pension under an approved scheme could not normally come into payment before actual retirement or leaving service.

Maximum lump sum

As with pension, commutation could either be on a basic or on an accelerated scale. The basic scale was 3/80ths of a member's final remuneration for each year of service up to a maximum of 40. Accordingly, the maximum commutation permitted after 40 years on the basic scale was 1.5 × final pensionable pay. An enhanced scale was permitted over 20 years (with lesser

broadly proportionate amounts for service of less than 20 years), when again
commutation of 1.5 × final remuneration was permitted:

Years of service to NRD	80ths of final remuneration
1–8	3 for each year
9	30
10	36
11	42
12	48
13	54
14	63
15	72
16	81
17	90
18	99
19	108
20 or more	120

Leaving service

A deferred pension equal to the ordinary early retirement pension based on
final remuneration at date of leaving service and revalued in deferment. This
was commutable within normal limits on retirement.

Early retirement

In accordance with HMRC's practice on discretionary approval, retirement on
pension was permitted at any time after age 50.

A ratio of completed service to potential service was applied, calculated in
accordance with the following formula:

$$N/NS \times P$$

where:

> P is the maximum pension approvable based on the employee's service
> to normal retirement date based on final remuneration to the date of
> retirement;

> N is the number of years of actual service completed, with a maximum
> of 40 years;

> NS is the number of years actually completed plus the number of years
> of potential service to normal retirement date, again limited to 40.

The maximum pension available was the maximum fraction of final
remuneration which the employee could have attained had he remained in

service until normal retirement date, but based on his final remuneration as at the date of leaving service.

Late retirement

Scheme rules could make provision for pension and lump sum benefits to continue to accrue in respect of pensionable service after normal retirement date. Pensionable service completed after normal retirement date could count to the actual date of retirement, and actuarial increases or increases in proportion to the rise in the cost of living were available. However, where the employee had less than 40 years' service, a pension of no more than two-thirds of final remuneration at the date of actual retirement was permitted. Where the employee had more than 40 years' service, an additional five years of pensionable service could be earned, giving a total pension of 45/60ths for an employee with 45 years' pensionable service.

Death-in-service cash sum

4 × final remuneration, or actual remuneration plus a refund of employee's contributions (with interest).

Death-in-service pension

2/3 × the maximum potential pension which could have been provided for the member at normal retirement date. This could be paid to a surviving spouse. In addition, pensions could be paid to the dependants of the member. The maximum aggregate benefit payable to a surviving spouse and dependants, or all dependants, was the member's own maximum pension as described above. In the absence of a surviving spouse the maximum pension payable to one dependant is the same as may be paid to a surviving spouse.

Death after retirement pension

2/3 × the maximum pension which could have been provided for the member at actual retirement, increased in line with RPI (no commuted lump sum was available). This could be paid to the surviving spouse. In addition to this benefit, or a lesser amount of benefit, pensions could be paid to the dependants of the member. The maximum aggregate benefit payable to a surviving spouse and dependants, or all dependants, was the member's own maximum pension as described above. In the absence of a surviving spouse the maximum pension payable to one dependant was the same as could be paid to a surviving spouse.

AVCs

The additional benefits purchased had to be paid in pension form, except that a commutation lump sum could be paid (subject to the overall limits) if the employee had entered into the AVC arrangement prior to 8 April 1987.

Surplus AVCs could be repaid to the employee after tax had been deducted which equated to a tax credit at the basic rate only.

1987 continued rights members

Maximum pension

The maximum rate of pension build-up was 1/30th of final remuneration for each year of pensionable service up to a maximum of 20 years. Accordingly, a pension of two-thirds of final remuneration could only be built up over 20 years as opposed to 10 for a pre 1987 continued rights member.

Maximum lump sum

Additional restrictions were imposed in order to peg the maximum rate of permitted accelerated accrual to the maximum permitted rate of accrual for pension purposes, again over a maximum 20-year period as follows:

(a)   if the member's pension benefits were calculated on an N/60ths basis, there could be no enhanced lump sum and the member would be entitled only to a basic-rate lump sum, ie of 3/80ths of final remuneration for each year of service up to a maximum of 40;

(b)   if there was an enhanced pension entitlement (limited to 1/30th of final remuneration for each year of pensionable service up to a maximum of 20), one took the percentage difference between the basic and the maximum permitted rate of pension accrual. The basic lump sum entitlement on the 3N/80ths basis was then increased by that same percentage.

Remuneration in excess of the 'permitted maximum', which for such members was £100,000, could not be brought into account in determining the maximum lump sum which could be produced by commutation.

Leaving service

Scheme rules could make similar provision for a deferred pension to be paid as applied to pre 1987 continued rights members.

Early retirement

Scheme rules could make similar provision for pension and lump sum benefits to be paid before normal retirement date as applied to pre 1987 continued rights members.

Late retirement

Scheme rules could make similar provision for pension and lump sum benefits to continue to accrue as applied to pre 1987 continued rights members.

Death-in-service cash sum

4 × final remuneration, or actual remuneration plus a refund of employee's contributions (with interest).

Death-in-service pension

Scheme rules could make similar provision for pension as applied to pre 1987 continued rights members.

Death after retirement pension

Scheme rules could make similar provision for benefits as applied to pre 1987 continued rights members.

AVCs

Scheme rules could make similar provision for AVCs as applied to pre 1987 continued rights members.

1989 members

Maximum pension

2/3 × final remuneration after 20 years' service. If service was less than twenty years, 1/30 × final remuneration for each year of service.

Maximum lump sum

Further lump sum restrictions applied to limit the permitted accelerated rate of commutation. They applied to members who joined a scheme established before 14 March 1989 on or after 1 June 1989 and to all members of schemes established after 14 March 1989. For such members, the permitted basis of commutation was 3/80ths for each year of pensionable service or a higher alternative maximum of 2 ¼ × the initial pension payable under the scheme. This initial pension was the pre-commutation pension payable for the first year (including pension arising from additional voluntary contributions), ignoring changes in that year and on the assumption that the employee would survive for that year, ignoring also any surrender of pension to provide benefits for survivors.

Scheme rules could make provision for pension and lump sum benefits to continue to accrue in respect of pensionable service after normal retirement date ie deferred benefits. Where a member was entitled to continued rights (meaning pre-17 March 1987 or pre-1 June 1989 continued rights), pensionable service completed after normal retirement date could count to the actual date of retirement, and actuarial increases or increases in proportion to the rise in the cost of living were available. However, where the employee had less than 40 years' service, a pension of no more than two-thirds of final remuneration at the date of actual retirement was permitted. Where the

247

employee had more than 40 years' service, an additional five years of pensionable service could be earned, giving a total pension of 45/60ths for an employee with 45 years' pensionable service.

Leaving service

The permitted benefits were:

(a)　a deferred pension equal to the ordinary early retirement pension based on final remuneration at date of leaving service and revalued in deferment;

(b)　a deferred lump sum of 2 ¼ × initial annual rate of actual pension (before commutation or allocation).

Early retirement benefits

The permitted benefits were:

(a)　a pension of 1/30 × final remuneration × years of service, subject to a maximum pension of 2/3 × final remuneration;

(b)　a lump sum of 2 ¼ × initial annual rate of actual pension (before commutation or allocation).

Late retirement

The position was as follows:

(a)　maximum pension could not exceed 1/30th of final pensionable pay for each year of pensionable service to a maximum of 20 years, with the date of actual retirement being substituted for normal retirement date;

(b)　benefits had to commence payment prior to age 75. No part of any pension benefit (pension or lump sum) could be paid before actual retirement or leaving service except guaranteed minimum pensions which had to be payable at state pension age subject to permitted deferral in the case of a late retiree remaining in pensionable service.

Death-in-service cash sum

4 × final remuneration, or actual remuneration plus a refund of employee's contributions (with interest).

Death-in-service pension

Scheme rules could make similar provision for pension as applied to pre 1987 continued rights members.

Scheme rules could make similar provision for benefits as applied to pre 1987 continued rights members.

The main regulations and orders which apply to the current tax regime

- the Employer-Financed Retirement Benefits (Excluded Benefits for Tax Purposes) Regulations 2006 (SI 2006/210);

- the Employer-Financed Retirement Benefits (Excluded Benefits for Tax Purposes) Regulations 2007 (SI 2007/3537);

- the Employer-Financed Retirement Benefits Schemes (Provision of Information) Regulations 2005 (SI 2005/3453);

- the Finance (No 2) Act 2005, Section 45 (Appointed Day) Order 2005 (SI 2005/3337);

- the Pension Benefits (Insurance Company Liable as Scheme Administrator) Regulations 2006 (SI 2006/136);

- the Pension Protection Fund (Tax) (2005–06) Regulations 2005 (SI 2005/1907);

- the Pension Protection Fund (Tax) Regulations 2006 (SI 2006/575);

- the Pensions Schemes (Application of UK Provisions to Relevant Non-UK Schemes) Regulations 2006 (SI 2006/207);

- the Pension Schemes (Categories of Country and Requirements for Overseas Pension Schemes and Recognised Overseas Pension Schemes) Regulations 2006 (SI 2006/206);

- the Pension Schemes (Categories of Country and Requirements for Overseas Pension Schemes and Recognised Overseas Pension Schemes) (Amendment) Regulations 2007 (SI 2007/1600);

- the Pension Schemes (Information Requirements – Qualifying Overseas Pension Schemes, Qualifying Recognised Overseas Pension Schemes and Corresponding Relief) Regulations 2006 (SI 2006/208);

- the Pension Schemes (Reduction in Pension Rates) Regulations 2006 (SI 2006/138);

- the Pension Schemes (Relevant Migrant Members) Regulations 2006 (SI 2006/212);

- the Registered Pension Schemes (Accounting and Assessment) Regulations 2005 (SI 2005/3454);

- the Registered Pension Schemes (Authorised Surplus Payments) Regulations 2006 (SI 2006/574);

- the Registered Pension Schemes and Employer-Financed Retirement Benefits Schemes (Information) (Prescribed Descriptions of Persons) Regulations 2005 (SI 2005/3455);

- the Registered Pension Schemes and Overseas Pension Schemes (Electronic Communication of Returns and Information) Regulations 2006 (SI 2006/570);

- the Registered Pension Schemes (Authorised Member Payments) Regulations 2006 (SI 2006/137) for demutualisation of insurance companies and members of qualifying pension schemes;

- the Registered Pension Schemes (Authorised Member Payments) (No 2) Regulations 2006 (SI 2006/571);

- the Registered Pension Schemes (Authorised Member Payments) Regulations 2007 (SI 2007/3532);

- the Registered Pension Schemes (Authorised Payments) Regulations 2006 (SI 2006/209);

- the Registered Pension Schemes (Authorised Payments – Arrears of Pension) Regulations 2006 (SI 2006/614);

- the Registered Pension Schemes (Authorised Payments) (Transfers to the Pension Protection Fund) Regulations 2006 (SI 2006/134);

- the Registered Pension Schemes (Audited Accounts) (Specified Persons) Regulations 2005 (SI 2005/3456);

- the Registered Pension Schemes (Block Transfers) (Permitted Membership Period) Regulations 2006 (SI 2006/498);

- the Registered Pension Schemes (Block Transfers) (Permitted Membership Period) (Amendment) Regulations 2007 (SI 2007/838);

- the Registered Pension Schemes (Bridging Pensions) Regulations 2007 (SI 2007/826);

- the Registered Pension Schemes (Co-ownership of Living Accommodation) Regulations 2006 (SI 2006/133);

- the Registered Pension Schemes (Defined Benefits Arrangements and Money Purchase Arrangements – Uprating) Regulations 2005;

- the Registered Pension Schemes (Discharge of Liabilities under Sections 267 and 268 of the Finance Act 2004 Regulations 2005 (SI 2005/3452);

- the Registered Pension Schemes (Enhanced Lifetime Allowance) Regulations 2006 (SI 2006/131);

- the Registered Pension Schemes (Enhanced Lifetime Allowance) (Amendment) Regulations 2006 (SI 2006/3261);

- the Registered Pension Schemes (Meaning of Pension Commencement Lump Sum) Regulations 2006 (SI 2006/135);

- the Registered Pension Schemes (Meaning of Pension Commencement Lump Sum) (Amendment) Regulations 2007 (SI 2007/3533);

- the Registered Pension Schemes (Minimum Contributions) Regulations 2005 (SI 2005/3450);

- the Registered Pension Schemes (Modification of the Rules of Existing Schemes) Regulations 2006 (SI 2006/364);

- the Registered Pension Schemes (Prescribed Interest Rates for Authorised Employer Loans) Regulations 2005 (SI 2005/3449);

- the Registered Pension Schemes (Prescribed Manner of Determining Amount of Annuities) Regulations 2006 (SI 2006/568);

- the Registered Pension Schemes (Prescribed Schemes and Occupations) Regulations 2005 (SI 2005/3451);

- the Registered Pension Schemes (Provision of Information) Regulations 2006 (SI 2006/567);

- the Registered Pension Schemes (Relevant Annuities) Regulations 2006 (SI 2006/129);

- the Registered Pension Schemes (Relief at Source) Regulations 2005 (SI 2005/3448);

- the Registered Pension Schemes (Restriction of Employer's Relief) Regulations 2005 (SI 2005/3548);

- the Registered Pension Schemes (Splitting of Schemes) Regulations 2006 (SI 2006/569);

- the Registered Pension Schemes (Splitting of Schemes) (Amendment) Regulations 2007 (SI 2007/793);

- the Registered Pension Schemes (Standard Lifetime and Annual Allowances) Order 2007 (SI 2007/494);

- the Registered Pension Schemes (Surrender of Relevant Excess) Regulations 2006 (SI 2006/211);

- the Registered Pension Schemes (Transfer of Sums and Assets) (Amendment) Regulations 2008 (SI 2008/1946);

- the Registered Pension Schemes (Unauthorised Payments by Existing Schemes) Regulations 2006 (SI 2006/365);

- the Registered Pension Schemes (Uprating Percentages for Defined Benefits Arrangements and Enhanced Protection Limits) 2006 (SI 2006/130);

- the Tax and Civil Partnership Regulations (SI 2007/493);

- the Taxation of Pension Schemes (Consequential Amendments of Occupational and Personal Pension Schemes Legislation) Order 2006 (SI 2006/744);

Appendix 2 *The main regulations and orders*

- the Taxation of Pension Schemes (Protected Rights and Pension Commencement Lump Sums) (Amendment) Regulations 2007 (SI 2007/829);

- the Taxation of Pension Schemes (Transitional Provisions) Order 2006 (SI 2006/572);

- the Taxes Management Act (Modifications to Schedule 3 for Pension Scheme Appeals) Order 2005 (SI 2005/3457).

HMRC Forms and Registration Procedure

MAIN FORMS:

- Registration for tax relief and exemptions
- Registration for relief at source
- Contracting out (Industry wide schemes)
- Contracting out (other schemes)
- Event report
- Accounting for tax return
- Registered pension scheme return
- Protection of existing rights
- Enhanced lifetime allowance (pension credit rights)
- Enhanced lifetime allowance (international)
- Declare as a scheme administrator of a deferred annuity contract

MAINTENANCE FORMS:

- Cessation of scheme administrator
- Pre-register as a scheme administrator
- Notify scheme administrator details
- Change of scheme administrator/practitioner details
- Authorising a practitioner
- Add scheme administrator
- Amend scheme details

HMRC published the following guide to procedures, entitled 'What can be done at A-Day?'. This remains a helpful checklist. Most of the actions are now available, and should be completed, online.

Action	Online Form Name	Online form available at A-Day	Who can submit the form online?	Paper Form Name and Number	Paper form available at A-Day	Who can sign the paper form?	Anything else?
1 Use Pension Schemes Online							
Register to use Pension Schemes Online:							
a) Pre-register to obtain an Activation Token and Scheme Administrator/ Practitioner ID.	Register new user	Yes	Only the Scheme Administrator or Practitioner can pre-register themselves	Pre-register as a Scheme Administration Practitioner APSS 161	Yes	Only the Scheme Administrator or Practitioner pre-registering	
b) Complete registration for the online service.	Register new user	Yes	Only the Scheme Administrator or Practitioner can complete registration	Not applicable	No	Not applicable	This can only be done online as it requires the user registering to create their password
2. Scheme Registration							
Register a new scheme for tax relief and exemptions	Register a new pension scheme	Yes	Scheme Administrator	Pension Scheme Tax Registration APSS 100	Yes	Scheme Administrator	
Elect to contract out of state second pension	Elect to contract out	No	Scheme Administrator or Practitioner	Registered Pension Schemes-Election to Contract-out APSS 101	Yes	Employer, trustee or person responsible for the day to day management of the scheme	

Elect to contract out of state second pension by industry wide scheme	Elect to contract out	Proposed release Autumn 06	Scheme Administrator or Practitioner	Registered Pension Schemes-Election to Contract-out for industry wide schemes APSS 102	Yes	Employer, trustee or person responsible for the day to day management of the scheme	
Register to operate relief at source or amend relief at source details	Register for Relief at Source or Amend Relief at Source	No Proposed release Autumn 06	Scheme Administrator or Practitioner	Relief at Source Details APSS 103	Yes	Scheme Administrator or Practitioner	
Send specimen signature(s) authorised to sign repayment claims	Not applicable	No	Not applicable	Relief at Source specimen signatures APSS 103A	Yes	Those authorised to sign repayments of tax relief at source on contributions to registered pension scheme	This form is optional for providing samples of authorised signatures.
Complete single registration form, to register for tax relief and exemptions, elect to contract-out and register to operate at tax relief at source	Register a new scheme	No Proposed release Autumn 06	Scheme Administrator	Pension Scheme Registration APSS 100A	Yes	Scheme Administrator	

Appendix 3 *HMRC Forms and Registration Procedure*

Action	Online Form Name	Online form available at A-Day	Who can submit the form online?	Paper Form Name and Number	Paper form available at A-Day	Who can sign the paper form?	Anything else?
Make your declaration as required under Section 270 Finance Act 2004 as the Scheme Administrator of a deferred annuity contract made on or after A-Day	Declare as Scheme Administrator for a deferred annuity contract	Yes	Scheme Administrator	Declaration as a Scheme Administrator of a Deferred Annuity Contract scheme APSS 108	Yes	Scheme Administrator	This is only used for deferred annuity contracts made on or after A-day
3. Scheme Administer/Practitioner Maintenance							
Amend your details provided at pre-registration for Pension Schemes Online (see 1 above)	View or amend your details	Yes	Scheme Administrator or Practitioner whose details are being amended	Change of Scheme Administrator or Practitioner user details APSS 153	Yes	The Scheme Administrator or Practitioner whose details are being amended	
4. Scheme Maintenance							
Amend the scheme name or the establisher/sponsor details of client reference	Amend Scheme Details	No Proposed release Autumn 06	Scheme Administrator or Practitioner	Amend Scheme details APSS 152	Yes	Scheme Administrator or Practitioner	
Amend contracting-out details	Not applicable	No	Not applicable	Contracting-out Maintenance APSS 155	Yes	Employer, trustee or person responsible for the day to day management of the scheme	

	Practitioner Management	Yes	Scheme Administrator	Authorising a Practitioner APSS 150	Yes	Scheme Administrator	
Scheme Administrator of a pension scheme wishes to authorise HM Revenue & Customs (HMRC) to deal with a Practitioner acting on their behalf							
(a) A Scheme Administrator who was the Administration of a scheme on 5 April 2006 wishes to have their details recorded on the pension scheme record, or	Add yourself as Scheme Administrator	Yes	Scheme Administrator	Add Scheme Administrator to a scheme APSS 151	Yes	Scheme Administrator	If the scheme record held by HMRC already shows a Scheme Administrator the known Scheme Administrator will need to associate the new/additional Scheme Administrator before this form can be processed (see below)

Action	Online Form Name	Online form available at A-Day	Who can submit the form online?	Paper Form Name and Number	Paper form available at A-Day	Who can sign the paper form?	Anything else?
(b) A Scheme Administrator who is appointed on or after A-Day (other than the Scheme Administrator of a new deferred annuity contract made on or after A-Day) should make their declaration as required under Section 270 Finance Act 2004							
The Scheme Administrator recorded against the HMRC record for the pension scheme needs to advise HMRC there is a new/additional Scheme Administrator for the scheme.	Scheme Administrator Management	Yes	Scheme Administrator recorded on the HMRC record for the scheme	Associate Scheme Administrator to scheme APSS 154	Yes	Scheme Administrator recorded on the HMRC record for the scheme	

This is to allow the new/additional Scheme Administrator to add their details to the pension scheme record (this allows them to view pension scheme information) and make their declaration as required under Section 270 Finance Act 2004							
The appointment of a Scheme Administrator of a scheme is terminated they need to report the cessation to HMRC	Scheme Administrator Management	No Proposed release Summer 06	Scheme Administrator that ceased	Cessation of Scheme Administrator APSS 160	Yes	Scheme Administrator that ceased	

5. Reporting and returns

The scheme has wound up this has to be reported to HMRC or The scheme has wound up and there are other events to report to HMRC as well	Event Report	No Proposed release April 07	Scheme Administrator or Practitioner	Events Report APSS 300	Yes	Scheme Administrator	
Claim in-year repayment of tax relief deducted at source from contribution	Not applicable	No	Not applicable	Relief at Source – interim claim APSS 105	Yes	Authorised signatory	Formerly the PP10

Appendix 3 *HMRC Forms and Registration Procedure*

Action	Online Form Name	Online form available at A-Day	Who can submit the form online?	Paper Form Name and Number	Paper form available at A-Day	Who can sign the paper form?	Anything else?
Make annual claim for repayment of tax relief deducted at source from contributors	Not applicable	No	Not applicable	Relief at Source – annual claim APSS 106 (Not available until October 2006)	Yes	Authorised signatory	Formerly the PP14
Make annual statistical return	Not applicable	No	Not applicable	Relief at Source – annual statistical return APSS 107 (Not available until October 2006)	Yes and magnetic media	Authorised signatory	Formerly the PP14 (Stats)
6. Enhanced LTA							
Protection of existing rights – Notification for Primary Protection & Enhanced Protection	To be advised	No Release date to be agreed	Individual or agent	Protection of existing Rights APSS 200	Yes	Individual	Forms can be substituted from 6th April 06 to 5th April 09
Enhanced LTA (Pension credit rights)	To be advised	No Release date to be agreed	Individual or agent	Enhanced Lifetime Allowance (Pension Credit Rights) APSS 201	Yes	Individual	
Enhanced LTA (international)	To be advised	No Release date to be agreed Spring 07	Individual or agent	Enhanced Lifetime Allowance (International) APSS 201	Yes	Individual	
Authorise Scheme Administrator to view LTA Certificate	To be advised	No Release date to be agreed	Individual or agent	Authorise Scheme Administrator to view LTA Certificate APSS 203	Yes	Individual	

Request by Scheme Administrator to view LTA Certificate	To be advised	No Release date to be agreed	Scheme Administrator	Request by Scheme Administrator to view LTA Certificate APSS 209	Yes	Scheme Administrator
7. International						
Qualifying Overseas Pension Scheme (QOPS) Notification	Not applicable	No	Not applicable	Qualifying Overseas Pension Scheme (QOPS) APSS 250	Yes	Scheme manager
Qualifying Recognised Overseas Pension Scheme (QROPS) Notification	Not applicable	No	Not applicable	Qualifying Recognised Overseas Pension Scheme (QROPS) APSS 251	Yes	Scheme manager
Report of benefit crystallisation events	Not applicable	No	Not applicable	Report of benefit crystallisation events APSS 252	Yes	Scheme manager
Report of payments in respect of relevant members	Not applicable	No	Not applicable	Report of payments in respect of relevant members APSS 253	Yes	Scheme manager
Individual election for a deemed benefit of crystallisation event	Not applicable	No	Not applicable	Individual election for a deemed benefit of crystallisation event APSS 254	Yes	Individual

SCHEME ADMINISTRATOR/PRACTITIONER ID

In addition to being required to complete registration for Pension Schemes Online these ID's are used to ensure as far as is possible that information is recorded against the correct record. For this reason many of the forms ask for the Scheme Administrator/Practitioner ID to make the link to the record. It is therefore recommended that if you did not take part in the recent pre-registration exercise you pre-register for Pension Schemes Online (see 1a) in the table above) and obtain a Scheme Administrator/Practitioner ID. For online submissions your user ID and password are linked to your ID (but knowing the ID is not enough to view the record or make submissions. The user ID and password are needed).

RPSM20000000 – Glossary

A

Active member An individual who has benefits currently accruing for or in respect of that person under one or more arrangements in the pension scheme.

Active membership period The active membership period begins with the date on which benefits first began to accrue to or in respect of the individual under the **registered pension scheme** or, if later, 6 April 2006, and ends immediately before the benefit crystallisation event or, if earlier, the date on which benefits cease to accrue under the scheme.

Alternatively secured pension Payment of income withdrawals direct from a money purchase arrangement to the member of the arrangement (who is aged 75 or over) and that meet the conditions laid down in *paras 12 and 13* of *Sch 28* to the *Finance Act 2004*.

Alternatively secured pension fund Funds (whether sums or assets) held under a money purchase arrangement that have been 'designated' to provide a scheme member (who is aged 75 or over) with an alternatively secured pension, as identified in *para 11* of *Sch 28* to the *Finance Act 2004*. Once sums or assets have been 'designated' as part of an 'alternatively secured pension fund' any capital growth or income generated from such sums or assets are equally treated as being part of the 'alternatively secured pension fund'. Similarly, where assets are purchased at a later date from such funds, or 'sums' generated by the sale of assets held in such funds, those replacement assets or sums also fall as part of the 'alternatively secured pension fund' (as do any future growth or income generated by those assets or sums).

Annual allowance The annual allowance is such amount, not being less than the amount for the immediately preceding tax year, as is specified by order made by the Treasury.

Annual allowance charge A charge at the rate of 40% in respect of the amount by which the **total pension input amount** for a tax year in the case of an individual who is a member of one or more **registered pension schemes** exceeds the amount of the **annual allowance** for the tax year.

Annual amount

For the purposes of *Part 4* of the *Finance Act 2004* the annual amount of a **relevant annuity** is the rate of annual income which the tables published for this purpose by the Government Actuary's Department show as available if:-

(a) a **relevant annuity** were purchased by the application of the sums and assets representing the member's pension fund valued at the relevant date: and

(b) the purchaser were the same age and sex as the member or dependant.

Annuity protection lump sum death benefit

A lump sum benefit paid following the death of a scheme member who died before age 75 and was in receipt of a either a **lifetime annuity** or **scheme pension** under a **money purchase arrangement**, and which does not exceed the limits imposed through *para 16 Sch 29 Finance Act 2004*.

Appropriate date

The earlier of a nominated date falling in the tax year immediately after that in which the last pension input period ended, and the anniversary of the date on which the period ended.

Arm's length bargain

A normal commercial transaction between two or more persons

Arrangement

A contractual or trust-based arrangement made by or on behalf of a member of a pension scheme under that scheme. A member may have more than one arrangement under a scheme.

Authorised employer payment

Authorised employer payments are payments made to sponsoring employers or former sponsoring employers as follows:

public service scheme payments,

authorised surplus payments,

compensation payments,

authorised employer loans,

scheme administration employer payments, and

any other payment prescribed by Regulations.

Authorised member payment

Authorised member payments are made to a current or former member of a registered pension scheme and are:

pensions that comply with the pension rules in *s 165 Finance Act (FA) 2004* or the pension death benefit rules in *s 167 FA 2004* (current members only),

lump sum payments that comply with the lump sum rule in *s 166 FA 2004* or lump sum death benefit rule in *s 168 FA 2004* (current members only), recognised transfers that comply with *s 169 FA 2004* (current members only),

scheme administration member payments,

payments in accordance with a pension sharing order or provision, and

any other payment prescribed by Regulations.

Authorised open-ended investment company

A body incorporated by virtue of regulations under *s 262* of the *Financial Services and Markets Act 2000* in respect of which an authorisation order is in force under any provision made in such regulations by virtue of *subsection (2)(l)* of that section.

B

Bank

One of the following a person within *s 840A(1)(b)* of the *Income and Corporation Taxes Act 1988 (ICTA)* (persons other than building societies etc. permitted to accept deposits), or a body corporate which is a subsidiary or holding company of a person falling within *s 840A(1)(b)* of *ICTA* or is a subsidiary of the holding company of such a person (subsidiary and holding company having the meanings in *s 736* of the *Companies Act 1985* or *Article 4* of the *Companies (Northern Ireland) Order 1986).*

Basis amount

The basis amount is the base calculation for determining the maximum level of **unsecured pension** or **alternatively secured pension** (and the **dependant** equivalents) payable from a **money purchase arrangement**. The basis amount represents the **annual amount** of lifetime annuity (or **relevant annuity**) income the **unsecured pension fund** or **alternatively secured funds** (etc) could purchase at the initial calculation and review points.

BCE

Benefit crystallisation event

Benefit crystallisation event

Is a defined event or occurrence that triggers a test of the benefits 'crystallising' at that point against the individual's available **lifetime allowance**. There are eight such events.

Block transfer

The transfer in a single transaction of all the sums and assets held for the purposes of (or representing accrued rights under) the **arrangements** under the **pension scheme** from which the transfer is made, which relate to the member in question and at least one other member of that pension scheme. Before the transfer the member must not have already been a **member** of the registered pension scheme to which the transfer was made for longer than 12 months before the date of transfer. If the receiving scheme is a personal pension scheme any period of membership is ignored if the member's rights under the personal pension scheme were solely contracted out rights. To be a single transaction all of the sums and assets must be transferred from the transferring scheme to only one receiving scheme. Two or more partial transfers to two or more different schemes cannot be a transfer in a single transaction; and the transaction must be made under a single agreement for a single transfer between the two schemes. It is not necessary that all of the sums and assets are all physically passed from the transferring scheme to the receiving scheme on the same day – there may be legal or administration reasons why this is not possible. However they should all be transferred in relation to the agreement to transfer and within a reasonable timescale.

Building society   This means a building society within the *Building Societies Act 1986*.

C

Cash balance arrangement   A type of **money purchase arrangement**. An **arrangement** is a cash balance arrangement where the **member** will be provided with **money purchase benefits**, but where the amount that will be available to provide those benefits is not calculated purely by reference to payments made under the arrangement by or on behalf of the member. This means that in a cash balance arrangement, the capital amount available to provide benefits (the member's "pot") will not derive wholly from any actual contributions (or credits or transfers) made year on year.

For example, the scheme may promise that on retirement, a specified amount will be made available to provide the member with benefits for each year of pensionable service. The specified amount might be an absolute amount, eg £5,000 per year of service, or might be a percentage of the member's salary for each relevant year of service. Optionally, the scheme might also guarantee a rate of investment return on the specified amount. The member knows what will go into the promised pot each year (regardless of any contributions actually made) and so can ascertain the amount that accrues in that promised pot each year. It is possible that in a cash balance arrangement the promised pot builds up entirely notionally year by year, being funded only at the end. So, during the build-up phase, the amount in any actual fund held in respect of the member (whether more or less than the amount in the promised pot) is irrelevant. And when benefits ultimately become due, the amount in the promised pot is funded and it is that amount that is used to provide benefits.

In a cash balance arrangement, some of the investment and mortality risk is transferred to the scheme (or, if there is one, the employer); the fact that all or part of the pot is guaranteed or promised means that the promised amount must be made available to provide benefits irrespective of the level of actual funds held.

Chargeable amount

The amount that crystallises for **lifetime allowance** at a **benefit crystallisation event** that is not covered by an individual's available lifetime allowance at that time, plus any 'scheme-funded tax payment'. The chargeable amount is the amount on which the **lifetime allowance charge** arises.

Charity lump sum death benefit

A lump sum benefit paid from a **money purchase arrangement** to a charity (as defined in *s 506 Income and Corporation Taxes Act 1988*) following the death of a scheme member (or a **dependant** of such a member) who is aged 75 or over which meets the conditions of *para 18, Sch 29* to the *Finance Act 2004*. Such a lump sum cannot be paid where there is still a surviving **dependant** of the member.

D

Deferred member

An individual who has rights under a pension scheme and who is neither an active member, nor a pensioner member.

Defined benefits

Benefits provided under a **pension scheme** that are calculated by reference to earnings or service of the member or any other factor other than by reference to an amount available under the scheme for the provision of benefits to or in respect of that member (so which are not **money purchase** benefits).

Defined benefits arrangement

An **arrangement** other than a **money purchase arrangement** that provides only **defined benefits**. "Defined benefits" are calculated by reference to the earnings or the service of the **member**, or by any other means except by reference to an available amount for the provision of benefits to or in respect of the member, (thus making the definitions of money purchase and defined benefit arrangements mutually exclusive). A defined benefit arrangement is, typically, a 'final salary' scheme, that is, one where the level of benefits paid is calculated by reference to the member's final salary and length of service with the employer. Contributions are often made to such an arrangement, and so there may be a pension fund or pot, but the benefits that may be paid are not calculated by reference to that fund or pot.

267

Defined benefits lump sum death benefit	A lump sum benefit paid from a **defined benefits arrangement** following the death of the scheme member before the age of 75 (and within two years of that date of death), and as defined in *para 13, Sch 29* to the *Finance Act 2004*.
Dependant	A person who was married to, or a civil partner of, the member at the date of the member's death is a dependant of the member. A child of the member is a dependant of the member if the child has not reached the age of 23, or has reached age 23 and, in the opinion of the **scheme administrator**, was at the date of the member's death dependent on the member because of physical or mental impairment.

A person who was not married to the member or was not in a civil partnership with the member at the date of the member's death and is not a child of the member is a dependant of the member if, in the opinion of the **scheme administrator**, at the date of the member's death the person was financially dependant on the member, the person's financial relationship with the member was one of mutual dependence, or the person was dependant on the member because of physical or mental impairment. |
Dependants' alternatively secured pension	Payment of income withdrawals direct from a **money purchase arrangement** to a **dependant** of a scheme member who is aged 75 or over, that meets the conditions laid down in *paras 26* and *27* of *Sch 28* to the *Finance Act 2004*.
Dependants' alternatively secured pension fund	Funds (whether sums or assets) held under a **money purchase arrangement** that have been 'designated' after the death of a scheme member to provide a particular **dependant** of that member (who is aged 75 or over) with a **dependants' alternatively secured pension**, as identified in *para 25* of *Sch 28* to the *Finance Act 2004*. Once sums or assets have been 'designated' as part of a 'dependants' alternatively secured pension fund', any capital growth or income generated from such sums or assets are equally treated as being part of the 'dependants' alternatively secured pension fund'. Similarly, where assets are purchased at a later date from such funds, or 'sums' generated by the sale of assets held in such funds, those replacement assets or sums also fall as part of the 'dependants' alternatively secured pension fund' (as do any future growth or income generated by those assets or sums).
Dependants' annuity	An annuity paid by an **insurance company** to a **dependant** of a scheme member following the death of that member

that meets the conditions laid down in *para 17, Sch 28* to the *Finance Act 2004*.

Dependants' scheme pension
A pension paid to a **dependant** of a member of a **registered pension scheme** following the death of that member, the entitlement to which is an absolute entitlement under the scheme and that meets the conditions laid down in *para 16, Sch 28* to the *Finance Act 2004*.

Dependants' short-term annuity
An annuity contract purchased from a **dependants' unsecured pension fund** held under a **money purchase arrangement** that provides that **dependant** with an income for a term of no more than five years (not reaching to or beyond their 75th birthday), and which meets the conditions imposed through *para 20, Sch 28* to the *Finance Act 2004*. This definition covers replacement assets purchased after the initial 'designation' from such funds, or any capital growth from or income generated by assets held in the fund (whether held at the time of 'designation' or where replacement assets).

Dependants' unsecured pension
Payments of income withdrawals direct from **a money purchase arrangement**, or income paid from a **dependants' short-term annuity** contract purchased from such an **arrangement**, to a **dependant** (who is aged under 75) of the scheme member who established the **arrangement** and that meets the conditions laid down in *para 20* and *23–24* of *Sch 28* to the *Finance Act 2004*.

Dependants' unsecured pension fund
Funds (whether sums or assets) held under a money purchase arrangement that have been 'designated' after the death of a scheme member to provide a particular dependant of that member (who is aged under 75) with a dependants' unsecured pension, as identified in *para 22* of *Sch 28* to the *Finance Act 2004*. Once sums or assets have been 'designated' as part of a 'dependants' unsecured pension fund', any capital growth or income generated from such sums or assets are equally treated as being part of the 'dependants' unsecured pension fund'. Similarly, where assets are purchased at a later date from such funds, or 'sums' generated by the sale of assets held in such funds, those replacement assets or sums also fall as part of the 'dependants' unsecured pension fund' (as do any future growth or income generated by those assets or sums).

E

Employer-financed retirement benefits scheme
This means a scheme for the provision of benefits consisting of or including relevant benefits to or in respect of employees or former employees of an

employer. However, neither a registered pension scheme nor a *s 615(3)* scheme is an employer-financed retirement benefits scheme.

EU member state   Any of the following –

Austria, Belgium, Bulgaria, Czech Republic, Cyprus, Denmark, Estonia, Finland, France, Germany, Greece, Hungary, Ireland, Italy, Latvia, Lithuania, Luxembourg, Malta, Netherlands, Poland, Portugal, Romania, Slovakia, Slovenia, Spain, Sweden, United Kingdom.

European Economic Area (EEA) investment portfolio manager   This means an institution which is an EEA firm of the kind mentioned in *para 5(a)*, *(b)* or *(c)* of *Sch 3* to the *Financial Services and Markets Act 2000* (certain credit and financial institutions), or qualifies for authorisation under *para 12(1)* or *12(2)* of that Schedule, or has permission under the *Financial Services and Markets Act 2000* to manage portfolios of investments.

Ex-spouse   An individual to whom **pension credit** rights have been or are to be allocated following a **pension sharing order**, agreement or equivalent provision.

F

Former approved superannuation fund   Any fund which immediately before 6 April 1980 was an approved superannuation fund for the purposes of *s 208 Income and Corporation Taxes Act 1970*, that has not been approved for the purposes of *Chap 1 Pt 14 Income and Corporation Taxes Act 1988* since 5 April 1980, and has not received any contributions since 5 April 1980.

Former civil partner   An individual to whom **pension credit** rights have been or are to be allocated following a **pension sharing order**, agreement or equivalent provision.

FSAVCS   A **registered pension scheme** that was originally approved by the Board before 6 April 2006 as a retirement benefits scheme by virtue of *s 591(2)(h) Income and Corporation Taxes Act 1988*, established by a pension provider or the trustees of an approved centralised scheme for non-associated employers to which the employer does not contribute and which provides benefits additional to those provided by a scheme to which the employer does contribute.

G

GAD   The Government Actuary's Department.

GAD tables   The Government Actuary's Department Tables on a single life basis.

GMPs   Stands for guaranteed minimum pensions and has the same meaning as in the *Pension Schemes Act 1993*.

270

H

Hybrid arrangement

An **arrangement** where only one type of benefit will ultimately be provided, but the type of benefit that will be provided is not known in advance because it will depend on certain given circumstances at the point benefits are drawn.

For example, a hybrid arrangement may provide the member with **other money purchase benefits** based on a pot derived from the contributions that have accrued over time, but subject to a **defined benefit** minimum or underpin. If the benefits provided by the money purchase pot at the point benefits are drawn fall below a certain defined level, for example 1/60ths of final remuneration for every year worked, that higher defined benefit will be provided. So the benefits will be either other money purchase benefits, or defined benefits.

When benefits are drawn, if the benefits actually provided are other money purchase or **cash balance benefits** then the arrangement will become a **money purchase arrangement**. And if the benefits provided are defined benefits then the arrangement will become a **defined benefits arrangement**.

I

Insurance company

Either a person who has permission under *Part 4* of the *Financial Services and Markets Act 2000* to effect or carry out contracts of long-term insurance, or a European Economic Area (EEA) firm of the kind mentioned in *para 5(d)* of *Sch 3* to the *Financial Services and Markets Act 2000* (certain direct insurance undertakings) which has permission under *para 15* of that Schedule (as a result of qualifying for authorisation under *para 12* of that Schedule) to effect or carry out contracts of long-term insurance.

L

Lifetime allowance

The lifetime allowance is an overall ceiling on the amount of tax privileged pension savings that any one individual can draw. The exact figure will be whatever the 'standard lifetime allowance' for the tax year concerned is or a multiple of this figure where certain circumstances apply.

Lifetime allowance charge

A charge to income tax that arises on any chargeable amount generated at a 'benefit crystallisation event'. The rate of charge is either 25% or 55%, depending on whether the 'event' giving rise to the charge was the payment of a lump sum or not. The scheme administrator

271

and member are jointly liable to the charge, except where the chargeable amount arises following the death of the member. Here, the recipient of the payment giving rise to the charge is solely liable.

Lifetime allowance excess lump sum   A lump sum benefit paid to a member of a **registered pension scheme** (who is aged under 75) because they have used up their available **lifetime allowance**, and which meets the conditions of *para 11* of *Sch 29* to the *Finance Act 2004*.

Lifetime annuity   An annuity contract purchased under a **money purchase arrangement** from an **insurance company** of the member's choosing that provides the member with an income for life, and which meets the conditions imposed through *para 3, Sch 28* to the *Finance Act 2004*.

M

Market value   The market value of an asset held for the purposes of a pension scheme is to be determined in accordance with *s 272* of the *Taxation of Chargeable Gains Act 1992* and *s 278(2)–(4) Finance Act 2004* (where dealing with a right or interest in respect of money lent directly or indirectly to certain parties).

Member   An individual who is either an active member, a pensioner member, a deferred member or a pension credit member of a pension scheme.

Money purchase benefits   Benefits provided under a pension scheme, the rate or amount of which is calculated by reference to an amount available for the provision of benefits to or in respect of the member (whether the amount so available is calculated by reference to payments made under the scheme by the member or any other person or employer on behalf of the member, or any other factor).

Money purchase arrangement   An arrangement is a money purchase arrangement if, at that time, all the benefits that may be provided to or in respect of the member under the arrangement are cash balance or other money purchase benefits.

N

Nominated date   This means in the case of a **money purchase arrangement** other than a **cash balance arrangement**, such date as the individual or **scheme administrator** nominates, or in the case of any other arrangement, such date as the **scheme administrator** nominates.

Non-group life policy   A policy of insurance under which the only benefits which may become payable are benefits payable in consequence, or anticipation of:

the death of the individual or

the death of one of a group of individuals which includes the individual (e.g. a policy which covers a number of individuals but only pays a benefit out on the first death or last survivor' death) or

the deaths of more than one of a group of individuals (eg a policy which pays a benefit out on the death of each of the individuals)

where the group includes the individual, and

the other members of the group are connected with the individual in accordance with *s 195A(8) FA 2004*.

Normal minimum pension age	This is
	age 50 for the period before 6 April 2010
	age 55 on or after 6 April 2010.

O

Occupational pension scheme	A pension scheme established by an employer or employers and having (or capable of having) effect so as to provide benefits to or in respect of any or all of the employees of that employer or employers, or any other employer (whether or not it also has effect so as to provide benefits to or in respect of other persons, or is capable of having such effect).
Other money purchase arrangement	A **money purchase arrangement** other than a **cash balance arrangement**
	An **arrangement** is an other money purchase arrangement where the member will be provided with **money purchase benefits**, and the amount that will be available to provide those benefits is calculated purely by reference to payments made under the arrangement by or on behalf of the **member**. This means that in an other money purchase arrangement the capital amount available to provide benefits (the member's 'pot') will derive wholly from actual contributions (or credits or transfers) made year on year.
	The **scheme administrator** or trustees may use the payments made under the arrangement to make investments of any kind on behalf of the member (for example, cash on deposit, shares, other investment assets, a life assurance policy on the member's death). As long as the pot ultimately used to provide benefits is wholly derived from the original payments, the arrangement is an other money purchase arrangement. The subsequent investment income and any capital gains are derived from

273

payments made under the arrangement, and they themselves become part of the member's pot.

It is a feature of other money purchase arrangements that the member bears all the investment and mortality risk. The scheme simply pays out whatever benefits the amount in the pot, including the proceeds of all the investments that have been made using the payments into the scheme, will support.

Overseas arrangement active membership period

This is the period beginning with the date on which the benefits first began to accrue to, or in respect of, the individual under the recognised overseas scheme arrangement or, if later, 6 April 2006 and ending immediately before the recognised overseas scheme transfer. If benefits ceased to accrue under the recognised overseas scheme arrangement before the transfer then it is this date on which the overseas arrangement active membership period is treated as ending.

Overseas pension scheme

A **pension scheme** is an overseas pension scheme if it is not a **registered pension scheme** but it is established in a country or territory outside the UK and satisfies the requirements in the *Pension Schemes (Categories of Country and Requirements for Recognised Overseas Schemes) Regulations 2004. (Regulations not finalised yet).*

P

Pension commencement lump sum

A lump sum benefit paid to a member of a registered pension scheme (who is aged under 75) in connection with an arising entitlement to a pension benefit (other than a short-term annuity contract), and which meets the conditions detailed in *paras 1–3* of *Sch 29* to the *Finance Act 2004.*

Pension credit

The pension sharing provisions in the *Welfare Reform and Pensions Act 1999 (WRPA)* introduced the 'pension debit' and 'pension credit'. The 'pension debit' is the amount by which the value of the original member's pension rights are reduced and the 'pension credit' the corresponding amount by which the **ex-spouse**'s or **former civil partner**'s pension rights are increased. *Section 29 WRPA* determines the value of the pension credit to be transferred to the ex-spouse or former civil partner.

Pension credit member

An individual who has rights in a pension scheme which are directly or indirectly attributable to pension credits.

Pension debit

The pension sharing provisions in the *Welfare Reform and Pensions Act 1999 (WRPA)* introduced the 'pension debit' and 'pension credit'. The 'pension debit' is the amount by which the value of the original member's pension rights are reduced and the 'pension credit' the corresponding amount by which the **ex-spouse**'s or **former civil partner**'s pension rights are increased.

Pension input amount

The amounts as arrived in accordance with *ss 230–237* of *Finance Act 2004*

Pension input period

This means the period beginning with the **relevant commencement date** and ending with the earlier of a **nominated date** and the anniversary of the **relevant commencement date**, and each subsequent period beginning immediately after the end of a period which is a **pension input period** (under either this or the earlier paragraph) and ending with the **appropriate date**.

Pension protection lump sum death benefit

A lump sum benefit paid following the death of a scheme member of a **registered pension scheme**, who died before age 75 and was in receipt of a **scheme pension** under a **defined benefits arrangement** and which does not exceed the limits imposed through *para 14 of Sch 29* to the *Finance Act 2004*.

Pension scheme

A pension scheme is a scheme or other arrangements which is comprised in one or more instruments or agreements, having or capable of having effect so as to provide benefits to or in respect of persons on retirement, on death, on having reached a particular age, on the onset of serious ill-health or incapacity or in similar circumstances.

Pension sharing order

An order or provision made as listed in *s 28(1)* of the *Welfare Reform and Pensions Act 1999* (or the *Welfare Reform and Pensions (Northern Ireland) Order 1999 (SI 1999/3147)*) following a divorce or the dissolution of a civil partnership.

Pension year

The period the maximum **unsecured pension** and **alternatively secured pension** limits apply to (and the **dependant** equivalents). In the legislation these are referred to as 'unsecured pension years' and 'alternatively secured pension years'. These periods run in consecutive 12-month periods from the point initial entitlement to such pensions actual arise under a **money purchase arrangement**. These periods are set at the point that initial entitlement arise, and cannot be changed from that point onwards (although the pension year the member or **dependant** dies or reaches age 75 will be deemed to end immediately before such an occurrence – these truncated 12-month periods are treated as a whole 12-month period for limit purposes).

Pensioner member   A member of a pension scheme who is entitled to the payment of benefits from the scheme **and** who is not an active member.

Personal pension scheme   A pension scheme previously approved by the Board of Inland Revenue under *s 631 Income and Corporation Taxes Act 1988.*

Personal representatives   In relation to a person who has died, this means (in the UK) persons responsible for administering the estate of the deceased. In a country or territory outside the UK, it means the persons having functions under its law equivalent to those administering the estate of the deceased.

Prescribed occupation   Any of the following occupations –

Athlete, Badminton Player, Boxer, Cricketer, Cyclist, Dancer, Diver (Saturation, Deep Sea and Free Swimming), Footballer, Golfer, Ice Hockey Player, Jockey – Flat Racing, Jockey – National Hunt, Member of the Reserve Forces, Model, Motor Cycle Rider (Motocross or Road Racing), Motor Racing Driver, Rugby League player, Rugby Union Player, Skier (Downhill), Snooker or Billiards Player, Speedway Rider, Squash Player, Table Tennis Player, Tennis Player (including Real Tennis), Trapeze Artiste, Wrestler.

Prescribed scheme   Any of the following schemes:-

The Armed Forces Pension Scheme, The British Transport Police Force Superannuation Fund, The Firefighters' Pension Scheme, The Firemen's Pension Scheme (Northern Ireland), The Police Pension Scheme, The Police Service of Northern Ireland Pension Scheme, The Police Service of Northern Ireland Full Time Reserve Pension Scheme.

Property investment LLP   A Limited Liability Partnership whose business consists wholly or mainly in the making of investments in land and the principal part of whose income is derived from that business.

Protected rights   As defined in *reg 3* of the *Personal and Occupational Pension Schemes (Protected Rights) Regulations 1996,* but should be read as including safeguarded rights, wherever appropriate.

Public service pension scheme   A pension scheme established by or under any enactment, approved by a relevant governmental or Parliamentary person or body, or specified as being a public service pension scheme by a Treasury order.

Q

Qualifying overseas pension scheme

An overseas pension scheme is a qualifying overseas pension scheme if it satisfies certain HMRC requirements. The scheme manager must notify HMRC that the scheme is an **overseas pension scheme** and provide evidence to HMRC where required. The scheme manager must also sign an undertaking to inform HMRC if the scheme ceases to be an overseas pension scheme and comply with any prescribed benefit crystallisation information requirements imposed on the scheme manager by HMRC. The overseas pension scheme must not be excluded by HMRC from being a qualifying overseas pension scheme.

Qualifying recognised overseas pension scheme

A **recognised overseas pension scheme** is a qualifying recognised overseas pension scheme if it satisfies certain HMRC requirements. The scheme manager must notify HMRC that the scheme is a recognised overseas pension scheme and provide evidence to HMRC where required. The scheme manager must also sign an undertaking to inform HMRC if the scheme ceases to be a recognised overseas pension scheme and comply with any prescribed information requirements imposed on the scheme manager by HMRC. The recognised overseas pension scheme must not be excluded by HMRC from being a qualifying recognised overseas pension scheme.

R

Recognised European Economic Area (EEA) collective investment scheme

This means a collective investment scheme (within the meaning given by *s 235* of the *Financial Services and Markets Act 2000*) which is recognised by virtue of *s 264* of that Act (schemes constituted in other EEA states).

Recognised overseas pension scheme

A recognised overseas pension scheme is an **overseas pension scheme** which is established in a country or territory mentioned in *reg 3(2)* of the *Pension Schemes (Categories of Country and Requirements for Recognised Overseas Schemes) Regulations 2006 – SI 2006/206*. An overseas pension scheme which is not established in such a country is a recognised overseas pension scheme if it satisfies the requirements prescribed in *reg 3(4)* of those regulations.

Recognised transfer

A transfer representing a member's accrued rights under **a registered pension scheme** to another **registered pension scheme** (or, in certain circumstances, to an **insurance company**) or a **qualifying recognised overseas pension scheme**.

277

Refund of excess contributions lump sum	A lump sum benefit paid to a member of a **registered pension scheme** because they have contributed more to the scheme than they are entitled to tax relief on, and which meets the conditions of *para 6, Sch 29* to the *Finance Act 2004*.
Registered pension scheme	A **pension scheme** is a registered pension scheme at any time when, either through having applied for registration and been registered by the Inland Revenue, or through acquiring registered status by virtue of being an approved pension scheme on 5 April 2006, it is registered under *Chap 2* of *Pt 4* of the *Finance Act 2004*.
Relevant administrator	For a **retirement benefits scheme**, former approved superannuation fund or relevant statutory scheme as defined in *s 611A Income and Corporation Taxes Act 1988* (ICTA), or a pension scheme treated by HMRC as a relevant statutory scheme, this is the person(s) who is/are the administrator of the pension scheme under *s 611A* of ICTA.

For a deferred annuity contract where the benefits are provided under one of the types of scheme above, or a retirement annuity, this is the trustee(s) of the pension scheme, or the insurance company which is a party to the contract in which the pension scheme is comprised.

For a Parliamentary pension scheme or fund, this is the trustees of the scheme or fund.

For a **personal pension scheme**, this is the person who is referred to in *s 638(1)* of the *Income and Corporation Taxes Act 1988*).

Relevant annuity	For the purposes of *Pt 4* of the *Finance Act 2004* (pension schemes etc) a 'relevant annuity' is a single life annuity without a guaranteed term.
Relevant commencement date	This means

a) in the case of a **cash balance arrangement** or a **defined benefits arrangement** or a **hybrid arrangement,** the only benefits under which may be cash balance benefits or defined benefits, the date on which rights under the arrangement begin to accrue to or in respect of the individual, or

b) in the case of a **money purchase arrangement** other than a cash balance arrangement, the first date on which a contribution within *s 233(1)* of *Finance Act 2004* is made, or

c) in the case of a **hybrid arrangement** not within paragraph (a), whichever is the earlier of the date mentioned in that paragraph and the date mentioned in paragraph (b).

Relevant consolidated contribution	A contribution made by way of discharge of any liability incurred by the employer before 6 April 2006 to pay any pension or lump sum to or in respect of the individual.

Relevant overseas individual

An individual who either does not qualify for UK relief on contributions paid to a **registered pension scheme** because they are not a "relevant UK individual" as defined in *s 178 Finance Act 2004*, or an individual who is not employed by a UK resident employer and only qualifies for UK relief on pension contributions because they were resident in the UK both during 5 years immediately before the tax year under consideration and when they became a member of the **registered pension scheme**.

Relevant UK earnings

This means

employment income,

income which is chargeable under Schedule D and is immediately derived from the carrying on or exercise of a trade, profession or vocation (whether individually or as a partner acting personally in a partnership), and

income to which *s 529* of *Income and Corporation Taxes Act 1988* (ICTA) (patent income of an individual in respect of inventions) applies.

Relevant UK earnings are to be treated as not being chargeable to income tax if, in accordance with arrangements having effect by virtue of *s 788* of ICTA (double taxation agreements), they are not taxable in the United Kingdom.

Relevant UK individual

An individual is a relevant UK individual for a tax year if

the individual has relevant United Kingdom (UK) earnings chargeable to income tax for that year,

the individual is resident in the UK at some time during that year,

the individual was resident in the UK both at some time during the five tax years immediately before that year and when the individual became a member of the pension scheme, or

the individual, or the individual's spouse, has for the tax year general earnings from overseas Crown employment subject to UK tax.

Relievable pension contribution

A contribution paid to a **registered pension scheme** by or on behalf of a member of that scheme, unless one or more of the following exceptions applies. A payment is not a relievable contribution if the member was aged 75 or over when the contribution was made, or

the contribution is paid by the member's employer, or

the payment is an age related rebate or a minimum contribution paid by HMRC to a contracted-out pension scheme under *s 42A(3)* or *s 43* of the *Pension Schemes Act 1993* or the corresponding Northern Ireland legislation or

it is a life assurance premium contribution in accordance with *s 195A Finance Act 2004*.

Retirement annuity contract	A retirement annuity contract or trust scheme previously approved by the Board under *Chap 3* of *Pt 14* of *Income and Corporation Taxes Act 1988*.
Retirement benefit scheme	A retirement benefit scheme is any of the following

a scheme which was approved under *Chap 1* of *Pt 14* of *Income and Corporation Taxes Act (ICTA) 1988*;

a relevant statutory scheme (as defined in *s 611A ICTA 1988*);

a scheme treated as a relevant statutory scheme; or

an old code scheme approved under *s 208 ICTA 1970* that has not received contributions since 5 April 1980.

RPI   Stands for the Retail Price Index, which is the index of retail prices compiled by the Office for National Statistics. Where that index is not published for a relevant month any substitute index or index figures published by the Office for National Statistics may be used. (See *s 279 Finance Act 2004*.)

S

Scheme administration employer payment   Payments made

by a **registered pension scheme** that is an **occupational pension scheme**,

to or in respect of a **sponsoring employer** or a former sponsoring employer

for the purposes of administration or management of the scheme.

Scheme administration member payment   Payments made by a **registered pension scheme** to or in respect of a member or a former member for the purposes of administration or management of the scheme.

Scheme administrator   The person(s) appointed in accordance with the **pension scheme** rules to be responsible for the discharge of the functions conferred or imposed on the scheme administrator of the pension scheme by and under *Pt 4* of *Finance Act 2004*. This person must be resident in an **EU member state** or in Norway, Liechtenstein or Iceland (EEA states which are not EU states). The person must have made the declarations to HMRC required by *s 270(3) Finance Act 2004*.

Scheme chargeable payment	Scheme chargeable payments are

any unauthorised payment by the pension scheme other than a payment that is exempted by *s 241(2) Finance Act 2004* from being a scheme chargeable payment (see list below), and

a payment that the pension scheme is treated as having made and classed as a scheme chargeable payment by *ss 183–184 Finance Act 2004* because of unauthorised borrowing.

The following unauthorised payments are not scheme chargeable payments.

The payment is treated as having been made by *s 173 Finance Act 2004* and the asset used to provide the benefit is not a wasting asset as defined in *s 44 Taxation of Capital Gains Act 1992*.

The payment is a compensation payment as defined by *s 178 Finance Act 2004*.

The payment is made to comply with a court order or an order by a person or body with the power to order the making of the payment.

The payment is made on the grounds that a court or any such person or body is likely to order (or would be were it asked to do so) the making of the payment.

The payment is of a description prescribed by regulations made by HMRC.

Scheme pension   A pension entitlement provided to a member of a **registered pension scheme**, the entitlement to which is an absolute entitlement to a lifetime pension under the scheme that cannot be reduced year on year (except in narrowly defined circumstances) and meets the conditions laid down in *para 2 of Sch 28* to *Finance Act 2004*.

Section 9 (2B) Rights   Rights derived through *s 9(2B)* of the *Pension Schemes Act 1993*.

Secured pension   Either a **lifetime annuity** or **scheme pension**.

Short service refund lump sum   A lump sum benefit paid to a member of an **occupational pension scheme** because they have stopped accruing benefits under the scheme and have less than two years of pensionable service under the scheme, and which meets the conditions of *para 5, Sch 29* to the *Finance Act 2004.*

Short-term annuity

An annuity contract purchased from a member's **unsecured pension fund** held under a **money purchase arrangement** that provides that member with an **unsecured pension** income for a term of no more than five years (not reaching to or beyond their 75th birthday), and which meets the conditions imposed through *para 6, Sch 28* to the *Finance Act 2004.*

Sponsoring employer

In relation to an occupational pension scheme means the employer, or any of the employers, to or in respect of any or all of whose employees the pension scheme has, or is capable of having, effect as to provide benefits.

Stand-alone lump sum

A lump sum benefit paid as a single **BCE** to a member (aged under 75) of a **registered pension scheme** that represents all the member's uncrystallised rights under the scheme. The lump sum must meet the conditions of *Arts 25–25D* of the *Taxation of Pension Schemes (Transitional Provisions) Order 2006 – SI 2006/572 –* as amended by the *Taxation on Pension Schemes (Transitional Provisions)(Amendment No 2) Order 2006 – SI 2006/2004.*

Standard lifetime allowance

The overall ceiling on the amount of tax-privileged savings that any one individual can accumulate over the course of their lifetime without taking any special factors into account that may increase or decrease the tax-privileged ceiling. For the year 2006–07, this amount is £1,500,000. The standard lifetime allowance for following tax years will be specified by an annual order made by the Treasury, and will never be less than the amount for the immediately preceding tax year.

T

Total pension input amount

The aggregation of the **pension input amounts** in respect of each arrangement relating to an individual under a registered pension scheme of which the individual is a member.

Transfer lump sum death benefit

A lump sum benefit paid from a **money purchase arrangement** for the benefit of another member of the same pension scheme following the death of a scheme member (or a **dependant** of such a member), who is aged 75 or over, which meets the conditions of *para 19, Sch 29* to the *Finance Act 2004.* Such a lump sum cannot be paid where there is still a surviving **dependant** of the member.

Trivial commutation lump sum	A lump sum benefit paid to a member of a **registered pension scheme** (who is aged under 75) because their pension entitlements (under both that scheme and other such schemes) are deemed trivial, and which meets the conditions of *paras 7–9* of *Sch 29* to the *Finance Act 2004*.
Trivial commutation lump sum death benefit	A lump sum benefit paid to a **dependant** of a scheme member of a **registered pension scheme** (who died before age 75) because that **dependant's** entitlement under that scheme is deemed trivial, and which meets the conditions of *para 20* of *Sch 29* to the *Finance Act 2004*.

U

Unauthorised employer payment	An unauthorised employer payment is a payment by a registered pension scheme that is an occupational pension scheme to or in respect of a sponsoring employer or a former sponsoring employer which is not an authorised employer payment, or anything which is treated as being an unauthorised payment to a sponsoring employer or former sponsoring employer under *Pt 4* of *Finance Act 2004*.
Unauthorised member payment	An unauthorised member payment is a payment by a registered pension scheme to or in respect of a member or a former member of that pension scheme that is not an authorised member payment, or anything which is treated as being an unauthorised payment to or in respect of a member or former member under *Pt 4* of *Finance Act 2004*.
Unauthorised payments charge	Tax due under *s 208 Finance Act 2004* on either **unauthorised member payments** or **unauthorised employer payments**. The rate of tax is 40% of the unauthorised payment.
Unauthorised payments surcharge	Tax due under *s 209* Finance Act that is paid in addition to the **unauthorised payments charge**. The tax will be due where total unauthorised payments go over a set limit in a set period of time of no more than 12 months. The rate of tax is 15% of the unauthorised payments.
Uncrystallised funds	Funds held in respect of the member under a **money purchase arrangement** that have not as yet been used to provide that member with a benefit under the scheme (so have not crystallised), as defined in *para 8(3)* of *Sch 28* to the *Finance Act 2004*. These are defined differently for **cash balance arrangements**. Here it is what funds there would be if the member decided to draw benefits on a

	particular date not the funds actually held in the cash balance arrangement at that time.
Uncrystallised funds lump sum death benefit	A lump sum benefit paid from a **money purchase arrangement** following the death of the scheme member before the age of 75 (and within two years of that date of death) from any **uncrystallised funds** the member held in that **arrangement** at the point of death, and as defined in *para 15, Sch 29* to the *Finance Act 2004*.
Unit trust scheme manager	This means one of the following

(a) a person who has permission under *Pt 4* of the *Financial Services and Markets Act 2000* to manage unit trust schemes authorised under *s 243* of that Act, or

(b) a firm which has permission under *para 4* of *Sch 4* to the *Financial Services and Markets Act 2000* (as a result of qualifying for authorisation under paragraph of that Schedule; Treaty firms) to manage unit trust schemes authorised under that section.

Unsecured pension	Payment of income withdrawals direct from a **money purchase arrangement**, or income paid from a **short-term annuity** contract purchased from such an **arrangement**, to the member of the **arrangement** (who is aged under 75) and that meet the conditions laid down in *para 6* and *8–10* of *Sch 28* to the *Finance Act 2004*.
Unsecured pension fund	Funds (whether sums or assets) held under **a money purchase arrangement** that have been 'designated' to provide a scheme member (who is aged under 75) with an **unsecured pension**, as identified in *para 8* of *Sch 28* to the *Finance Act 2004*. Once sums or assets have been 'designated' as part of an 'unsecured pension fund' any capital growth or income generated from such sums or assets are equally treated as being part of the 'unsecured pension fund'. Similarly where assets are purchased at a later date from such funds, or 'sums' generated by the sale of assets held in such funds, those replacement assets or sums also fall as part of the 'unsecured pension fund' (as do any future growth or income generated by those assets or sums).
Unsecured pension fund lump sum death benefit	A lump sum benefit paid from a **money purchase arrangement** following the death of the scheme member before the age of 75 from any **unsecured pension fund** the member held in that **arrangement** at the point of death, and as defined in *para 17, Sch 29* to the *Finance Act 2004*.
Untraceable member	A member of a registered pension scheme who cannot be traced prior to their 75th birthday.

V

Valuation assumptions	The valuation assumptions in relation to a person, benefits and a date are assumptions

if the person has not reached such age (if any) as must have been reached to avoid any reduction in the benefits on account of age, that the person reached that age on the date, and

that the person's right to receive the benefits had not been occasioned by physical or mental impairment.

W

Winding-up lump sum	A lump sum benefit paid to a member of an occupational pension scheme because the scheme is being wound-up and their accrued benefits under the scheme are deemed 'trivial', and which meets the conditions of *para 10, Sch 29* to the *Finance Act 2004*.
Winding-up lump sum death benefit	A lump sum benefit paid to a **dependant** of a member of an **occupational pension scheme** because the scheme is being wound-up and their accrued benefits under the scheme are deemed 'trivial', and which meets the conditions of *para 21, Sch 29* to the *Finance Act 2004*.

Summary of the investment rules for pre A-Day of SSASs and SIPPS

SSASS

Loans

- Loans to members were not allowed;

- Loans to employers were permitted, but with restrictions where controlling directors were involved (see below);

- Maximum amount – 50% of scheme assets;

- Frequency – the pattern and frequency of loans to employers, compared to the scheme contribution history, dictated whether HMRC SPSS viewed the arrangements as satisfactory;

- Purpose – for proper business purposes only, investment in luxury items, eg private cars, would jeopardize approval;

- Interest rate – a commercially reasonable one, by general reference to the Clearing Bank Base Rates (CBBR);

- Tax deduction – interest payments allowed gross;

- Capital repayment – preferably built into a series of interest and capital repayment instalments;

- Liquidity – loans could not be approved, that would impede the financial liquidity of the scheme's purpose in paying benefits;

- Security – evidence from a bank that terms and conditions were similar, if loan was made at less than CBBR + 3%.

Property and land

Another attractive feature of the investment facilities with a SSAS was the capability to invest in property and land, in particular to purchase from an employer and then lease it back to them. Summarised below are the main features. The permitted (or otherwise) categories of sale and and purchase transactions were:

Permitted properties, vendors and purchasers

Land or property, freehold or leasehold, comprising;

- commercial/industrial property;

- residential property, if held indirectly via unit trust, where no scheme members occupied the property. Other exceptions applied where non-connected persons (eg caretakers) occupied the property;

- residential property forming an integral part of the business premises, occupied by independent party on commercial terms;

- agricultural property and land;

- forestry and woodlands;

- commercial/industrial property held abroad;

- permitted vendors/purchasers included the principal company and associated companies – regardless of their participation in the scheme;

- unconnected third parties;

- transactions of property owned by the trustees before 15 July 1991.

Classes of vendor, purchaser and property not permitted

- members or their relatives;

- partnerships involving members;

- residential property, other than the permitted cases mentioned above;

- residential property held abroad.

All transactions were reportable within 90 days of completion, whether involving cash sales or not.

Substantial gains in the value of property could in exceptional cases arise where for example, planning permission became available to change the nature and purpose of the property, giving rise to surpluses within the scheme, long before any subsequent sale or development at a later date. Actuarial advice in such circumstances could lead to refunds having to be made to the employer, incurring a charge of 35%.

Environmental law and health and safety law were further major considerations for the trustees in relation to such investments.

Unquoted shares, other investments and borrowings

Share ownership within participating and associated companies was another feature of SSAS investment that came under scrutiny by HMRC SPSS. Shareholdings in unconnected unquoted companies were also controlled under the SSAS regulations as transactions of this nature could be misused, to create tax avoidance measures. The regulations specifically prohibited any transactions between the scheme trustees and any of the members or their families.

HMRC monitored share transactions under powers contained in *ICTA 1988, Pt XVII, s 703 et seq*. Referral to HMRC technical division was made in connection with a transaction for clearance, if there was any doubt that tax rules might be infringed.

Another aspect of tax avoidance through transactions in shares related to inheritance tax. Given the nature of transactions in unquoted companies it was frequently the case that family relationships would exist between vendor and purchaser, so the shares could be transferred at an artificial price, thus reducing or avoiding tax. HMRC SPSS would therefore refer the details of a transaction to the shares valuation division, for verification of the true value of shares transferred. Clearance from that division enabled ownership of such shareholdings to be accepted as investments under a SSAS.

In order to satisfy liquidity requirements for payment of benefits, share ownership within a SSAS was permissible while there was at least one active member in the scheme, but once the final member retired, measures to discontinue share ownership took effect, with a time limit of 5 years for their ultimate disposal.

Similarly to transactions in property, share transactions were reportable to HMRC SPSS within 90 days of execution, under SSAS regulations.

Special provisions related to holdings in unquoted companies acquired before 5 August 1991 and dealings in shares with members, where the scheme acquired them before 15 July 1991, and restrictions were placed on non-income producing assets and certain other investment.

Trading and self-assessment

The range of trustee activity that could be construed as trading was very wide, but the range of such activities that was permissible within a SSAS was limited, generally to ensure that tax avoidance schemes were not involved, but also to ensure that tax on profits from permitted trading was properly assessed and paid. Judgment whether a transaction was taxable was in the hands of the local inspector of taxes.

The intentions of the trustees in their purchases and sales of investments was the key to whether an activity would be classed as trading. HMRC SPSS view was that where there was an organised effort to generate profit, this would create taxable income. Carrying out development work for example, on a property with a view to disposal, would constitute such effort.

Investments in the stock market by trustees, although they could involve short-term acquisition and disposals of shares when markets were volatile, did not amount to trading, in HMRC SPSS view. This type of activity only attracted their attention if 'bond washing' or 'dividend stripping' could be identified.

Stock lending activities were permissible transactions, common in larger pension schemes. The fees had been taxable up to 2 January 1996, but thereafter became exempt from tax.

From 6 April 1996, self-assessment applied to the trustees of all self-administered pension schemes, which included SSASs. Even if a scheme did not generate any chargeable income under this regime, the requirement to submit a return was nevertheless obligatory, with the imposition of a fine for failure to submit them within the annual deadline of 31 January following the relevant tax-year end.

The scheme administrator was not subject to this regime. The administrator was however, required under the reporting regulations, to submit details annually, listing chargeable events including refunds of contributions to members on withdrawal in the year and commutation payments on retirement where a taxable element was included, ie on grounds of triviality or serious ill-health.

SIPPS

The main attraction of SIPPS was for the company director, self-employed partner, or sole proprietor to purchase commercial property, such as offices, which could be let on arm's-length terms to the member's business. The purchase could be funded not just from the fund itself, but from borrowings and/or transfer payments brought in from previous pension arrangements. The member could decide on his own investments, subject to HMRC requirements, either as a trustee of his/her own SIPPS fund or by instructing the trustee. Such control was not available with an insured personal pension unless it was of the self-managed variety. However, a SIPPS was mainly funded by personal contributions by the member (in the absence of an employer's contribution for self-employed taxpayers and the general reluctance of employers to make contributions on behalf of their employees to personal pensions).

The facility to take income withdrawals from a SIPPS after retirement and up to age 75, within certain parameters, was undoubtedly a distinct advantage. It was more flexible than either the more common facility under a SSAS to defer the purchase of annuities to age 75, where the level of pension could be maintained, subject to sufficiency of funds, or the less used facility introduced in PSO Update No 54, which was also available to all types of money purchase retirement benefits schemes. The main areas of greater flexibility were those in relation to 'phased' income withdrawals and death benefits. It was also advantageous to director members of retirement benefits schemes who wished to continue in an executive capacity but also draw retirement benefits where this would not be permitted under the rules of the retirement benefits scheme, and to escape the 5% maximum self-investment requirement for occupational schemes.

The main list of investments that could be held, directly or indirectly, for the purposes of a SIPPS were:

- Stocks and shares listed or dealt in on a recognised stock exchange;

- Futures and options, relating to stocks and shares, traded on a recognised futures exchange;

- Depository interests;

- Units in authorised unit trust schemes;

- Units in unit trust schemes which:

    (a) were an unauthorised unit trust whose gains were not chargeable gains by virtue *of s 100(2)* of the *Taxation of Chargeable Gains Act 1992,* and

(b)   did not hold any freehold or leasehold interest in residential property other than that specified under (i) and (ii) below;

   (i)   property which was, or is to be, occupied by an employee, whether or not a member of the self-invested personal pension scheme or connected with a member of the scheme, who was not connected with his employer and was required as a condition of his employment to occupy the property, and

   (ii)   property which was, or is to be, occupied by a person who was neither a member of the self-invested personal pension scheme nor connected with a member of the scheme in connection with the occupation by that person of business premises held as an investment by the scheme;

- Eligible shares within the meaning of *s 638(11)* received by the self-invested personal pension scheme as contributions to the scheme;

- Shares in an open-ended investment company;

- Interests (however described) in a collective investment scheme that was either a recognised scheme or a designated scheme within the meaning of *s 86* or *s 87* of the *Financial Services Act 1986*;

- Contracts or policies of insurance linked to insurance company managed funds, unit-linked funds or authorised in accordance with *Article 6 of Council Directive 79/267 (First Council Directive on Direct Life Assurance)*;

- Traded endowment policies transacted with a person regulated by the Financial Services Authority;

- Deposits in any currency held in deposit accounts with any deposit-taker;

- A freehold or leasehold interest in commercial property where the interest was acquired from any person other than a member of the scheme or a person connected with him, or the interest is acquired from a member of the scheme or a person connected with him in circumstances in which *reg 9(3)* applies;

- Ground rents, rent charges, feu duties or other annual payments reserved in respect of, or charged on or issuing out of, property, except where the property concerned was occupied by a member of the scheme or a person connected with him.

Index